WOMEN'S POWER AND
SOCIAL REVOLUTION
Fertility Transition
in the West Indies

FRONTIERS OF ANTHROPOLOGY

Series Editor:
H. RUSSELL BERNARD, *University of Florida*

The **Frontiers of Anthropology** series is designed to explore the leading edge of theory, method, and applications in cultural anthropology. In rapidly changing times, traditional ways in which anthropologists work have been transformed, being influenced by new paradigms, methodological approaches beyond the use of participant observation, and field settings beyond the world of primitive peoples. Books in this series come from many philosophical schools, methodological approaches, substantive concerns, and geographical settings—some familiar to anthropologists and some new to the discipline. But all share the purpose of examining and explaining the ideas and practices that make up the frontiers of contemporary cultural anthropology.

Books in This Series

FAMILY VIOLENCE IN CROSS-CULTURAL PERSPECTIVE
by **DAVID LEVINSON,** *Vice President*
Human Relations Area Files, New Haven
Frontiers of Anthropology, Volume 1
ISBN: 0-8039-3075-5 (cloth)　　　ISBN: 0-8039-3076-3 (paper)

WOMEN'S POWER AND SOCIAL REVOLUTION
Fertility Transition in the West Indies
by **W. PENN HANDWERKER,** *Humboldt State University*
Frontiers of Anthropology, Volume 2
ISBN: 0-8039-3115-8 (cloth)　　　ISBN: 0-8039-3116-6 (paper)

WAREHOUSING VIOLENCE
by **MARK S. FLEISHER,** *Washington State University*
Frontiers of Anthropology, Volume 3
ISBN: 0-8039-3122-0 (cloth)　　　ISBN: 0-8039-3123-9 (paper)

CAPITAL CRIME
Black Infant Mortality in America
by **MARGARET S. BOONE,** *George Washington University,*
School of Medicine and Health Sciences
Frontiers of Anthropology, Volume 4
ISBN: 0-8039-3373-8 (cloth)　　　ISBN: 0-8039-3374-6 (paper)

WOMEN'S POWER AND SOCIAL REVOLUTION
Fertility Transition in the West Indies

W. PENN HANDWERKER

Frontiers of Anthropology   Volume 2

SAGE PUBLICATIONS
The Publishers of Professional Social Science
Newbury Park   London   New Delhi

To my parents, who made it possible.

For information address:

SAGE Publications, Inc.
2111 West Hillcrest Drive
Newbury Park, California 91320

SAGE Publications Ltd.
28 Banner Street
London EC1Y 8QE
England

SAGE Publications India Pvt. Ltd.
M-32 Market
Greater Kailash I
New Delhi 110 048 India

Printed in the United States of America

Library of Congress Cataloging-in-Publication Data

Handwerker, W. Penn.
   Women's power and social revolution : fertility transition in the
West Indies / W. Penn Handwerker.
      p.   cm. — (Frontiers of anthropology : v. 2)
   Bibliography: p.
   Includes index.
   ISBN 0-8039-3115-8.   ISBN 0-8039-3116-6 (pbk.)
   1. Fertility, Human—Barbados. 2. Demographic transition—
Barbados. 3. Women's rights—Barbados. I. Title. II. Series.
HB966.5.B35H36   1988
304.6′32′0972981—dc19   88-18567
                                                              CIP

FIRST PRINTING 1989

Contents

Foreword

Cultural anthropology is changing quickly, adding new methods of data collection and analysis, and new problems to the repertoire of the discipline. Until recently, cultural anthropologists relied almost entirely on participant observation as *the* method of data collection, and on qualitative exposition of results. Today, in addition to participant observation, anthropologists commonly use more formalized methods for the collection of quantitative data; and, in addition to qualitative methods of data analysis, they use statistical techniques and nonmetric scaling. Until World War II, anthropologists studied almost exclusively non-Western peoples, particularly preliterate societies. Beginning a half century ago, anthropologists extended their use of participant observation to the study of small agriculturalists and fisherfolk—what came to be called "peasant" societies.

Now, anthropologists have turned their attention to the study of occupational groups and of modern bureaucracies, as well as to the study of social problems like family violence, teen pregnancy, drug abuse, civil war, and forest depletion. The study of new problems has led to the development of new theories, and anthropologists are finding new ways to apply the discipline's theories and findings—in helping to determine the historical legitimacy of Indian tribes, for example, or in building better workplace environments, or in marketing new commercial products. The Frontiers of Anthropology series explores all the exciting edges of the discipline, and provides an outlet for some of the most creative and controversial work in the field.

In this volume, Penn Handwerker describes a deductive theory that takes on the issue of process in social change. We tend to think of social change as a series of steps, from one social *type* to another. The types are more or less stable, until some force for change produces an evolutionary transition that results in new types. What is most interesting, of course, and most difficult to understand, is the process by which change occurs. That is, what are the underlying forces of social change? How are those forces brought into being in the first place? Once they occur, how do they effect change in people's thinking and behavior?

Handwerker's ambitious theory is an important step in answering these questions. He suggests that the social types that we have conceptualized are, in fact, ephemeral. For Handwerker, social and cultural change arise out of a built-in human process of innovation and an attempt by people to use new ideas and behaviors to improve their material well-being and their access to resources. It is tempting to think of human beings as rational, economic maximizers. But, in Handwerker's view, the patterns and the rationality that we document in social and cultural processes are not generated by people who are prescient, rational maximizers. The observable fact is that people make a lot of mistakes about what is really in their own best economic interests. The rationality and patterning of social and cultural life arises after the fact and reflects people's ability to correct their mistakes.

Handwerker's theory is based on two primitive axioms: (1) that people, like all other living things, require regular inputs of energy and nutrients; and (2) that new ideas and new forms of behavior arise through a random process. Nonrational processes generate rational social and cultural patterns because selection must favor any idea or behavior that improves or optimizes resource access. (Selection, of course, is something that we see after the fact, too.) Cultural evolution and social change thus reflect changes in the cost structure of resource access and changes in power relationships as measured by a variable he calls K. Changes in the cost structure of resource access may be brought about by changes in ecological or demographic parameters, or by innovative ideas and behavior. Handwerker's theory thus brings together perspectives argued by Adam Smith, Karl Marx, and Charles Darwin.

Handwerker applies his theory to revolutionary changes that have taken place in the character of social and family relationships, and in fertility behavior—changes that have accompanied the industrial revolution and are therefore not evident universally, particularly not (yet) in the Third World. These changes include: the depersonalization of social relationships; a rise in women's status; marked changes in men's and women's roles that emphasize the equality of the sexes; overt, not merely symbolic, conflict between men and women as they vie for access to resources; the breakdown of the traditional family, characterized by overt conflict between parents and children; and a dramatic decline in fertility, to or even below population replacement levels.

Handwerker deduces that cost differentials in access to resources generate social inequalities and that those same cost differentials reflect uncompetitive resource access opportunities. Women's status is low when they must optimize their access to resources by relying on their husbands, parents, and children; women equalize their power, relative to their parents, their husbands, and their children to the extent that they are free to gain access to resources independently. Women have a lot of children when childbearing optimizes resource access; and women have few or no children when childbearing impedes resource access. Childbearing impedes resource access when both women and men have independent access to well-paying employment. Independent access to well-paying employment reflects increasing levels of competition in the world economic system. These levels of competition are manifested in social conflict and in depersonalization of social relations.

Handwerker tests his resource access hypothesis against standard socialization and modernization hypotheses, and against Caldwell's Westernization theory of fertility transition. This test is conducted with a combination of both individual-level and societal-level ethnographic and statistical data from Barbados, an island that experienced a revolution between 1950 and 1980 in social and family relationships. The findings of Handwerker's test convince him that his deductive theory does, in fact, generate concrete guidelines for the formulation and implementation of national and international development policy.

Readers will find some of his conclusions and the recommendations that follow from his conclusions, to be controversial. For example, the theory put forward in this book suggests that we have overplayed the role of purpose and intention in human behavior, especially fertility behavior. Furthermore, if the analysis of the Barbados case extends to other nations in the developing world, schooling by itself does not bring about fundamental social and economic change. Further, from the results of Handwerker's test, relying on family planning programs may be the worst way to control population growth. Educational programs have little direct influence on the number of children a woman chooses to have, only on the spacing of those children.

From Handwerker's theory and the test he provides, whether or not women in the Third World (or in poverty pockets in our own society, for that matter) limit their fertility depends on whether children make it easier or more difficult for women to improve their lives materially. Having children as a vehicle for economic success is characteristic of uncompetitive economies that restrict access to resources. Until it is possible for women to use their own skills and abilities to improve their lives, independently of their husbands, their parents and their children, the modern transition to low fertility will not occur. And unless the world is saved by some new technology, as yet unknown, the result will be an expansion of the current, obscene reality of widespread starvation.

— *H. Russell Bernard*
University of Florida

Acknowledgments

The fieldwork on which this study is based was funded by the National Science Foundation in two small grants, one for the summer of 1985 (BNS-8507605) and one for the summer of 1986 (BNS-8520445). I am most grateful for this support, but the opinions, findings, conclusions and recommendations expressed in this study are those of the author and do not necessarily reflect the view of the National Science Foundation. I am also grateful for the useful comments provided both by the NSF referees and by the NSF review committee. Their comments contributed in important ways to the development of the ideas expressed here, both by bringing some of my ideas into closer focus and by raising some important issues that I had not explored. They deserve more praise than they usually receive.

Readers acquainted with the demographic literature will find much here familiar, for many of the views I express were first proposed by Jack Caldwell. I merely repackage them. Readers acquainted with the literature on cultural change also should find familiar ideas, for many of the views I express were first proposed by Homer Barnett. These, too, have been repackaged. The specific manner in which I have repackaged these ideas, and others, owes much to conversations and correspondence with Verne Dorjahn. I am grateful to all three.

Over the years a number of people have patiently listened to my speculations and have provided important feedback. These include (in alphabetical order): Russ Bernard, Donna Birdwell-Pheasant, Caroline Bledsoe, David Cleveland, Paul Crosbie, Corrine Glasne, Mary Granica, Henry Harpending, Brian Hayden, Barry Isaac, Ruth Kornfield, Bill Murphy, Mary Odell, Ted Ruprecht, Peter and Jane Schneider, Debra Schumann, Peter Weil, and my undergraduates at HSU. Robert Dunnell, David Cleveland, Paul Crosbie, Henry Harpending, Ruth Kornfield, Ted Ruprecht, Carolyn Sargent, Peter Weil, Ron Wetherington and Ed Wilmsen read drafts of selected chapters and provided helpful feedback. Conversations with Phil Morgan have been short but formative. Bill Harger and Mary Ann Luedtke read the manuscript with the proverbial fine-toothed comb. If you find the language used well, thank them. The Sage referees provided unusually good suggestions and criticisms. I am grateful.

Sidney Greenfield read early versions of Chapters 3 and 4 and made very helpful suggestions. It was at his urging, and to my great benefit, that I reviewed the literature on the history of English family relationships and fertility.

Dennis Conway provided information and suggestions concerning research on Barbados before I visited the island. These were to prove instrumental to the success of this research. The faculty and staff of the University of the West Indies (Cave Hill) and the Institute for Social and Economic Research, particularly Dr. Graham Dann and Dr. Joycelin Massiah, generously shared their time and facilities. The research on which this book is based could not have been completed without the equally generous assistance of Dr. DeLisle Worrell and Clyde Mascoll of the research department of the Barbados Central Bank, Eric Staughn and Alyson Forte of the Barbados Statistical Service, Clyde Gollop of the Barbados Family Planning Association, and the staff at the Barbados National Archives.

Of equal importance has been the friendship, assistance and encouragement of Peter and Babs Johnson, Angela and John Cropper, Bill Baucom, Neville Selman, and Cecilia Karch. Jan Ward, Andrea Edey, Marilyn Paton-Robinson, Cheryl and Sharon Giles, and Wilfred Callender expressed great interest in and enthusiasm for the research reported on here, willingly shared their knowledge and experience, and set me straight when I strayed off the path. So did a large number of other Barbadians who it would be inappropriate to name individually. These include both men and women, from their twenties through their eighties, who ranged from the unemployed to highly-placed business executives and professionals, who patiently gave of their time and perspectives. They made my fieldwork on Barbados an extraordinary experience. I am profoundly in their debt.

Few research projects owe more to accompanying family members than has this one. Leslie, Kate, and PennElys, my fieldwork family, made it a joy to be in the field, and their presence eased my way into social contacts and relationships that would have been inaccessible had I been a single male in the field. This book has been influenced fundamentally by my mate, Leslie, and by all six of our children: Ian, Pilar, Mish, Liesl, Kate, and PennElys, from whom I have learned much.

Finally, this book owes more than it can express adequately to Se Wilson, Emmanuel Saingbe, and Victor Chumbe, West Africans who provided insights. May their children enjoy the freedoms they envisage.

—W. Penn Handwerker
Trinidad, CA

—1—

POWER AND THE
WORLD REVOLUTION

This book outlines a deductive theory of power from which the properties of social relationships follow as logical consequences. This theory is grounded on one assumption whose truth is self-evident (that all forms of life require regular inputs of energy and nutrients), and one proposition whose truth logically follows (selection must favor cultural and behavioral properties that improve or optimize resource access). The theory is Darwinian in the sense that it posits that novel concepts and behavior, like novel genes, appear randomly and are subject to selection on the basis of specific criteria. However, Marx's core claims follow as logical consequences and we are led to a kind of class analysis when we apply the theory. Moreover, this theory reveals that the ideas of Marx complement those of Adam Smith in important ways. Deductions from the theory lead to the conclusion that we have misconstrued the nature of social change and its relation to historical processes. Applications of the theory yield clear guidelines for the formulation and implementation of certain aspects of national and international development policy.

This theory also leads to the conclusion that changes in women's power relationships with men, their children, and their parents distinguish this moment in human history, and that they explain revolutionary changes in the ways in which individual women and men, and entire generations, relate to one another—an increasing equality and conflict both between men and women and between generations, a depersonalization of social relationships, and changes in moral evaluations in which the use of social relationships to justify material assistance shifts from being morally right to being morally wrong. Changes in women's power relationships are predicated on fundamental changes in women's ability to gain access to resources. These changes also explain the revolution in reproductive behavior and the transition from high to low fertility that accompanies the world social revolution.

THE ORIGINS OF THE MODERN WORLD
AND THE NATURE OF SOCIAL CHANGE

The source or sources of the modern world and the nature of our transition into it are among the most perplexing theoretical and policy issues in the social sciences. We have studied the modern world revolution almost since its inception and have long recognized some of its major components. We have developed increasingly sophisticated frameworks with which to study those components. But we have been frustrated consistently in our attempts to document the precise temporal interrelationships among them.

The contemporary world social revolution and the demographic transition from high to low birth and death rates that accompanies it have their origins some 200 years ago. In about 1750 the populations of Western Europe, which had for centuries experienced high levels of mortality and fertility, began to experience a decline in mortality, and after 1850, a decline in fertility. Infant mortality levels commonly near or above 25% in the early 1700s fell to around 1% by the 1980s; total fertility rates of 5-9 fell to below replacement levels. These changes occurred as the world industrial system matured, as cities grew in size and number and as farm populations declined, as literacy rates rose and as the length of time people spent in formal educational settings increased, as individuals lived better and as they experienced increasing personal freedoms and both social and geographical mobility.

The demographic transition also is widely thought to have accompanied a transformation in families—from relatively complex extended family units that functioned as economic production units, to smaller, nuclear family units that function as economic consuming units. Jack Caldwell (1982), for example, argues that these changes entail a nucleation of family obligations and expenditures in which the conjugal bond takes precedence over other social relationships, parent-child relationships take precedence over all relationships external to the nuclear family, and the moral economy of parent-child relationships emphasizes what parents owe their children rather than what children owe their parents. These distinctive changes in social relationships and their associated moral qualities signal the emergence of a conjugal family system of the kind William Goode discussed in his book *The World Revolution and Family Patterns* (1963). Such a family system is marked by the emergence of individual freedoms—to choose a spouse on the basis of mutual attraction, to establish a residence independently of one's parents, to support oneself with minimal assistance and interfercnce from kin outside the nuclear family and, together with one's spouse, to make decisions about how many children to have.

The high fertility of traditional societies is presumed to reflect a scarcity of children brought about, at least partially, by high fetal, infant, and early childhood mortality. The low fertility of modern societies is presumed to reflect a potential excess of children, which may be brought about by many different factors (Easterlin, 1978; cf. Notestein, 1945; Davis, 1963; Heer, 1983; Easterlin, 1983; Easterlin and Crimmins, 1985). For example, improvements in public health care might create a potential excess supply of children by increasing both the number of pregnancies that can be brought to full term and the number of children who survive to adulthood. Likewise, education and increased consumption of mass media might create a potential excess of children because they make people (perhaps especially women) aware of a greater range of opportunities and options for behavior; thus educational processes—whether through formal schooling or media consumption—may "break down" or "weaken" traditions and customs to create a "modern" perspective on the world in which people come to expect behavioral change. Education may also create new tastes and preferences and thus may increase the opportunity costs of bearing and raising children. Simultaneously, education may increase child-rearing costs because it places emphasis on the quality of children rather than on their numbers. Educated people, who become aware of greater personal opportunities as well the disadvantages of large families, also can be expected to have greater access to (and experience lower relative costs for) effective forms of contraception and abortion. The availability of new goods and services, and the growth of per capita income that makes such goods and services increasingly available, plausibly operates in much the same way: (1) they may make one aware of a greater range of opportunities and options for behavior, (2) they may reduce costs of effective forms of contraception and abortion, (3) they may increase the opportunity costs of having children, especially for women, (4) they may create new tastes and preferences, thus (5) they may create increased child-rearing costs. Caldwell (1982) proposes that mass Westernized education and the consumption of Westernized mass media exerts the most profound effect—it transforms the structure and moral economy of family relationships. Dramatic reductions in fertility occur when the moral economy of parent-child relationships place an emphasis on what parents owe children rather than on what children owe parents.

These influences are interdependent and may influence fertility through many different paths. Increasing levels of education lead to increased levels of mass media consumption and both factors can increase the effectiveness, the diffusion rate, and/or the effective application of new public health practices, including the acceptability of using fertility control technologies. Increasing levels of per capita income make health care, fertility control technologies, education, and mass media more accessible. And, of course, increasing levels of education lead to increased levels of per capita income. Improving public health can contribute to rising levels of per capita income and increased levels of education. Urbanization increases the spatial concentration of all of these factors and reduces access costs for both new services (health services included) and new goods (fertility control technologies included).

The prevailing social and demographic paradigm is still based on the distinction between traditional and modern societies explicated by Marx, Durkheim and Weber, and the research problem is still taken to be understanding the nature of the two and of the transition between them. The world of the past is construed as a stable one in which behavior and beliefs were fixed by custom. The transition to the modern world is construed as a secular transformation that replaced custom with the rational pursuit of individual interests and that ushered in the first major period of sustained social change in human history; as entailing a transition from premarket (tribal and peasant) subsistence economies run by reference to fixed norms of reciprocity to market economies run by reference to the profit motive; and as manifested in a transition from societies characterized by inequalities and run by oligarchs—kings, emperors, barons, chiefs, bishops, priests, or autocratic heads of extended families—to societies marked by individual religious, political, and economic freedoms, and by social equalities. In short, the modern social and demographic revolution is construed as integral to a broad and highly interdependent process of modernization and Westernization. The modernization paradigm constitutes our understanding of contemporary development processes, on which we both formulate and carry out development policy.

This conception of the origins of the modern world presumes that social change, like cultural evolution, entails the derivation of new forms out of historical antecedents. This conception of social change and the nature of human history originated as a way of talking about the transition from a "feudal" to a "capitalist" society in Western Europe, which were presumed to be qualitatively different and mutually exclusive social formations.

The supposition that there is an historical separation of social formations has proved to be too facile. Indeed, it does not even fit the type-case on which it was originally constructed, England. In *The*

Origins of English Individualism, Alan MacFarlane notes that "if we use the criteria suggested by Marx, Weber and most economic historians, England was as 'capitalist' in 1250 as it was in 1550 and 1750. That is to say, there were already a developed market and mobility of labour, land was treated as a commodity and full private ownership was established, there was very considerable geographical and social mobility, a complete distinction between farm and family existed, and rational accounting and the profit-motive were widespread" (1978: 195-196; cf. Braudel, 1979 for a more general account of Western Europe).

People whose material well-being is vitally dependent on reciprocity, like the Kpelle of West Africa (Bledsoe, 1980), tend to display an acute sense of the political-economic realities of the gift and the market forces that surround it. The "profit motive" thus, arguably, is implicit in all patterned material reciprocities. Much the same may be claimed for "capitalism," for all people use resources ('capital' in its elemental sense) to produce resources ('capital' in its technical sense) that can be used to produce other resources. Thus in a fundamental sense all production and exchange—including the creation and management of social reciprocities—is "capitalist," although both production and exchange vary in their scope, their scale, the means by which they are carried out, the speculation and risk they entail, and in the power relationships by which they are organized. Similarly, oligarchs exist in the world today— as heads of governments, corporations, and families. Indeed, in- dustrialization creates inequalities—new social, economic, and political elites. Individual religious, political, and economic freedoms have existed in the past, as have the importance of personal achievement, the pursuit of self-interest, and openness to innovation. The nuclear family preceded industrialization in Europe. The extended family has facil- itated industrialization or has emerged as its concomitant, at least in some parts of the world. The English have had a "modern" conjugal family system for more than 600 years that has coexisted with very high levels of marital fertility (MacFarlane, 1986).

The modernization paradigm thus captures the social dynamics of the last few hundred years only imperfectly. Ambitious research programs like Princeton's European Fertility Project (e.g., Coale and Watkins, 1986) set out to document a clear conception of the transition from what Peter Laslett called "the world we have lost" to the world we gained from our ancestors. They succeeded mainly in obscuring the differences between them and in casting doubt on the empirical validity of the prevailing conception of the origin of the modern world. The ambiguities of the modernization paradigm may reflect an erroneous presumption about the nature of social change.

CULTURAL EVOLUTION AND SOCIAL CHANGE

What if men and women do not think and act in ways that are fixed by socialization or convention? What if their childhood and adult experiences provide cultural prototypes that they can use to construct and negotiate social relationships in particular social interactions (e.g., Comaroff and Roberts, 1981)? In short, what if the properties of social relationships exist independently of space and time coordinates, even if their construction, maintenance, and change are grounded in concrete cultural and historical processes? If these speculations are correct, new social forms cannot develop out of historical antecedents. They must develop in circumstances with specific properties that exist independently of specific antecedent social relationships. Social change, unlike the historically continuous process of cultural evolution, thus must exhibit temporal and spatial *discontinuity*.

In his book *Innovation* (1953), Homer Barnett describes a model of human thinking processes that suggests that the genes that create human brains and thus dictate how we think do not dictate which perceptions will be related to which memory traces, or in which way. We thus think "intelligently" (e.g., Sternberg, 1985) and do not change our behavior merely because we sense material stimuli with particular physical qualities. On the contrary, we construct conceptual models of reality by inference because the genes that control the processes by which concepts form do not control the conceptual outcome of those processes. We thus possess a built-in mechanism—the very process by which people experience material stimuli—that continuously generates new and unexpected ways to look at and act in the world.[1]

People are subject to the constraints that bear on all living things. *Life* may be usefully defined as an open energy system controlled by nucleic acids. By definition, all forms of life require regular inputs of energy and nutrients. *Resource* is a cover term that encompasses all energy and nutrients and all pathways by which they can be acquired. It follows that selection must favor any property that improves or optimizes resource access, that selection will concentrate conceptual and behavioral innovations that do so, and that selection will build relatively advantageous means of acquiring resources and will eliminate innovations that interfere with the process of resource acquisition. It follows that novel cultural forms evolve out of cultural prototypes and that customs change whenever conceptual and behavioral innovations or changes in climatic, edaphic, or biotic parameters change the cost structure of resource access. It also follows that power is a function of the cost structure of resource access, and that the properties of social relationships arise independently of specific antecedent social forms as functions of power. The changes in social relationships and reproductive behavior that mark this moment in human history thus must reflect specific power relationships grounded on specific resource access cost structures.

PARAMETERS OF COMPARATIVE SOCIAL HISTORY

Chapter 2 will demonstrate for any set of resources that power is a function of the variable K, which is the ratio of the number of channels by which people gain access to those resources relative to the size of the population that seeks access to those resources. Cultural evolution is one component of ecosystem change and, like changes in climatic, edaphic, and biotic parameters, it creates new resources and resource access channels and so changes the costs attached to both. Selection for conceptual and behavioral properties that improve or optimize resource access operates through power relationships to create the properties of social relationships—hierarchy, equality, coercion, corruption, exploitation, competition, cooperation, reciprocity, and the extent to which social relationships are personalized. Social change is thus fundamentally different from cultural evolution, which modifies historically specific prototypes to create new cultural forms (see Barnett, 1953, 1961, 1983). By contrast, social change entails temporal and spatial discontinuity that reflects differences in resource access costs and the power relationships captured by the variable K.

This theory thus provides a foundation for understanding how and under what circumstances social groups of varying kinds come into being and change, and why, and under what circumstances social relationships exhibit or change particular characteristics. This theory applies to any social behavior (e.g., risk-taking), social relationship (e.g., friendship, male-female interaction), social group (e.g., families, bureaucracies), or social system (e.g., slavery, international, political, and economic relationships).[2] When we link these deductions with specific historical data, we can understand why cultural evolution produces social change and, occasionally, social revolutions, as in the change from hunting and gathering to agriculture some 10,000 years ago, and from an agricultural to an industrial and industrializing world over the past few hundred years, and we can explain the social revolutions that accompanied each. For example, we can explain why hunting societies tend to be characterized by flexible social units, an egalitarian ethic, and cooperation; why agricultural societies tend to be characterized by more rigidly defined social groups, hierarchy, exploitation, corruption, and coercion; and we can stipulate the circumstances in which these generalizations do not hold. This book thus develops the argument that the contemporary world social revolution is best understood from a comparative perspective on human history that is both broad and deep, for it has its origins in cultural changes that have been common to all of the revolutions that have marked human history since the advent of the Upper Paleolithic some 30,000 years ago—it is a fundamental change in resource access and in the social power relationships that follow from a particular resource access cost structure.

RESOURCE ACCESS, POWER AND FERTILITY TRANSITION

The resource access hypothesis developed in this book conceives parent-child relationships, like all other social relationships, as mediated by the costs incurred by individuals when they try to gain access to resources through one or another resource access channel (see Handwerker, 1983, 1986a, 1987).[3] This means that

- fertility transition occurs when women are freed from economic dependency on their children;
- women may achieve this freedom by direct governmental manipulation of resource access costs, as recently in China and Singapore;
- women may also achieve this freedom once well-paying employment opportunities open to them as well as to men, and
- these employment opportunities open to women when economic power is decentralized and creates competition that selects employees more on the basis of personal skills and competence than on the basis of personal relationships with employers.

The resource access hypothesis thus conceives fertility transition and the revolution in social relationships that precipitate it as one effect of a fundamental change in the costs that attach to resources and to means women can use to gain access to resources, and thus as one effect of a fundmental change in women's power. Fertility transition is *not* conceived as the outcome of a highly interdependent process of "modernization" (e.g., Bulatao and Lee, 1983a, 1983b; Easterlin and Crimmins, 1985) in which rising standards of living, new goods and services, reduced mortality, higher levels of education, urbanization, and improved health facilities and services reduce the (real and psychic) costs of using fertility control technologies and increase the motivation to use them. Likewise, fertility transition is *not* conceived as the outcome of a "Westernization" of family values brought about by mass education (e.g., Caldwell, 1982). Chapter 2 will show that the claims of the resource access hypothesis are consistent with what we now know about the historical experience that served as the cultural prototype of the modernization paradigm, that of England, the world's first industrial nation.

The resource access hypothesis provides a parsimonious explanation of fertility transition that uses a small set of independent variables, and it suggests new ways to think about the factors that the modernization and Westernization hypotheses implicate in fertility transition, such as industrialization, education, urbanization, new goods and services, rising opportunity costs, women's work opportunities, and family planning programs. The resource access hypothesis redefines how those factors operate, and thus may explain both why those factors have *appeared* to be determinants of fertility transition and why empirical research on those determinants has yielded ambiguous results. Thus declines in infant mortality cannot bring about fertility transition because mortality dissociates from fertility for women who have experienced the personal changes in perspective that characterize transition. Increases in education can change women's and men's perspectives on the world and can provide post hoc rationalizations for restricted fertility. However, education will have no bearing on fertility transition in the absence of conceptual and behavioral innovations that create means by which education can be used to access strategic resources. To bear on fertility, increasing levels of education must be accompanied by increasing economic rewards. There will be increasing returns from education only in the presence of competition that selects for both employer and employee productivity.

Urbanization may be generated by economic and social processes that produce fertility transition, but urbanization has no independent effect on fertility because the increasing population density through which urban centers are identified is unrelated to the criterion that selects for unrestricted or restricted childbearing. Similarly, rising standards of living may be generated by an economic system charac-terized by new and competitive resource access channels. The creation of those new resource access channels should change women's power relationships with their spouses, parents, and children, and thus lower fertility. But rising standards of living should increase fertility. More-over, parents with large families may be those who best access the new goods and services by which rising standards of living are defined. Female labor participation rates have no bearing on fertility transition in the absence of economic and social processes that create new and competitive resource access channels. These rates are highest, and approximate 100%, in preindustrial and protoindustrial populations, such as those in historical England or contemporary Africa.

Family planning programs (and related "reductions" in fertility regulation costs) cannot bring about fertility transition, because the mere use of contraception or abortion (or the intentional spacing of births) may be used either to maximize completed family size or to restrict fertility. Women's placement in resource structure selects for one or the other optimization strategy. Even if women use contraception and abortion to restrict their fertility, however, they may do so only because of oppressive economic circumstances, and fertility will rise when economic conditions improve. The application of contraception and abortion brings about fertility transition only when women are freed from dependency on their children. One might conceptualize this factor as "rising opportunity costs," but one would be wrong to do so—rising opportunity costs are the *effect* of a fundamental change in women's power and resource access.

This means that policymakers who want to promote fertility transition but who do not want to manipulate directly the cost structure of resource access have to create a resource structure in which women and men can find well-paying employment on the basis of their individual skills and competence. This theory thus has clear policy implications that can provide intelligent guidance to development policy discussion and implementation.

We shall test these claims with a combination of ethnographic, historical, and both micro-level and macro-level statistical data on Barbados. The Barbadian study constitutes an intensive examination of a completed social revolution and fertility transition in which data could be collected from the women and the men whose behavior both antedated and created those social and behavioral revolutions. Both micro- and macro-level data are systematically integrated. Clearly stated alternative hypotheses are submitted to rigorous statistical evaluation.

AN ISLAND IN THE SUN

Barbados is a small speck on our globe that is known in North America and Europe, if it is known at all, as a vacation spot that has produced several world class cricket players. Barbados is a coral limestone outcropping of the South American continental shelf. The island is about 40 km long and 25 km wide and lies at 13^0 10' N. Latitude and 59^0 33' W. of Greenwich, approximately 150 km east of St. Vincent and the fault line along that most of the Caribbean islands have emerged, and approximately 275 km north of Trinidad and the northern coast of South America. In contrast to the sharp relief features of the Antilles chain of islands, which often rise to more than 1,000 meters within a few miles from the coast, Barbados is characterized by low, rolling hills (its highest point is only 300 meters), and extensive areas of level ground.

Rainfall averages more than 125 cm annually on all but the northeastern tip of the island in the parish of St. Lucy, and on the southeastern and southwestern coasts in the parishes of St. Philip, Christ Church, and St. Michael. Some rain usually falls every month of the year, but mainly from June through December, in hurricane season. The fortunes of the island have been influenced significantly by erratic rainfall and hurricanes.

The limestone soaks up the rain, filters the water, and deposits it in large, readily accessible reservoirs sealed by a clay substrate. Underground streams percolate to the surface at springs on the leeward side of the island. Even today, Barbados enjoys a large supply of water. The island averages more than 3,000 hours of sunlight annually. Its mean daytime temperature of around 27^0 C fluctuates little over the course of the year, and is moderated considerably by NE trade winds that blow year-round. More than 250,000 people now live on this rock of some 166 square miles, making it, with more than 1,506 people per square mile, one of the most densely inhabited regions of the world.

Barbados was colonized by the English early in the seventeenth century and was densely populated scarcely half a century after the first settlers landed. In that short span of time, Barbados was transformed by the plantation system and slavery into the first major monocropping sugar producer of the West Indies. Careful examination of its early history illuminates the processes that led to the growth of a world industrial system. Careful examination of its recent history illuminates the fundamental transformation in social relationships, morality, and reproductive behavior that we examine in this book.

In England, as in Western Europe generally, these changes extended over nearly a century. On Barbados, these changes were telescoped into a period of only about 30 years. Whereas in the 1950s, Barbadian family relationships were characterized by sharp sexual and generational inequalities, in the 1980s younger Barbadian women were experiencing spousal relationships characterized by a growing ideology of equality, and they were insisting on equality with their mates and with their parents. Whereas in the 1950s Barbadian women experienced fertility levels restricted only by constraints on their own fecundity and by constraints on their sexual activity implicit in their spousal unions, in the 1980s younger Barbadian women were bearing children at a rate approximately half that of their mothers and grandmothers. Period total fertility rates fell from around 5.0 in 1955 to a low of about 2.0 in 1980 (Guengant, 1985; see Figure 1.1).

Within the Caribbean, Barbados has been among the first to experience the changes that swept England a century earlier. Barbados shares with other countries of the Caribbean a common history, and we may use her experience to help guide our understanding of the circumstances in which other Caribbean countries may be similarly transformed. More important, the greater depth of information available for Barbados can help us to identify precisely some of the sources of the modern world social revolution—more so, indeed, than an analysis of English history itself.

Chapters 3 and 4 will provide an ethnographic and historical account of the contemporary world social revolution as it has been manifested on Barbados. The bulk of the data reported in these and subsequent chapters were collected during six months of intensive field research. The numerical data reported in these chapters derive from a simple random sample of 436 women from all except the highest income class (over BDS\$65,000 annually) who belonged to a series of five-year age cohorts from 20-24 through 60-64 (see appendix). Data summarized in these chapters reveal that the Barbadian family system has been a re-creation of the English family system in the West Indies, subject to the structural peculiarities of the plantation system and the sugar economy. The Barbadian data thus provide grounds by which we can better understand the recent history of English family relationships and the English fertility transition.

Chapters 5, 6, 7, and 8 will report explicit, rigorous tests that directly compare the explanatory power of the resource access hypothesis with the explanatory power of standard social theory and Caldwell's Westernization alternative. Micro-level and macro-level models of the Barbadian fertility transition are developed on the basis of the reasoning outlined in the ethnographic and historical chapters. The micro-level model accounts for about 62% of the variance in individual fertility. The macro-level model accounts for about 97% of the variance in period total fertility rates from 1950 through 1980 and very accurately reproduces the historical trends in Barbadian fertility. Tests reveal that

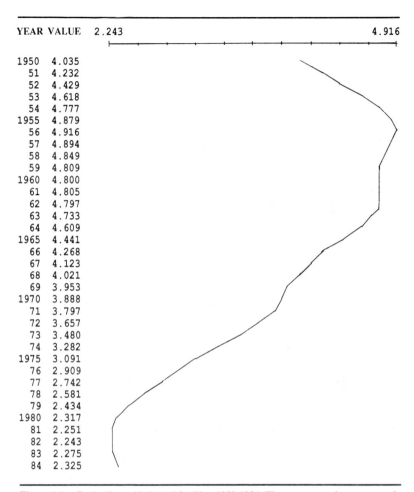

YEAR	VALUE	2.243	4.916
1950	4.035		
51	4.232		
52	4.429		
53	4.618		
54	4.777		
1955	4.879		
56	4.916		
57	4.894		
58	4.849		
59	4.809		
1960	4.800		
61	4.805		
62	4.797		
63	4.733		
64	4.609		
1965	4.441		
66	4.268		
67	4.123		
68	4.021		
69	3.953		
1970	3.888		
71	3.797		
72	3.657		
73	3.480		
74	3.282		
1975	3.091		
76	2.909		
77	2.742		
78	2.581		
79	2.434		
1980	2.317		
81	2.251		
82	2.243		
83	2.275		
84	2.325		

Figure 1.1:   Barbadian period total fertility, 1950-1984. Three-year moving average of sample estimates.

model specifications consistent with either standard social theory or Caldwell's Westernization alternative do not have empirical support.

The final chapter of this book (Chapter 9) will discuss theoretical and policy implications and will place the findings of this research into perspective with development issues. It is commonly assumed that in LDCs family planning programs are essential for reducing the birth rate, and that they achieve this goal, perhaps primarily, by providing women and couples greater freedom of choice. Family planning programs thus contribute simultaneously to development and to human rights progress. The data reviewed in this book reveal that this viewpoint is one of the great myths of development. It attributes to family planning programs goals they cannot, and should not be expected to accomplish, while it simultaneously ignores the real development and human rights impact those programs can and do have. Like all myths, this one contains elements of truth. Like some myths, this one is potentially dangerous. The danger is that it can lead to development policies and programs that inhibit rather than promote development and human rights progress—either by throwing money at family planning programs, and thus constraining programs aimed at job promotion or educational reform, or by inappropriately cutting family planning program funding and constraining the human rights progress those programs help realize.

The myth and its counterdevelopment implications are perpetuated by the modernization paradigm that informs contemporary population policy. The modernization paradigm perpetuates the myth because it fails to recognize that the real revolution in contemporary world affairs is one that has been common to all of the revolutions that have marked human history—as Marx argued, it is a fundamental change in power and resource access.

NOTES

1. Thus I believe that the previous serious attempts to conceptualize cultural evolution in Darwinian terms—by Cavalli-Sforza and Feldman (1981), Boyd and Richerson (1985), and even Rindos (1985, 1986), who otherwise foreshadows several points implicit in the approach advocated here—take directions that are fundamentally incorrect. These conceptual approaches reify cultural traits and thus cannot conceptualize the creativity (the process we call "intelligence" and its genetic foundation) that automatically generates the properties of human thought, behavior, and social relations.

2. We can also use this theory to integrate Marx's core ideas with neoclassical economics or descriptions of Parsonian value-consensus, and to explain such diverse phenomena as fiscal corruption, human fertility, and the spatial configuration of marketplaces. We can explain not only the effects of a particular preference function, but also why that preference function came into being, and we can specify the circumstances under which it should change. This theory also applies to biological evolution. We shall discuss some of its implications for the fossil record, especially those related to the origins and evolution of intelligence and culture, in another context (Handwerker, in press).

3. Carl Mosk's *Patriarchy and Fertility, Japan and Sweden 1880-1960* (1983) makes an argument very close to the one developed here. My argument extends Mosk's by generalizing its applicability (by differentiating the resource access positions of men and women) and by deriving it from a broader evolutionary theory that rejects rather than integrates standard modernization theory.

—2—

SOURCES AND SOCIAL IMPLICATIONS OF POWER

Power corrupts. Absolute power corrupts absolutely.

—Lord Acton

A fish gets rotten from the head.

—Kru Proverb

People are subject to the constraints that bear on all living things. One of these is the necessity to obtain regular inputs of energy and nutrients. This means that people, like all life forms, cannot exist without some means by which they can detect and can interact with changes in the material world they inhabit. Genes construct mechanisms we know as "senses," which permit living things to keep track of changes in the world in which they live. Genes also construct mechanisms that permit living things to alter their biological and behavioral state in the presence of significant environmental changes. The process we call "intelligence" is one such mechanism. People must construct conceptual models of material reality by inference because the genes that control the processes by which concepts form do not control the conceptual outcome of those processes.

Thus the manner in which our brains process information about the material world generates an unceasing flow of conceptual and behavioral novelty. Cultural innovations, like genetic innovations (mutations), do not occur randomly in the strict sense that all possible new ideas or behaviors are equally probable, as Barnett (e.g., 1953) makes clear. Cultural innovations, like genetic innovations, arise out of specific prototypes, and the direction of cultural evolution, like the direction of biological evolution, is channeled by evolutionary history. Cultural and biological innovations occur randomly only insofar as they are *unexpected*—we cannot predict which biological or cultural prototype will change, in which way, or when it might do so. We can know only that innovations occur all the time and that, in an otherwise ad hoc historical process, they contribute to patterned cultural, social, and biological change because they are subject to selection on the basis of criteria that must be implicit in the definition of life itself.

Perhaps the vast majority of these new perspectives and behavioral strategies are not very useful, and many constitute errors of varying magnitude. Selection favors any innovation that improves or optimizes resource access. But it does not follow that innovations that optimize or improve resource access will occur. Nor does it follow that individuals will correctly identify and choose to use those innovations that improve or optimize resource access. However, it does follow that selection favors the individuals, groups, or organizations that rectify their mistakes most rapidly. Consequently, selection concentrates conceptual and behavioral innovations that optimize or improve resource access, builds relatively advantageous means of acquiring resources, and eliminates innovations that interfere with the process of resource acquisition.

Selection conceived in this way operates by reference to the costs attached to various resources and to the means (the channels) by which they may be accessed. Changes in selective pressures are changes in the access costs of one resource relative to others. The presence and intensity of selective pressures thus may be measured as cost differentials. Changes in resource access costs come about when people create new ways to think about and act in the world, when ecological parameters change, and when populations grow, decline, or when they experience change in their age or sex structure or their fertility, mortality, or migration parameters. The ways to conceptualize the world and the behavioral strategies that optimize or improve resource access change accordingly.

Culture does not evolve exclusively by selection, of course. Conceptual or behavioral innovations that do not significantly change the cost structure of resource access are selectively neutral. Significant portions of religious and artistic content often qualify for this status, and these and other selectively neutral aspects of culture contribute to the extraordinary cultural diversity of our species. Any adequate explanation of human beliefs and behavior must be ad hoc and historical, at least in part, because cultural changes arise unexpectedly out of cultural prototypes. Explanations for cultural innovations that are selectively neutral must be almost solely ad hoc and historical.

By contrast, conceptual and behavioral stability and *systematic* changes in concepts and behavior occur because some beliefs and actions change the cost structure of resource access in significant ways. The distinctive realism, mercantile settings, and focus on ordinary people of Rembrandt, Vermeer, and other seventeenth-century Dutch artists, for example, clearly reflects the rise of the Netherlands as a wealthy colonial trading power. Chartres and other gothic cathedrals just as clearly reflect the worldly power of the Church in Europe during the late middle ages (Adams, 1957). As Weil (1986b) shows in his analysis of changes in the ideology and composition of four Mandinka masks, public dimensions of both religion and art are unlikely to be selectively neutral (cf. Harris, 1966). Consequently, these aspects of both religion and art undergo change that mirrors selection processes that operate on other aspects of culture. Selection eliminates the mistakes and concentrates the conceptual and behavioral innovations that optimize or improve resource access to maintain existing cultural and social patterns or to create regularities in cultural and social change.

Conceptual and behavioral innovations drive evolution, as do changes in climatic, edaphic, and biotic parameters, because they create new resources and resource access channels and thus change the costs attached to both. This is true whether the cultural dimension in question evolved by selection or was selectively neutral for its innovator. For example, the arbitrary whims of people in power, whether university administrators or government officials, may have no perceptible effect on their ability to access resources, and thus may be selectively neutral. Those whims can radically alter the selective pressures to which other people are subject, however. A decision to hire women for positions formerly filled only by men significantly alters the economic and power relationships women enjoy with men, their children, and their parents.

This chapter shows how selection creates social relationships with different properties. I will demonstrate for any set of resources that power is a function of the variable K, which is the number of channels by which people gain access to those resources relative to the size of the population that seeks access to those resources. Selection for cultural and behavioral properties that improve or optimize resource access operates through power relationships to create hierarchy, equality, coercion, corruption, exploitation, competition, cooperation, and reciprocity. When we link theoretical deductions with specific historical and ethnographic data, we can explain why particular social relationships exhibit their distinctive properties. We can also explain the revolution in reproductive behavior that constitutes the modern fertility transition.

DEFINITIONS

Resources are the energy and nutrients necessary for life, the foods that provide energy and nutrients, and the things, behavior, concepts, or

other forms of life that facilitate resource access. "Money," "land,"
"labor," "education," "berries," "hoes," "axes," "nets," "cattle," "horses,"
"husbands," "wives," or "friends" all may constitute a "resource,"
depending upon the time and place one analyzes.

The theory of power and social relationships economy outlined in
this chapter is concerned specifically with two properties of resources:
(1) the means by which they can be accessed, and (2) the access costs (in
energy, money, time, or other pertinent measures) attached to one or
another means or one or another resource. Any means by which a
resource can be accessed can be thought of as a "channel" to that
resource. Resource access channels may be sets of activities, a person or
people, a social organization, or some combination of activities, people,
and organizations. For example, when husbands or wives are resources,
the activities that constitute "marriage" would be a resource access
channel. The activities involved in producing spears, bows and arrows,
nets, or digging sticks may be resource access channels. A "job" is both
an access channel to resources and a resource. Access channels to the
resource of a job may include the activities that constitute "education," a
school organization, individual teachers, employers, friends, or relatives.

Let "gatekeeper" refer to individuals or organizations that function
as resource access channels. For example, hunters may be differentiated
by skill—one person may be an exceptional tracker, another may be
able to make finely balanced arrow points, another may have the ability
to mediate the interests of people in the camp and to summarize
effectively the group consensus, and another may have special abilities
to communicate with the supernatural. Each person would function
relative to others in the camp as a gatekeeper for particular resources. In
a community of farmers, parents possess rights in land and thus function
relative to their children as gatekeepers of the resource of land.
Husbands and wives characteristically function relative to each other as
gatekeepers of specialized labor resources. Schools and teachers, or
employing organizations and employers, function as gatekeepers for
still other kinds of resources.

In the following pages I will outline a system for analyzing social
relationships and will identify a small number of specific deductive and
testable hypotheses. The following remarks are by no means comprehensive. For clarity of exposition, suppose for the moment that any
set of resources (R), any set of gatekeepers, and any set of resource
seekers are homogeneous. All theoretical deductions are made as *ceteris
paribus* claims, of course. Pertinent complications and qualifications
may be added when they are appropriate for particular analyses.

POWER AND SOCIAL HIERARCHY

Selection operates by reference to the access costs attached to various resources and to the channels by which they may be accessed. Changes in relative access costs change the selective advantage of one or another resource or one or another resource access channel. Changes in relative access costs create patterned changes in social relationships and behavior because selection will favor the cultural and behavioral innovations that optimize or improve resource access.

It follows that both gatekeepers and resource seekers will tend to optimize or improve their access to any pertinent resource set (R). Because gatekeepers can levy access costs on resource seekers, the population of resource seekers (P) that uses a given access channel constitutes a resource for gatekeepers. Hence, gatekeepers can optimize their resource access only by continuing to serve as channels to R, and can improve their resource access only by serving this function for larger numbers of resource seekers. It follows that the power of a gatekeeper (with respect to R) varies directly with P.

Selection will favor maximizing the level of resource access costs and, in the absence of constraints, this maximizing tendency will drain resources from resource seekers. Resource seekers can only optimize or improve their resource access by using the lowest resource access costs. The creation of new access channels (C) implies a reduction in the expected number of resource seekers per channel. The creation of new resources has the same effect. Hence, increases in C create opportunities for those seeking access to R to by-pass resources or resource channels with high access costs. Increases in C thus create competition among gatekeepers and the power of a gatekeeper (with respect to R) varies inversely with C. Because gatekeepers who maintain high resource access costs can be by-passed, competition among gatekeepers constitutes selective pressure for lower resource access costs.

It follows that the access costs attached to various resources and to the channels by which they may be accessed vary with K, the ratio of the channels by which individuals gain access to resources (C) to the population seeking access to those resources (P):

$$K = C/P$$

Hence, for resource set R, power is a function of K. The power of gatekeepers varies inversely with K. The power of resource seekers varies directly with K. If there is only one resource seeker for each resource, K will equal 1.00. As the number of resource seekers grows relative to the number of gatekeepers, K will approach a limit close to 0.00.

Let "hierarchy" refer to power differentials between two or more individuals with respect to R. It follows that the existence and importance of hierarchical social relationships are inverse functions of this ratio (K) of resource channel gatekeepers to the population of resource seekers. Where K = 1.00, there are no gatekeepers who control access to resources, and hierarchy in social relationships is absent (that is, social relationships are strictly egalitarian). As this ratio departs from unity, there emerges hierarchy in social relationships, identified by the presence of gatekeepers who control access to resource set R.

Gatekeepers exist in all social groups, however. When each person in a social unit functions as a gatekeeper for a distinct resource R_i, K_i will approach 0. However, if every person needs access to all resources and if all R_i are equally important, K for the aggregate set of resources approximates 1.00 and social relationships tend to be egalitarian.

This condition is met or approximated frequently in living hunter-gatherer communities. These communities do not occupy regions that are rich in resources, and their strategic subsistence problem is to match population size and movements to resources that fluctuate in time and space and over which people have little or no control. Individuals typically cannot, by themselves, gain access effectively to all the resources they need. We can expect that each person will tend to attach the highest possible resource access costs to the resources for which they act as gatekeeper, and that each will tend to seek resources they need through the channels with the lowest possible resource access costs. Because nearly everyone functions as a gatekeeper for resources of approximately equal importance that nearly everyone else needs, however, selection will favor roughly equal access costs for all resources and K approximates 1.00 for the aggregate set of resources. Consequently, among living hunter-gatherers we tend to find minimal hierarchical differentiation on the basis of age and sex, predominantly egalitarian social relationships based on balanced material reciprocities, and corruption (e.g., failing to share food equitably), exploitation (e.g., seeking an inequitably large share of food) or coercion rare. When prehistoric hunter-gatherers occupied regions much like those occupied by living hunter-gatherers and faced equivalent strategic subsistence problems, we would expect that their communities would be organized likewise.

These conditions are met to some degree and in some situations in all societies. Settled cultivators, like hunter-gatherers, are not self-sufficient for example. Marriage creates the basic agricultural labor unit, a husband and wife. However, marriage creates only a minimally adequate division of labor and labor force. Either husband or wife may fall sick or be injured during a crucial time in the farm cycle and the results would be disastrous. Selection favors the creation and effective management of material reciprocities with other adults.

In Africa, for example, husbands and wives function as gatekeepers relative to each other for very important resources. Husbands commonly function as gatekeepers for land, and wives function as gatekeepers for the bulk of the labor skills necessary for effective food production, processing, and consumption. Family dynamics, consequently, express material reciprocities. Indeed, "husband" cannot be identified independently of obligations for providing land, clearing the forest, burning the field, and otherwise striving to make a large, productive farm; "wife" cannot be identified independently of obligations to bear many healthy children, to plant the field, harvest and process food, and to make decisions that assure that her family is well-fed, to assist her parents and in-laws should they run short of food, and to see to it that the household can offer significant quantities of food to its guests. Private husband-wife interactions may exhibit marked egalitarian qualities.

More generally, in Liberia, as in much of Africa, there are two primary forms of social relationships. One form carries with it an underlying admonition and obligation to assist; the other carries with it a latent threat and is identifiable in the absence of the first form. To establish or to maintain positive relationships, it is necessary to use one's wealth (cattle, chickens, spouses, children, people who work on one's farm, houses) to maintain fairly regular material flows of goods and/or services. A person who does not participate in these material reciprocities will be suspected of being a competitor who either seeks to block material flows to the other person or seeks to act in ways that could embarrass the other. Such actions alienate an individual from the support network of reciprocal material obligations that bind people together.

Of course, material resources are scarce and participation in material transaction networks is selective. The initiation of material flows (gift giving) creates additions (either patrons or clients) to existing social networks. For example, influential elders and chiefs acquire large numbers of wives from people who present one of their daughters as a gift in exchange for support for their own projects or goals.[1] On a smaller scale, the traditional gifts of a white chicken and a white kola nut that are given, for instance, to the father of a prospective wife, function in an equivalent way. The cessation of material flows severs linkages of mutual assistance. The process of selectively creating social networks thus creates its complement—networks of opposing and potentially hostile people and organizations. Because all people selectively create and change the constituents of the social networks to which they belong, all organizations (including kin groups) are subject to change, and all are subject to competitive processes by which individuals seek both to control their own network of supporters and clients and to subvert opposing individuals and their networks of supporters and clients (see, e.g., Murphy, 1980, 1981). The effect is that individuals who seek to create and maintain adequate levels of material well-being necessarily and continually compete over the scarce support relationships on which that well-being is contingent (e.g., Bledsoe, 1980, 1988; Murphy, 1988). One's bargaining position is determined by K.

An increase in K means either a reduction of resource seekers or the creation of new access channels. Increases in K increase the power of resource seekers relative to gatekeepers. Selective pressures generated by increases in K may exist solely for gatekeeper individuals. However, if gatekeeper organizations are subject to selection, their component individuals also must be subject to selection. The relative success of organizations subject to competition will be contingent on the performance of their managers and workers and both managers and workers will be subject to selective elimination on the basis of their contributions to organizational goals.

For example, medieval English towns emerged as trading centers in an open, competitive economy. They did not originate as independent, self-governing units. On the contrary, they belonged to a lord and yielded substantial portions of his income. Self-governing bodies of freemen arose around nuclei provided by the officials who administered revenues and the merchant organizations that represented those whose activities generated the revenues. Self-government was widely achieved only in the late thirteenth and fourteenth centuries, and on terms that provided long-term compensation to the lord. But towns were communities of freemen in which wage- or self-employment provided an avenue to escape manorial bonds long before they achieved self-government. The quality and prices of their products and their location in regional and national distribution systems determined the wealth of towns, of their governing officials, and, before self-government, of their lords. Consequently, as J. L. Bolton remarks in *The Medieval English Economy, 1150-1500,* "If the goods its artisans produced were shoddy, men would not come to market to buy them. Towns felt they had a duty to search out and prosecute inferior or fraudulent work" (1980: 140). Toward that end, towns and cities exercised strict quality controls and closely supervised working conditions that could lead to poor workmanship.

Similarly, throughout much of contemporary West Africa work cooperatives function as one among several channels by which a farmer can gain access to labor. In Liberia, work cooperatives are not permanent organizations, although the membership of particular cooperatives may extend over several farming seasons. Instead, they are called for particular tasks (e.g., brushing the farm, planting, weeding, harvest). Depending on the task and the region of the country, their membership may be exclusively men, exclusively women, or both men and women. Members are drawn from among kin and friends, normally from among those who farm in the same area. Work cooperatives characteristically have appointed leaders who organize and direct work. However, anyone may organize a work cooperative. Because there are a relatively large number of channels by which one can obtain labor, the pertinent resource channel ratio is relatively high and members are subject to selection on the basis of their work effectiveness. It is by consensus that the people who are members of a particular cooperative work group agree to help one another perform a task that can be done more efficiently and enjoyably by a group than by individual effort. Continued participation presupposes that people committed to perform cooperative labor fulfill their obligations. A person who does not is ridiculed and ostracized, and may be fined by the leader of the work cooperative. If appropriate apologies and restitution are not made, such a person will not be allowed to participate in a cooperative in the future.

Conversely, as K diminishes, the greater the power of gatekeepers and the greater the tendency for gatekeepers to enrich themselves at the expense of the powerless (resource seekers). For instance, when men in hunting and gathering societies control access to resources that are more important than those controlled by women, women's status tends to decline (e.g., Hayden et al., 1986). More generally, K diminishes and social hierarchy intensifies when an individual or an organization controls access to a particularly important resource or to a broad class of important resources. Selection favors individual or group control of particular resources, and thus creates competition (see Hayden, 1986), when they are regularly available in large quantities. In the presence of reliable and highly productive sites, selection will favor relatively permanent settlement and diminishing K. As K diminishes, corporate groups and social hierarchy emerge. We find these social patterns among recent living hunter-gatherer societies, most notably the Indians of the Northwest Coast of North America, who exploited the rich fisheries of the region. These patterns may have developed among interior plateau groups more than 3,000 years ago (Hayden et al., 1985). Similarly, archaeological evidence associated with Natufian sites in the Middle East prior to 9,000 B.C. reveals a society of settled and socially stratified hunters and seed collectors who exploited rich stands of wild plants.

The emergence of fully agricultural societies, however, ushered in a world revolution in social patterns because agriculture creates, by cultivation or animal husbandry, highly productive and relatively reliable resource sites. Living hunter-gatherers characteristically are mobile and structurally flexible because resource location and timing fluctuate. Particular sets of resources may occur in very high quantities, but only seasonally, and quantities will fluctuate from year-to-year owing to factors over which people have little or no control. No individual and no group can reasonably expect to have access to adequate resource supplies over any extended period of time. Consequently, selection favors individual and camp mobility. Selection also favors the creation and maintenance of intergroup social relationships (visiting and marriage) and loose or nonexistent group boundaries that permit people to move easily from camp to camp, or to fission, in response to fluctuations in resource access. The variable K remains high, and selection does not favor individual or group control of particular resources. Among settled cultivators, however, the strategic subsistence problem is not where and when to find resources, but to gain access to the right kind of land in appropriate amounts and to obtain sufficient labor of the right kind at the right time. K diminishes in the presence of these fundamental changes in resources and in resource access channels, and there emerge more rigidly defined social groups, such as corporate kin groups, hierarchy, exploitation, corruption, and coercion.

An extraordinary historical sequence in the Tehuacan Valley of Mexico, for example, documents the transition from mobile hunters of horses, antelope, deer and, perhaps, mammoths prior to 8000 B.C. through the origins of agriculture (see MacNeish, 1978, 1981). The first clear evidence of extensive interregional trade, occupational specialization, social stratification, and the emergence of what may have been corporate kinship groups appears about 1500 B.C. during the first period at which the people in this valley produced enough food by agriculture to support themselves in permanent villages throughout the year. By about 900 B.C., agricultural technologies were transferred a short distance to the north, to the Valley of Mexico (Sanders, 1976). Irrigation techniques may have been developed in the Valley of Mexico by 450 B.C., at about the same time that they appeared in the Tehuacan Valley. Within the northern portion of the Valley of Mexico, a series of small villages appear in the archaeological record about 250 B.C., with a combined population of perhaps 1,500 people. Within about 100 years, these villages integrated into the city of Teotihuacan, with a population of 20,000-30,000 who occupied an area of some 10 km². Before its fall in 750 A.D., Teotihuacan grew to encompass an area of more than 20 km² and a population of 125,000-200,000, and to control a state whose influence was felt throughout Mesoamerica (see, e.g., Cowgill, 1983, Millon, 1976, 1981, Sanders et al., 1979, Sanders and Santley, 1983). Teotihuacan became the preeminent urban center in the New World, and may have been the largest city that the world had ever known, including Rome at the height of its glory.

During the earliest phases of its growth, Teotihuacan developed and was supported by new agricultural technologies, including the extension of irrigation and terracing. There is evidence that the city's growth was tied to regional warfare and to the growth of a monopoly over one of the major sources of obsidian in Mesoamerica. There is also evidence of a significant centralization of authority and occupational specialization. The construction of significant public buildings took place during this phase, but major public architecture, including the construction of 23 temple complexes, the enlargement of the Sun Pyramid twice and the beginning of construction on the the Moon Pyramid, took place during the period from 1 A.D. to 150 A.D. The remaining monumental architecture, including the construction of a large block of public buildings, the completion of the Moon Pyramid, refinements to the Sun Pyramid, and the construction of the Temple of Quetzalcoatl, occurred during the following 50-year period. These growth phases were marked by major development in the obsidian industry. These growth phases also may have been marked by the first development of *chinampas*. These were small agricultural islands constructed by building alternating layers of mud and vegetation to a level of a few inches over the level of the shallow lakes in the Valley of Mexico. *Chinampas* exhibit extraordinarily high productivity because they can be cropped continuously by the use of separate seed beds, irrigation from natural seepage and hand watering, and regular replenishment of their naturally high nutrient content.

Although the city did not grow in area after about 200 A.D., its wealth, power, and population did. The period from about 200 A.D. to 450 A.D. was marked by extensive urban renewal. Poor quality wattle and daub construction that characterized earlier phases of growth were replaced by stone-walled "concrete" and plaster-surfaced apartment complexes. Murals and facades were added to the massive public buildings. Ethnic enclaves were formed. These are much like the Hausa enclaves in Yoruba cities that we find today in West Africa and, like the Hausa communities, may have constituted communities of stranger-traders. At the city's height, there were as many as 400 obsidian workshops, and there was marked specialization among these producers. There were, in addition, extensive specialization in other craft specialties. These changes were accompanied by significant changes in food production, including the development of an extensive network of canals and reservoirs for irrigation. These finds are mute evidence of the growth of a highly complex division of labor, political and trading relationships that extended as far south as Belize, and profound differences in and centralization of power and wealth. Charlton (1978, 1984) argues that these changes were predicated on the creation of a vertically and horizontally integrated monopoly over the production and distribution of obsidian tools. The growth of Teotihuacan profoundly changed the political and economic landscape not only of the Valley of Mexico, but all of Mesoamerica, which was integrated through interregional trade and ritual networks in ways that may have mirrored, in one region, the economic integration of the contemporary world.

HISTORICAL AND REGIONAL VARIATION

The variable K fluctuates historically in all human societies. Among agricultural societies, however, K almost invariably is lower than among hunting societies. When K is relatively high, competition is high, the presence of performance constraints reduces the power of gatekeepers, and coercion, exploitation, and corruption are relatively minor. When, however, K is low, competition is muted and the absence of performance constraints means that the power of gatekeepers is largely unrestrained. The effect is improvement of the well-being of gatekeepers at the expense of resource seekers.

The manorial system of the Middle Ages provides a classic example of a system with a low ratio of gatekeepers to resource seekers. In England, exploitation of the peasantry increased as the latter population grew over the course of the twelfth, thirteenth, and early fourteenth century. In the eleventh and in the early part of the twelfth centuries, there was not a clear distinction between farmers who worked land they held freehold and manorial tenants. Manorial tenants included villeins and cottars. Villeins farmed anywhere from 15 to 120 acres, depending on the quality of the soil, and were further divided into status groups based on the amount of land they leased. Cottars had only a house and a few acres of land, and relied on wage labor to make ends meet. Villeins might own some land, even cottars could aspire to land ownership, and freemen might lease land. Manorial requirements varied. A monastic community, for example, might produce primarily to feed itself. More commonly, produce from demesne lands both fed the lord and his household and was sold at market to provide cash for other goods and services. With the exception of absentee landlords or lay lords whose activities did not allow them to manage their agricultural estate directly, lords demanded labor services from their villeins in direct proportion to the amount of land they leased, not money payments. There was no countrywide judiciary and access to courts did not differentiate free from unfree.

However, the spread of royal courts in the late 1100s raised the question as to who would have access to them, and this occurred as the English population appears to have grown rapidly. Prices for food and land values rose, and production for the market became increasingly profitable just when living expenses were rising. By the middle of the twelfth century there was a widespread substitution of money payments for labor services. Many lords, who themselves held land by tenantry from the king, subleased their manors, sometimes to villeins, and thereby created an increasingly complex social and economic order. This tendency was reversed by the late twelfth century as lords began to work demesne lands directly, and they began to redefine and extend their demands to encompass, for instance, money rents for land, fines for the marriage of a daughter or for her "immoral" behavior, death duties, and a fine to succeed to an inherited tenancy. Villeins were denied access to any court other than their lord's. Villeins thus became bound to the manor (see Bolton, 1980: 19-22), unable to buy, sell or sublet their tenancies, unable to purchase land and so escape their bonds, and unable to leave the manor without the lord's permission. Villeins were compelled to allow the lord to use their equipment. They were also compelled to use and to pay for the use of the lord's mill to grind grain and of the lord's oven to bake bread, their staple food. By the thirteenth century, the free were effectively and clearly set apart from the unfree.

The manorial system that developed on the basis of decreases in K brought about by a growing English population withered away over the later portions of the fourteenth and the fifteenth centuries when depopulation from the Black Death created new resource access channels and competition among landlords. The death of from one-third to one-half of the English population left land vacant and created significant labor shortages. Real wage levels, which had fallen over the thirteenth and most of the fourteenth centuries, rose to levels they were not to reach again until the late nineteenth century. Villeins deserted their villages or did not pay their rents.

K varies cross-sectionally from one region of a country to another and from one segment of society to another, as well as historically. For example, the manorial constraints that bound villeins were not uniformly as severe as those described earlier, even in the early fourteenth century just prior to the Black Death. In substantial portions of thirteenth and early fourteenth-century England, an extraordinarily active market in land and in tenancies arose among smallholding freemen and villeins in response to the rise of food prices that increased the value of agricultural land and that led landlords to exert more control over their manors (MacFarlane, 1978). The gatekeeper position of manors was undermined in the presence of large numbers of freemen who bought and sold land at will. In these circumstances, Bolton notes (1980: 24),

> [landlords] had, in a sense, to bow to the inevitable. Ely Abbey in the twelfth and thirteenth centuries was content to see the creation of substantial numbers of free or semi-free tenants on newly assarted land. In the bishop's hamlet of Elm near Wisbech there were 7,000 acres of cleared land in 1251, of which 1,500 were held by ten free tenants, and 2,400 by censuarii, rent payers performing a few boon and carrying services. The result was that by the thirteenth century manors in East Anglia consisted of a nucleus of demesne and villein land surrounded by a sea of free or semi-free rent-paying peasants of so many kinds that definition is all but impossible.

In Cornwall in the southwest, the growth of tin mining weakened the manorial gatekeeper position and provided, likewise, for the emergence of leaseholding, free tenants.

Similarly, manorial exploitation was not limited to landlords. Barbara Hanawalt (1986: 121) points out that the villeinage had its own gatekeepers:

> Domination of village offices, such as juror, capital pledge, ale taster, and so on, not only offered social prestige but gave the office-holder a greater opportunity to manipulate competitors and further his own ends. In case of arrest, the officeholder could use his ties to ensure acquittal. In addition, some money could be made in petty corruption. So important were these positions that the primary village families jealously guarded access to these village offices and became village oligarchs.

What was true for a village was true also for towns and cities of England, particularly London (Bolton, 1980: 143-149). Town and city office-holders were not elected by popular vote and could not otherwise be held accountable for their management of city affairs. They controlled access to key services and resources and they used their positions to further enrich themselves. Where K has been very low at other times and places—in Chicago and New York City at various times over the past century, in the United States after Andrew Jackson's election, and in the Philippines, Liberia, Panama, and other contemporary Less Developed Countries—much the same can be said, of course (Handwerker, 1987).

INTERGENERATIONAL RELATIONS

K consistently appears to be very low in one realm of nearly all agricultural societies: intergenerational relations. Passage into adulthood tends to be defined by reference to marriage and economic independence. Selection favors the creation and effective management of material reciprocities with other adults, as just indicated. However, effective management of these relationships is significantly improved by exploiting children, who take on a gatekeeper function they do not possess in the context of hunting and gathering. Whereas children are ineffective producers in mobile hunting and gathering economies, they can contribute to productive tasks from early childhood in agricultural communities (Bradley, 1987). For example, Barbara Hanawalt's study *The Ties That Bound* (1986) reveals for English peasant households of the fourteenth and fifteenth centuries that by age 2-3 children's activities already conformed to the adult sexual division of labor—girls accompanied their mothers and boys accompanied their fathers. By age 4-5, children began to perform minor household chores, such as babysitting or fetching water. By age 6-12, children began to engage in real work that could supplement the family income in significant ways. Children of these ages collected vegetable foods, hunted, and fished, and boys of these ages could substitute for women in many farm tasks. Children took on adult work responsibilities during their teens.

The labor contributions that children make to the economy of their parents in nonindustrialized agricultural settings is widely and well-documented. These contributions do not necessarily wither with the development of an active wage-labor market, as occurred in England soon after the Norman conquest if not earlier. Hanawalt remarks "One of the most significant contributions a wife could make to the household economy [of the English peasantry during the fourteenth and fifteenth centuries] was the bearing and training of children" (1986: 148) because villeins could thereby significantly reduce their labor costs.

Cottars were not the only ones competing for wage-earning possibilities. Wealth villagers with plows, carts, and other equipment often hired themselves and their equipment to make extra money. Furthermore, if primary or secondary villagers had more than enough labor for their own fields, they sent some of their adolescent children to work for wages elsewhere [p. 115].

Debra Schumann's (1986) study of a contemporary Tzeltal Maya community in southern Mexico reveals, likewise, that families with the largest number of children were those who were most able to take advantage of wage labor and commercial agricultural opportunities.

Richard Wall's (1985) study of Colyton, a parish in southwest England, in 1851 reveals the same pattern for farmers, and extends this finding to the homes of laborers and craftsmen. Sons remained in school longer than did daughters, and the children of craftsmen remained in school longer than did the children of laborers. But nearly all the sons and daughters of both occupational groups were employed by age 14, and some began working by age 7 or 8. Possibly one-fifth of the sons under age 20 and about one-half of the daughters were employed by their parents. Even when they were not so employed, children's wages can be expected to have augmented significantly the household income. David Levine's (1977) study of nineteenth-century English communities reveals, likewise, that the labor contributions of children were critical for early industrial workers, perhaps especially for framework knitters (also see Eric Ross, 1986).

Children's gatekeeper functions extend beyond the labor services they provide when they are young, of course. As a Tzeltal Mayan observed, "Children cost when they are young, but as they grow older, they begin to give it back to you. And when you are old, they take care of you" (Schumann, 1986: 149). Levine (1977) suggests that this may have been true also for English protoindustrial workers (p. 81):

> Since domestic workers had nothing of value except their innate physical skills, their earnings tended to decline as they reached later middle age. In that their children would themselves create individual units of production, workers from the older generation would be provided for in their declining years. They could slot themselves into their children's domestic production units at precisely the time when the younger generation's families were suffering the most adverse dependency ratios.

Moreover, when children marry and establish their own households, the assistance they provide their parents may increase rather than decrease. For example, Tacitus comments that, among the Germanic tribes of northern Europe around 98 A.D., "The larger a man's kin and the greater the number of his relations by marriage, the stronger is his influence when he is old. Childlessness in Germany is not a paying profession" (Tacitus, 1948: 118). The same can be said for Africa. A woman's husband will show respect for his wife's parents by working on their farm, by helping them pay taxes, and by giving them gifts. A man's wife will show respect for her husband's family by helping them with household chores and by working on their farm. Through marriage, pawning or wardship, children open up additional avenues for support for their parents (or their foster parents) by providing alliances with other families. Recent economic and political changes in Africa have not altered children's role (see, e.g., Cleveland, 1986; Dorjahn, 1986; Handwerker, 1986c; Weil, 1986a; Bledsoe and Isiugo-Abanihe, forthcoming).

Personal material well-being in most agricultural societies thus depends heavily on the control parents exercise over children and on the control a senior generation exercises over its juniors. In most regions of the world, parents have maintained control over their children by functioning as gatekeepers for the strategic resources of land, labor (especially that provided by marriage and the birth of children), and the supernatural. Hierarchical subordinates—whether clients or children—are frequently explicitly conceptualized as wealth. This is as true of nineteenth century Russian serfs who lived in large, multifamily households (Czap, 1983) as it is of contemporary African smallholders who live predominantly in nuclear family households. Among the Grebo of Liberia, in West Africa, for example, daughters are especially prized. As one man commented to me as recently as 1984,

> A man with 10 daughters is a wealthy man. When each marries, he will get both a cow and a son-in-law to work on his farm. By the time all daughters are married, he will not have to work any more. He can simply visit each daughter in turn, and he will be well cared for as long as he lives.

Thus, even in agricultural societies that otherwise exhibit marked egalitarian characteristics, the relationships between parents and children and, more generally, between a parental generation and its junior, tends to be marked by clear hierarchy, exploitation, and coercion.

PROPERTIES OF SOCIAL PHENOMENA

Nearly all social behavior and social relationships can be described by reference to a small set of social properties. These are: power, hierarchy, equality, exploitation, corruption, coercion, cooperation, competition, and reciprocity. The degree to which social relationships are personalized or impersonal constitutes another basic property of social relationships. Like the preceding attributes, this quality of social phenomena also is subject to selection.

The behavior of both resource seekers and other gatekeepers can reduce an individual's resource access and, in their attempt to optimize resource access, both gatekeepers and resource seekers are mutually dependent. Gatekeepers can raise resource access costs; other gate-keepers can lower resource access costs; and resource seekers can be expected to seek lower access costs. Barbara Ward (1960) pointed out many years ago that the ability to anticipate correctly the behavior of others decreases the likelihood that their behavior will reduce one's resource access. It follows that selection will favor behavioral and cultural innovations that increase knowledge of these others. Such knowledge can be acquired by direct, personal interaction. Selection will favor (1) the formation of social relationships based on personal knowledge and (2) cultural and behavioral innovations that facilitate the formation of personalized social relationships. Innovations that meet this criterion include the commonly observed phenomena of food and information sharing and the provision of mutual assistance of various kinds—in short, cooperation that stems from personal relation-ships based on material reciprocities (cf. Axelrod and Hamilton, 1981).

Cooperation between resource channel gatekeepers reduces the competition that stems from increases in resource channels (C), but the ability to create and maintain cooperative reciprocities entails costs. It follows, for resource channel gatekeepers, that the selective importance of such relationships with other gatekeepers varies directly with the number of resource access channels (C) to a limit set by the costs of creating and maintaining those ties, and inversely thereafter. Conversely, for gatekeepers the selective importance of reciprocities based on personal relationships with resource seekers varies inversely with the selective importance of such relationships with other gatekeepers.

For example, studies of retailers in Liberian market places in 1970 revealed varying degrees of gatekeeper cooperative reciprocity (e.g., Handwerker, 1973, 1979), as have similar studies of small-scale retailing throughout the world (e.g., Mintz, 1964, Davis, 1973). Adjacent traders looked after the goods of each other if one had to be absent, traders sold to each other at wholesale rather than retail rates, and, as one trader explained, "so that people will not buy only from one person," they set prices together when it was possible. However, it was possible to set prices together only when a small set of traders dealt in the same line of foodstuffs or merchandise. As the number of such traders increased, traders pointed out that "we do not know the people that spoil our prices because the sellers are too many." It was only in the small groups that price reductions could be traced to individuals who then could be "disciplined." Cooperative price setting was possible only rarely. Most traders used price and service concessions to minimize the risks of trading in a highly competitive environment. Price and service concessions were granted primarily as personal material reciprocities—a trader's "good customers" received these concessions so long as they regularly made purchases from the trader.

Personal social relationships between gatekeepers and resource seekers reduce resource channel access costs. It follows that the intensity of exploitation varies inversely with the formation of personal social relationships based on reciprocity (see Handwerker, 1987). Because the intensity of exploitation varies directly with K, it follows that, for resource seekers, the selective importance of reciprocities based on personal social relationships with gatekeepers varies inversely with K. Sidney Mintz and Eric Wolf, for instance, have shown in a classic study of ritual coparenthood (1950) that such ties were created hierarchically at the height of European feudalism and in Latin American villages that exhibited a strong hierarchical organization. Conversely, such hierarchical relationships broke down as the European feudal system crumbled and were not important in Latin American villages that did not have a strong hierarchical organization.

SOCIAL STRUCTURE AND SOCIAL DYNAMICS

All social relationships and social groups exhibit all of the properties of social relationships at one time or another and in various combinations. The distinctive qualities of particular social relationships and particular social groups are distinctive configurations of these qualities that were created and display patterned change by selection. Social properties come into being and change with shifts in resources and in the access costs attached to particular resources and resource access channels. These changes occur because intelligent people naturally generate new ways of conceiving and acting in the world, and selection favors those innovations that improve or optimize resource access.

It follows that, at a particular point in time and space, resource set R can be characterized by specific relationships among gatekeepers and between gatekeepers and resource seekers. These relationships will exhibit particular degrees and configurations of power, hierarchy, equality, exploitation, corruption, coercion, competition, cooperation, and reciprocity based on personal relationships. Let "resource structure" refer to these relationships and their properties. Selection will concentrate important conceptual and behavioral innovations. Hence, we can expect that people will tend to believe that what they do is morally appropriate. Let "moral economy" refer to the beliefs and behavior that people use to gain access to resources.

Social relationships with a distinctive configuration of properties should exhibit a characteristic equilibrium at an identifiable point E, if there occurs no change in resources or in resource access channels. Thus we shall find some degree of consensus in values and behavior at particular points in time and space. These conjunctions of value-consensus and behavior have been the focus of ethnographies since anthropologists first conducted field studies. But we may have misjudged their significance, for equilibria of these kinds are ephemeral.

Over any historical sequence we will observe conceptual and behavioral innovation. Selection will favor those that improve or optimize resource access—namely, innovations that both create and maintain gatekeeper positions and innovations that create new resources and new resource access channels and thus subvert existing gatekeeper positions and power. As Marx observed, analysis will reveal conflict between resource gatekeepers and resource seekers if we look closely at social relationships over any historical period. Social relations are created and changed by the parties to the relationship, through explicit or hidden negotiation or other means of competition (e.g., Comaroff and Roberts, 1981, Bledsoe, 1980, Murphy, 1988). Historical dynamics reflect conflict between gatekeepers who wish to consolidate and extend their position and resource seekers who have their own interests. These interests frequently can best be served by subverting the position of gatekeepers. Historical change is driven by behavioral and conceptual innovations that arise as the necessary outcome of the way in which our brains process information, by changes in climatic, edaphic, biotic, and human demographic parameters, and by selection, which must concentrate innovations that optimize or improve resource access, and thus builds relatively advantageous means of acquiring resources and eliminates innovations that interfere with the process of resource acquisition.

POWER RELATIONSHIPS AND HIGH FERTILITY

Parent-child relationships are mediated by the costs attached to resources and to resource access channels, as are all social relationships. Parents can be expected to occupy hierarchicaly superior positions to the extent to which they monopolize the channels by which children can access resources. If, simultaneously, children occupy positions as resource channel gatekeepers (as they do in nearly all nonindustrialized agricultural societies), childbearing will constitute an investment activity. Parents can improve or optimize resource access only if they maximize fertility or completed family size. Fertility will be largely determined by intermediate fertility variables other than contraception and abortion, and fertility levels will be "high" (the exact level of which will be a function of the determinants of the other intermediate fertility variable parameters). Because selection can be expected to concentrate important conceptual and behavioral innovations, we can expect that the moral economy of childbearing and parent-child relationships will stipulate mutual obligations. Because K is large for parents and small for children, however, we can expect that the obligations children have to their parents should take precedence over the obligations parents have to their children.

The varied interests of men and women may overlap, but they never constitute identical sets, and women always function as gatekeepers for the resource of children. Women's power relative to men rises when children function as important resource channel gatekeepers for both men and women, as in most African societies. Women's power relative to men falls when children function as important resource channel gatekeepers only for women. Thus high fertility occurs as one effect of the costs that attach to resources and the means *women* can use to gain access to resources. Childbearing constitutes an investment activity for women when their material well-being is dependent on their spouses, children, and parents.

For example, English marital fertility rates fluctuated between 9.25 and 9.69 between 1600 and 1800 (Wrigley and Schofield, 1983) and plausibly were equally as high during earlier centuries. We know that various means of contraception and abortion were both known and used in England very early. However, the demographic data reveal that fertility control was not widely or effectively practiced.

This was not because fathers wanted large families. In his book, *Marriage and Love in England, 1300-1840* (1986), Alan MacFarlane shows that English men could not count children as one of their investments for as far back as we have clear records.[2] Prevailing opinion held that people who had too many children brought economic hardship upon themselves. Ownership and property rights were individualized in England, parents could disinherit children, and children could do likewise. Consequently, children could not be counted on to support their elderly parents when a manorial organization, a guild, the Church Poor Relief, or the State failed to do so adequately. Children were known to steal their mothers' inheritances, to cheat their elderly fathers, and to send an aged mother out to beg for bread. Husbands commonly made provision for the care of their wives in their wills, and retirement contracts made with children or, more often, with strangers, were commonly used to secure an adequate living in old age.

MacFarlane's account of English family relationships reveals that the power of men was high relative to their parents, especially their fathers. Men generally found that their fathers' gatekeeper functions dissipated once they became adults because the structure of the English economy allowed men avenues for social and economic mobility independently of parents. They in turn could serve only minor gatekeeper functions for their adult children. When fathers looked to their adult children for economic assistance, of course, there could be very sharp conflict. But, generally, fathers did not expect economic assistance from their adult children and they sought to secure their own material well-being through their own efforts. Marriage could provide a life companion, but, as MacFarlane points out, for men, children were not essential to a marriage.

This was not true for English women, who could perform important gatekeeper functions for their children, especially their daughters, well into adulthood. Women, who were dependent largely on husbands for their economic well-being during their youth, looked to their mothers and children for both emotional and economic support throughout their lives.

Women's dependence on their children and spouses was made clear as early as 600 A.D. in England's earliest law code, that of Aethelbert of Kent, which stipulated that a widow shall inherit one-half of the goods left by her husband, but only if she had born a living child (Briggs, 1983: 50). Miriam Slater's study of the Verney family correspondence (1984), an extraordinary series of documents that spans several centuries and 12 generations, reveals that seventeenth-century women of the gentry viewed marriage very differently from men. Ladies may have enjoyed a relatively comfortable level of living as children, but marriage was the only effective means they had of maintaining or improving their material well-being. As Slater (1984) remarks, "In the society of the upper gentry there were few career options for younger sons, but there was only one for daughters" (p. 80). Spinsters were a drain on family resources and, family affections notwithstanding, they received from their brothers or fathers as little as the law allowed.

This was not a novel development and it was not one restricted to the seventeenth century. Eileen Power (1975: 40-41) reports that a similar pattern existed several centuries previously. Marriage was itself both social and economic career. A fifteenth-century woman, like Margaret Paston, organized and managed significant portions of her husband's manor and substituted for him in his absence, even seeing to the military defense in the event of an attack. In the late Victorian period, ladies of the upper and middle classes organized households that employed a small army of servants and managed annual budgets of several thousand pounds sterling, in addition to engaging in the social "calling" rituals by which such households established, maintained, and changed their social and economic status (Dyhouse, 1986). Jane Lewis (1984: 3) reports that English women continued to equate spinsterhood with social failure as recently as the early twentieth century. Spinsterhood and social failure continued to be so equated because spinsterhood meant economic failure. As Cicely Hamilton observed (1909), marriage itself was a woman's trade.

From very early in English history, women could own land and buy and sell it at will; women worked alongside their husbands, whether they were farmers or artisans; and women could work independently of men. Many women, especially those in the lower social orders, worked all of their lives. But this "freedom" was severely circumscribed. Married women were legally subordinated to their husbands and did not acquire substantive control over their income and property until the late nineteenth century. English statute legalized wage discrimination on the basis of sex as early as 1388 (Hanawalt, 1986: 151). The independent employment options for women were, in fact, relatively few. Hanawalt's account of peasant women in late medieval England (1986: 141-155) reveals that the primary employment opportunities for unmarried women were domestic service (in an urban center, on a manor, or in the home of a brother) and prostitution. Women's independent work opportunities increased with the industrial revolution of the eighteenth and nineteenth centuries, but only in minor ways. In addition to domestic service and prostitution, women could also find employment in textile manufacturing. However, the market for female labor could be flooded more easily than could the labor markets for men because it was so narrow. Consequently, women's wages not only were subject to legal constraints, they were also subject to significant market constraints (Prior, 1985). Hanawalt (1986: 151) points out, moreover, that while peasant women of the fourteenth and fifteenth centuries "could bring suit on their own, they had no access to magisterial roles and seldom even used attorneys." Women's options for attaining a relatively satisfactory standard of living by themselves, consequently, were negligible. If ladies could improve their material well-being by marriage, women low in the English social hierarchy were likely to find that marriage improved their livelihood substantially more, at least when they were young. As recently as the late nineteenth and early twentieth centuries, the average wage of such women was below subsistence levels (Lewis, 1984: 3).

John Burnett (1982) has edited and provided a synthesis of about 800 autobiographies that described what people remembered of their childhood, education, and families over the period 1820 to 1920. Burnett points out that there were many hardworking and caring husbands and fathers, but he also observes that fathers are remembered all too commonly as "a drunkard, often thoughtless and uncaring of wife and children, bad tempered and selfish, but occasionally overgenerous and sentimental" (1982: 233). Fathers spent most of their time away from the home. Men were expected to work and to provide for their families and their time with their children was reduced by the time they spent working. However, after work or when they were unemployed, men spent their time away from home drinking with friends and in the company of women other than their wives. When men were home they rarely shared in household chores. Consequently, they had time to play with the children. But they also took the lion's share of the family resources, and they abused their wives. More often than not, men alienated their children and wives, and were perceived as irresponsible. This was particularly true for the vast majority of the English population, those in the lower levels of the social hierarchy. Consequently, sons adopted a protective role toward their mothers from an early age; if necessary, they physically restrained their fathers during parental arguments. Mothers, by contrast, are remembered as being overburdened with work. Mothers were remembered occasionally as nagging and demanding, and thus, not always warmly. But whereas children developed relationships with their fathers that are generously described as "remote," they developed close emotional relationships with their mothers. Mothers are remembered consistently as performing innumerable, onerous chores without thought of themselves and often at great sacrifice, especially when they were deserted by their husbands.

Retirement contracts appear to have been quite important to men, whose activities tended to alienate their children and who might serve only minor gatekeeper functions for their children. However, mothers tended to develop strong emotional ties with their children. If their children did not otherwise provide for them adequately when they grew old, women could use their estates to secure a good retirement contract for themselves, either with their children or with someone else. But mothers tended to look to their children for critical support in their old age and most children appear to have acknowledged the debt. As Ralph Houlbrooke notes (1984: 195), during the period from 1450 to 1700,

Children were widely looked upon as a possible source of support in old age despite the existence of a long tradition of cautionary tales warning parents not to depend on them. . . . Although few elderly couples, save in the upper ranks of society, lived in the same household with their married children, many of the widowed elderly, especially women, found a refuge under a filial roof. As grandparents, the old in turn often proved a useful source of assistance in childcare.

Standish Meacham (1977) and Diana Gittins (1986) document an equivalent pattern for the late, nineteenth and early twentieth centuries. Moreover, the greater volume of data available for this recent time period permits them to show that grandmother-daughter-grandchildren linkages provided essential family continuity, mutual care, and economic support. Women frequently spent a portion of their early married years living in their mothers' homes and they took care of their mothers when the latter grew old. During the years they lived in separate households, mothers and daughters sought each other's company and support whenever circumstances permitted. Working class mothers who raised respectable daughters who married promising young men raised their own status and economic circumstances along with that of their daughters. By contrast, men were expected to take care of themselves and were cared for by their children only irregularly. All too often, as Jill Quadagno (1982: 150) reports, for men "retirement meant a choice between unemployment and pauperization."

Thus it is understandable, as MacFarlane observes, that women were quite anxious to marry and, indeed, that they perceived a great deal of competition for eligible males. For many men, marriage often was very disadvantageous and offered little more than companionship or partnership. On average, men married very late, only in their late twenties, and significant numbers of men never married at all. The average age at marriage rose and fell over the centuries with fluctuations in resource access because, for men, marriage itself was a consumption expenditure for which they had to accumulate sufficient resources. By contrast, for women, marriage was an investment activity and often constituted the only real chance they had to secure a reasonable livelihood. Similarly, men might be interested only marginally in having children, and might indeed come to look upon subsequent pregnancies as merely adding to their burdens. But for women childbearing could secure additional income in their youths and children provided security they otherwise might not have as they grew old. To understand why English women bore children throughout their reproductive careers, it is sufficient to observe that without children their lives would be very bleak indeed.

POWER RELATIONSHIPS AND FERTILITY TRANSITION

Childbearing becomes a consumption activity when children do not function as important resource channel gatekeepers, as the case of English fathers makes clear. When children do not function as resource channel gatekeepers, parents can optimize resource access only if they sharply restrict their childbearing. Because the parental gatekeeper position would be subject to selection for lower resource access costs, parental demands on children can be expected to moderate. Because selection can be expected to concentrate important conceptual and behavioral innovations, we can expect that the moral economy of childbearing and parent-child relationships will continue to stipulate reciprocity. But because K diminishes for parents and increases for children, we can expect that parents will come to believe that childbearing should not take precedence over other activities and that the obligations they have to their children should take precedence over the obligations their children have to them.

Caldwell (1982) argues that these changes in the moral economy of childbearing and parent-child relationships may uniquely identify the phenomenon of fertility transition. The resource access hypothesis leads to the same conclusion, but modifies it in ways that are revealed in the historical record for England. In historical England, these relationships between the value of K and the moral economy of parent-child relationships reflected differences in the power of men and women relative to each other, their children and their parents. English *total* fertility was relatively low because men had to balance the costs of rearing children with the advantages of a wife and, consequently, many men never married, and those who did married very late in life. English *marital* fertility was very high because childbearing was an investment activity for English women. A population's total fertility can decline dramatically only to the extent that *women* adopt these views of moral economy and this will happen only when women's power rises dramatically relative to men, their children, and their parents.

Thus fertility transition occurs as one effect of a fundamental transformation of the costs that attach to resources and to means *women* can use to gain access to resources. Childbearing may shift from an investment to a consumption activity by direct governmental manipulation of the costs that attach to existing resources and resource access channels. Childbearing also shifts from an investment to a consumption activity with an increase in K that stems from the emergence of new and competitive resource access channels.

When men have served as resource gatekeepers for women, as they have in both England and the Caribbean, such an increase in K simultaneously creates conflict between women and men. Moreover, an increase in aggregate K reduces the selective importance of personal social relationships among resource seekers. Consequently, such an increase in K brings about a general depersonalization of social relationships, and the use of social relationships to justify material assistance shifts from being morally right to being morally wrong. Such an increase in K thus brings about a revolution in the ways in which individual women and men, and entire generations, relate to one another. These are the changes in social relationships and fertility that characterize the modern world revolution.

These conditions began to be met in England during the latter half of the 1800s. Late Victorian England was a country of immense wealth that was distributed extraordinarily inequitably. By 1914, England had undergone fundamental social and economic transformations. England's industrial revolution over the late 1700s and the early 1800s was accomplished on the basis of legislation that protected infant industries from international competition and that permitted real wages to fall to less than half their level in 1507-1508. The maturation of English industrialization was accomplished by providing goods and materials that Germany and the United States used to fuel their own industrial revolutions, by investing in railway development in Latin America and India, and so by creating a market for English manufactures and reducing the costs of imported raw materials, and where possible, as in India and the West Indies, by suppressing industries that might have competed with English firms. Barriers to international competition were brought down in the name of free trade when English products no longer needed protection. England's industrial economy thus matured as it became increasingly dependent on international trade, which fueled the industrial development of other countries.

By the mid- to late-1800s, England began to encounter significant economic competition from the United States, Germany, and, by the early twentieth century, even from Japan. Both technological changes and competition selected for industrial centralization, the growth of firms with increasingly complex organization, and higher workforce educational requirements. The demands of Empire, made most clear perhaps by the Crimean War debacle, led to the establishment of a system of open competitive examinations for civil service placement in 1870, just prior to England's greatest imperial expansion—over the period 1880 to 1914. Universal education was made compulsory through the primary grades by 1876. Patronage and clientship became more restricted both in the areas of social and economic life to which they could be applied and in the rewards they could accrue. Real wages rose consistently after the mid-1800s. By the late 1800s, the husband-as-breadwinner family model had become an ideal for families throughout the English social hierarchy and the ability to provide all of the income necessary for maintaining a wife and children had become a key component of a man's reputation. Not having to work had become the mark of respectability for a wife. Improvements in health care brought about a significant reduction in both morbidity and mortality. Women experienced significantly expanded resource access opportunities in the context of an economy and political system that was subject to increasing competition from international sources. The Married Women's Property Acts of 1870 and 1882 guaranteed women's rights to property whether it was acquired prior to marriage or afterward, even though they did not succeed in giving married women the legal status of single women. Organized feminist movements emerged in the face of men's opposition to women's new resource access opportunities. English marital fertility began to fall by the late 1800s and fell precipitously during the first decades of the twentieth century.

English marital fertility fell as the structure of the English economy diversified and became more competitive. Fertility did not fall pre-cipitously or uniformly because the structural changes that eliminated childrens' gatekeeper functions for their mothers varied with time and place and by occupational and social position. Rising incomes and new goods and services continued to be accessed best through children for significant sectors of the English population, both urban and rural, well into the early twentieth century. Declining levels of infant and early childhood mortality merely improved the economic circumstances of such families. Ellen Ross (1986) shows that working class mothers in London worked their children hard when they were young and expected very specific financial returns when their children matured and began to work on their own. Their children appeared generally to look forward to the day when they could contribute materially to the support of their mothers, which is not unlike the view taken by many young people in Africa even today. In part, English children took it upon themselves to assist their mothers because it was their duty. In part, also, they took pride in attaining a mark of adulthood. This was especially true for boys, who were expected to become family breadwinners. Ellen Ross comments (1986: 87-88):

> Henry John Begg's formulation of his boyhood dream "to help" might stand for many others: "That was my one prayer, if I could only find some money or get hold of some money to help my mother. Yes. I used to feel so

very very sorry for poor old mum you know. Perhaps I'd see her sitting there crying, you know, well, don't know what her trouble was you know." Will Crooks, describing his childhood in the 1850s and 1860s in Poplar, recounts a vivid memory of waking up at night to see his mother crying "through wondering where the next meal is coming from," as she explained. The boy whispered to himself: "Wait till I'm a man! Won't I work for my mother when I'm a man!" Indeed when, at age thirteen, he earned his first half sovereign, he came running home with it: "Mother, mother, I've earned half a sovereign, and all of it myself, and its yours, all yours, every bit yours!" The words of a Pentonville girl, born in 1896 are very similar, yet she was the sixth child, clearly not the first to take a paid job. After working for 3/6d as a "learner" in a garment factory for six months, she finally graduated to better earnings. "Oh—the first—the first time I earned ten bob. Oh, I had a little thin—ten shilling piece—wasn't I half pleased when I brought it home to my mum. She gave me sixpence out of it."

Women in this situation did not limit their fertility or did so only in minor ways (e.g., Woods and Smith, 1983).

The English fertility transition began first, some time in the late Victorian period,[3] primarily in the mid- to upper levels of the social and economic hierarchy. Women married to men who were pursuing a meritocratic career ladder found, like their husbands, that they could look forward to a financial security that middle- and upper-class women of earlier generations could not. Resource access through children was severely circumscribed. In part, this was because children had to pass through increasingly longer unproductive periods of formal schooling. In part, this was because, once they began their own careers, children began to find that personal social relationships of patronage and clientship could not be counted on to create marked improvements in their careers. Mothers' resource access through personal relationships created by their children, which is still of vital importance in much of Africa (Handwerker, 1987), became decreasingly important in an economy in which competence was becoming the criterion for employment and promotion. This change in the structure of the English economy freed middle- and upper-class women from dependence for resource access on their children but did not alleviate their dependence on their husbands (see, e.g., Dyhouse, 1986). However, as education became an increasingly important criterion for career and income placement and advancement, such women found that they could contribute to the career advancement of their husbands and thus to their own standard of living from their youth to their old age, by reducing the number of children they bore.[4]

English fertility began to fall rapidly, however, only after the turn of the century when women, like men, found that they could look forward to genuine careers, even if those careers paid much less than the ones available to men. Women in the upper and upper middle classes found that they could create careers for themselves in the professions. Women in the lower middle classes and in the working classes began to experience the structural changes that had been experienced earlier by women higher in the English social order, for their husbands' incomes rose and their husbands' occupations began to offer career tracks and regular increases in pay. Moreover, these women found that they too could create careers for themselves—for example, in teaching, midwifery, and nursing. Women's employment did more than merely maintain subsistence. Lavinia Church, along with other women teachers (Copelman, 1986), found that her own employment generated a rising standard of living. Increasing proportions of women found that childbearing had ceased to be an investment activity. Childbearing now restricted one's ability to work, whether in a factory or in pursuing a career or in securing a satisfactory level of economic well-being from one's husband's income. Fertility fell because childbearing had finally become a consumption activity for women as well as for men.

It is important to emphasize that childbearing was not transformed from an investment activity to a consumption activity merely because worker participation rates for women increased. As indicated earlier, nearly all women were productive workers most of their lives through most of English history. Women's worker participation rates prior to 1800 almost certainly were markedly higher than they were in the early twentieth century. Childbearing ceased to be an investment activity because the character of the economy and the character of the work and its remuneration had changed profoundly and had eliminated children's gatekeeper functions for their mothers.

The gatekeeper functions of children were not eliminated because restrictions were placed on the use of child labor or because education was made compulsory (cf. Gittins, 1982). Child labor laws date to 1847 and compulsory education laws date to 1876. As previously indicated, children retained their gatekeeper functions for their mothers well into the twentieth century, at least in some sectors of the English population. These gatekeeper functions were eliminated by the structural changes that marked the maturation of England's industrial economy.

The maturation of the industrial economy was marked by increases in K and, consequently, by increases in the level of competition to which English firms and the English government was subject. Selection for concepts and behavior that optimize or improve resource access meant that material well-being became contingent on the criteria of educational accomplishments and competence. The income flows accessible to mothers through their children necessarily and correspondingly diminished. High fertility came to affect adversely the material aspirations of parents for themselves, their children, and/or both. The moral economy of childbearing and parent-child relationships changed, and fertility transition was initiated.

Standard social theory interprets fertility transition as integral to a broad and highly interdependent process of societal modernization encompassing changes in health care, per capita income, education, industrialization, and urbanization. Jack Caldwell's wealth-flows theory interprets fertility transition as the outcome of an equally broad process of Westernization stemming from the onset of mass education and increases in mass media consumption. The resource access hypothesis holds, to the contrary, (1) that fertility transition is independent of most of these processes; (2) that, of the processes identified by standard transition theory, only industrialization may bring about transition; but (3) that industrialization can bring about transition only when it is characterized by the presence of new and competitive resource access channels available to both men and women; (4) that reversal of the relative obligations of (and the flow of wealth between) parents and children does, indeed, distinguish fertility transition from other kinds of fertility declines; but (5) that this reversal stems not from Westernization but from the emergence of new and competitive resource access channels.

Historical data on English family relationships and fertility support these claims (contra Smith, 1981; and Cleland and Wilson, 1987; see Woods, 1987; Robinson, 1987). English marital fertility declined as English society "modernized" and as mass public education was established. But English fertility did not fall because of a broad and highly interdependent process of "modernization." Fertility decline can be traced specifically to the elimination of the gatekeeping functions of children, which transformed childbearing from an investment to a consumption activity for women. The elimination of the gatekeeping functions of children for their mothers can be traced to very specific changes in the economy—an increasing dependence on international trade in an increasingly competitive environment, legislation that allowed property rights for married women, and the proliferation of educational opportunities for women and for men that led to increasingly well-paying employment for both. Similarly, English fertility did not fall because mass public education was established or because the average level of education rose. Women who began to limit their family sizes were those who could use education to free themselves from their prior dependence on the gatekeeping functions of their children. Most English women did not experience these changes until long after the establishment of mass public education.

Historical data of the kind reviewed here do not permit a clear, comparative test of the contrasting claims of the modernization hypothesis, Caldwell's Westernization hypothesis, or the resource access hypothesis outlined in this chapter. Data on the social changes and fertility transition on Barbados over the period 1950 to 1980 do.

NOTES

1. Tacitus (1948) reported a similar phenomenon for the otherwise monogamous German tribes during the first century A.D. (p. 115).

2. The historical data on England reviewed in the latter portion of this chapter are reported on more fully in Handwerker (1988a).

3. All accounts of the English fertility transition date the origins of fertility decline to the late Victorian period. Various dates, from 1850 to 1880, have been suggested. The data, however, are ambiguous. For example, the men whom Banks (1981) identifies as "pioneers" in family limitation are also the men whose extra-marital escapades might have led them to be "pioneers" in infecting their wives with gonorrhea, a disease that may have reached significant proportions in the late Victorian period. Whereas male symptoms of the disease tend to be unmistakable, women's symptoms may be minor or may be confused with other abdominal ailments. The prevalence of venereal disease can be expected to reduce marital fertility and may well explain the declines in fertility that Banks and others have documented. Fertility declined slowly over the late 1800s, but whether this decline can legitimately be equated with a marital fertility transition will not be clear until or if fertility decline from venereal disease can be estimated.

4. Middle- and upper-class English women's resource access positions and experiences were varied and, even now, cannot be unequivocally documented. We need much more detail of the kind Jeanne Petersen's (1984) study of the Paget women reveal. Women's resource access position, rather than their husbands', was the deciding factor in the English fertility transition nonetheless. For example, we can expect that middle- and upper-class women who remained dependent on their children for resource access subverted their husbands' attempts to limit family size.

—3—

MUTUAL EXPLOITATION
OF WEAKNESS

BARBADIAN FAMILY RELATIONSHIPS IN THE 1950s

Barbadian family relationships during the 1950s displayed the characteristics that are commonly attributed to West Indian family organization. Outside of the upper class, family relationships have been characterized by (1) weak conjugal bonds, (2) the relative absence of stable nuclear family units, (3) weak bonds between fathers and children, and (4) strong bonds between mothers and children (e.g., Clark, 1966; R. T. Smith, 1956; M. G. Smith, 1962; Gonzales, 1969; Horowitz, 1967a, 1967b; Slater, 1977; Otterbein, 1965; cf. Henry and Wilson, 1975). These structural features tended to be manifested in a developmental cycle of visiting unions, consensual cohabitation, and legal marriage. Both men and women took part in a relatively large number of spousal relationships in which women were expected to remain faithful to husbands but in which it was unrealistic to expect husbands to reciprocate. Women were economically dependent on men. In their youth they depended on financial support from spouses; in their old age they depended on financial support from sons and (through their daughters) their sons-in-law. Legal marriage was contingent on men's ability to provide a house and the specific advantage of legal marriage was material: Marriage legitimized women's inheritance rights and the inheritance rights of (at least some of) their children; marriage assured that men's property would be well cared for when they migrated off the island to find work. Although most people might eventually contract legal marriages, these tended to occur late in life. Because of the shortage of men, many women could not establish such relationships and instead established long-lasting visiting unions with men who were married legally or consensually. Consequently, most childbearing—from 40 to nearly 80% of all births in any one year over the last 30—has occurred outside of legal marriage.

THE FAMILY LIFE COURSE

Sidney Greenfield (1961, 1966) very nicely traces the life course of relationships between men and women in the 1950s and in the process clearly delineates the character of spousal and parent-child relationships. This section on the family life course relies almost exclusively on Greenfield's report of fieldwork he carried out in a village in the parish of St. George during 1956-1957. In sections that follow, data I collected in 1985 (see the appendix) are used to expand on Greenfield's account. In these latter sections, I cite Greenfield's report to demonstrate the correspondence between his data and mine.

First Relationships

Barbadian standards of propriety meant that daughters should be shielded from the parentally unwanted interest of young men. The only acceptable meeting grounds for young men and women were church social gatherings. These meetings were known to the young women in Greenfield's field site as "Meet-hims" because it was at these gatherings that women in their teens came to know and become interested in particular young men. Contacts made initially at "Meet-hims" led young people to arrange secret meetings elsewhere, where they could come to know one another better. The normal course of relationship development led to secret meetings at the girl's home when her parents were away. These meetings tended to initiate sexual relationships.

Sexual relationships, of course, tended to precipitate pregnancies. If the girl did not get pregnant, the couple might separate and the course of male-female relationships began anew with different partners. However, pregnancy brought the developing relationship to a turning point, for the couple had to consider seriously their ability to assume adult parental responsibilities. Moreover, parents became involved. As elsewhere in the Caribbean, the discovery of the first pregnancy was accompanied by parental anger, recriminations, beatings, and threats to throw the girl out of the house. Parental anger was followed by family reconciliation.

If the young man did not want to continue the relationship, he might deny responsibility and simply sever the relationship. If the young man acknowledged that he was the father but he was in no position to assume the adult responsibilities of husband and father, the child might be fostered either by his parents or by the parents of the mother. If the child was fostered by a grandparent(s), the young couple was relieved of their parental responsibilities. Simultaneously, however, they relinquished their parental rights. Some young mothers chose to keep the child. A young mother without spousal support normally continued to live with her parents, but she had to find work to help with household expenses or she had to establish a relationship with a man who would agree to support her financially. She shared the support money with her mother.

Visiting Unions

If the couple agreed to continue their relationship after the woman became pregnant, the couple might marry legally. The costs of a traditional Barbadian wedding were very high (Greenfield, 1966: 101) and marriage normally required that the man provide a home (Greenfield, 1966: 90-94) for himself, his wife, and child. Very few young men could afford to marry, and this option was rarely chosen. The normal course of events was for the young man to "be friendly" with the young woman. He would formally request the approval of the young woman's father, and would promise to support and care for the woman and the child. He continued to live at his own home, but he slept with the woman in her parents' house. To provide regular cash support for his child and spouse, the young man's earnings began to be split between his spouse and his mother, whom he had helped support since beginning work.

In their teens and early twenties, young men were heavily dependent on the cooking, washing, ironing, and other services provided by their mothers. Mothers, in turn, expected monetary support from their sons. A son's establishment of a visiting relationship with a woman directly threatened his mother's material well-being and created a period of sharp stress for spousal relationships. Mothers frequently tried to break up relationships developed by their sons. They would find fault with the son's spouse, question the girl's morals, suggest that the girlfriend was seeing other men, and cater to their son's preferences in food and care. The degree of stress the mother generated tended to correspond with the degree to which she was dependent on her son's income. Since such income added significantly to most mothers' well-being, the danger mothers-in-law posed to spousal relationships became widely understood. As a young woman commented to me in 1985,

> There is a saying—I've heard it *a lot*: "Mothers-in-law break up most marriages." The mother be tellin' the man he forgettin' her! and the wife be tellin' the man "when are you going to grow up and cut the apron strings!"

A woman, now in her sixties, remarked that soon after she began living with her first husband, her "man's mother came over, knocked on her door, and started making trouble, saying the man is for her; he is her son and he owes her." Young women, of course, believed that a man owed his spouse, not his mother, once he established a serious relationship with a woman. Women's parental obligations were not abrogated by a union, and were met with money women earned independently of their spouses and with household money provided by spouses.

Persistent and severe criticism commonly was successful and the spousal relationship—and the support provided the woman and her child— dissolved. Consequently, a single woman with children had to struggle along on meager wages or with parental assistance until she could establish a visiting relationship with another man. Some young women actually preferred the status of daughter, especially if their fathers were well-off, and were quite content to seek only visiting relationships with men. If a woman was an only daughter, she might even be required to remain at home to look after her parents. These situations were exceptional, however.

Not all unions were subjected to severe maternal criticism. The mother-in-law might die or she might have adequate material support either from her spouse or from an older son. The spousal relationship continued to develop in these circumstances. The young woman began "to do" for her man—to cook for him, to wash and iron his clothes, and to provide the other domestic services. The young man would move into the house of his wife's parents. This movement marked a significant change in the union, for it meant that sons would cease to provide their mothers with significant portions of their income and it meant that daughters who formerly shared spousal support money with their own mothers ceased doing so. These changes transformed a visiting relationship into a consensual union. The social unit that was formed by these changes functioned as a distinct economic and family unit, even though it shared a roof with the wife's parents.

Consensual Unions

The formation of a consensual union created new relationships between a man and his in-laws that eventually led to another period of stress. Initially, a man's in-laws might be very sympathetic with the plight of the young couple—they, after all, may have shared the same circumstances when younger. Moreover, when he moved in with his in-laws, the young man extended his commitment to their daughter and grandchildren. In exchange for rent-free housing, he undertook to support both fully.

However, standards of male accomplishment dictated that one man should not be subordinate to another and that a man should demonstrate his ability to support a spouse and children by providing independent housing (cf. Wilson, 1973). Over time, fathers-in-law would come to resent having another family in the same house and sons-in-law would come to resent their dependence on in-laws. Grumbling from a woman's parents would find expression in her own dissatisfaction of having to remain in her parents' house.

If the young couple had saved enough money to construct their own home, they would do so and move into it. In the more likely event that they had not accumulated sufficient savings for this purpose, parental discontent and grumbling often led young men to avoid their in-laws whenever possible, and to spend much time away from the house. Men who removed themselves in this way tended to establish a relationship with another woman. This second relationship might be only a visiting relationship. However, such relationships frequently developed into regular consensual unions in which the man moved in with the second spouse. This was especially likely if she had a house or was less demanding than the first spouse. Movement out of the first spouse's house into the house of the second effectively dissolved the first union. When the union dissolved, financial support from the former spouse might decline and become intermittent. More likely, financial support ceased altogether. The former spouse then was forced to work to support herself and her children until she could establish a visiting or consensual union with a new mate.

However, the couple might obtain a house either by inheritance or by borrowing enough money to construct one, and so be able to establish an independent residence. Marriage was out of the question if the couple went into debt to construct their own house. The woman was expected to work to help pay off the indebtedness. She was also forced to work to assist with the household finances of a growing family if her spouse's employment and income remained low and intermittent. A man's authority within the family unit declined to the extent to which his spouse became economically independent. If he remained unemployed or marginally employed when sons began to work, the earnings they passed to their mother could make her fully independent of her spouse. In these circumstances, practical authority for the household shifted from a woman's spouse to herself.

Legal Marriage

If the couple did not go into debt to construct their house, their newly independent status often was marked by their legal marriage. As Greenfield (1966) remarked,

> One of the primary motivations for legal marriage appears to be the desire to insure the property rights of the conjugal partner and children. It is significant that in cases of intestacy in the absence of lawful heirs, all property reverts to the siblings of the deceased and their lawful descendants, with illegitimate children of the property owner receiving nothing [p. 99].

During the 1950s, Barbadian law defined all children borne outside of legal marriages as illegitimate. Children borne to a couple prior to their marriage were not legitimized by the subsequent marriage. To become legitimized, their births had to be reregistered and few people went to the trouble to do so. Marriage did, however, ensure the inheritance rights of wives. Moreover, men often took advantage of contract farm labor in the United States or sought to emigrate to England. In their absence, a legal wife with interests in the property would see to it that the house was well cared for and passed on to their children (cf. Dirks and Kerns, 1976).

It was a source of intense pride to Barbadian men if they could fully and adequately support their families through their own efforts. If the couple married legally the woman commonly remained at home as a housewife. It was not looked down upon for a woman to work outside the home so long as that was her choice. Her income was hers alone; her husband was expected to provide all the expenses for running the home by providing her with a portion of his weekly pay.

NUMERICAL DELINEATION OF THE LIFE COURSE

Table 3.1 presents the average proportions of a year women aged 50 or over in 1985 spent in different forms of marital unions. Women of these ages are those who both began and ended their reproductive careers during the 1950s and thus their reports fairly summarize the experience of Barbadian women during this period.

These data reveal that during the 1950s a woman under age 20 was likely to spend little time in a sexual union of any kind. As Greenfield reported, spousal relationships at this age were predominantly visiting unions. The dramatic decline in the average time not spent in a spousal

TABLE 3.1
Yearly Union Durations and Age-Specific Fertility in the 1950s

Union Type	15-19	20-24	25-29	30-34	35-39	40-44	45-49
Legal	.039	.207	.417	.539	.617	.613	.624
Consensual	.042	.154	.222	.239	.187	.161	.128
Visiting	.382	.459	.270	.132	.108	.092	.062
Out of Union	.537	.180	.091	.090	.088	.134	.186
ASFR	.151	.234	.228	.179	.110	.024	.008

Aggregate total fertility: 4.67 children

union by the early twenties indicates that women who had not become involved with men in their teens did so afterwards. As these women became involved with young men, the average period of time spent in visiting unions rose. Women who had been involved with men in the late teens, however, began to experience the changes in spousal relationships Greenfield documented. Significant proportions of these women married legally or transformed the visiting relationship to a consensual union.

The average period of time spent in different forms of unions from the late twenties through the end of the reproductive period reflects the relative economic circumstances of men and women. The relative proportion of time spent out of union was minimal from women's late twenties through their late thirties. By this period of a woman's life, she was likely to have significant help from children who had been born when she was a teenager or in her early twenties. Assistance from children brought about the economic independence Greenfield mentioned and thus reduced the need for a spousal relationship. The relative proportion of time spent uninvolved in a spousal relationship increased sharply in a woman's early forties and rose further by the end of her reproductive span.[1]

The proportion of time that women spent in visiting relationships declined dramatically between the early and the late twenties and fell consistently thereafter. The men whom women become involved with tended to become interested in the more durable unions that women sought. The persisting incidence of visiting unions primarily reflects the skewed sex ratio that made it impossible for all women to establish monogamous spousal relationships (cf. Marino, 1970).

The proportion of time spent in consensual unions peaked in the early thirties, fell dramatically in the late thirties, and declined consistently thereafter. The proportion of time spent in legal marriages, however, doubled between the early twenties and the late twenties, rose until the late thirties, and remained fairly stable through the end of the reproductive period. The incidence of legal marriage reflected, as Greenfield suggests, the relative economic circumstances of men. A period of consensual union tended to be bypassed at these older ages because the men involved with these women were older and, thus more likely than younger men to be able to transform visiting unions directly into legal marriages. Simultaneously, these were the years in which women whom had been involved in consensual unions realized circumstances in which they could become legally married. The persistence of consensual unions, of course, primarily reflected the continuing poor economic circumstances of some men.

BARBADIAN RESOURCE STRUCTURE
AND SOCIAL RELATIONSHIPS

Barbadian family relationships during the 1950s reflected specific islandwide power relationships predicated on a resource structure shaped by the demands of sugar production and by ramifications on Barbados of the growth of a world sugar market. Barbados was settled in the mid 1620s by planters who were among the earliest English inhabitants of the New World. The island was uninhabited and covered with forest and bush when the English arrived, although both Arawak and Carib Indians had left traces of their earlier occupation. Initial attempts to produce tobacco and cotton were unprofitable. However, with Dutch technical assistance, planters began to grow sugar cane. By 1650, Barbados had become the first major sugar producer of the emerging British empire and its fortunes were tied inextricably to sugar for the next 310 years. As early as 1680, the island had become home to 70,000 people. Nearly the entire island had been brought under cultivation.

Sugar Cane

Sugar cane is a tall perennial grass that appears to have been domesticated originally in India. It grows best when there is abundant sunshine, uniform warm temperatures, and relatively abundant rainfall that is distributed fairly evenly over the year. Sucrose, a dissachiride that consists of glucose and fructose, occurs in solution as a high proportion of the pithy portion of the stem, and can be extracted by crushing the pith. Crystallized sugar is produced by controlled boiling and evaporation of the water in which the sucrose is dissolved. The evaporation procedure yields molasses as a by-product. Molasses, when distilled, yields rum.[2]

Sugar cane is propagated originally from cuttings and matures in 10 to 18 months. On Barbados, cane usually has been planted in November and December and has been harvested between January and May, about a year and a half later. Sugar cane will grow for 10-15 years, however. Like other grasses, cane will grow from stubble (ratoons). However, ratoon productivity declines over time.

Sugar cane thus shares with certain other crops—for example, rubber, cocoa, coffee, tea, and coconuts—several key properties: (1) there is a significant delay between the time when the crop is planted and the time when it can be harvested; (2) there is a delay between the time when it can be harvested and the time when the yield is maximized; and (3) there is a period of declining yield. Cane has a related property, namely that its sucrose yield drops precipitously after it is cut. It must be processed rapidly for a maximum yield. Processing also adds significantly to the unit value of the crop, and tremendously reduces transportation costs. Sugar cane processing, however, requires a significant capital investment. Thus sugar cane, like these other crops, does not lend itself to significant commercial production solely by smallholders. It is a crop that requires large amounts of both labor and capital for optimal productivity. The commercial production of sugar cane, like rubber, cocoa, coffee, tea, and coconuts, selected for the plantation mode of agricultural production that came to dominate Caribbean island economies.

Plantations

Plantations are New World adaptations to the commercial production of one or two crops with the properties previously noted, although their cultural prototypes emerged in the Mediterranean (see Grigg, 1974). Plantations are a combination of self-contained community, factory, and agricultural estate, and thus provide a comprehensive political and economic framework for the lives of the people who are part of them. The corporate structure of the plantation means that the activities of the organization will be directed by a small number of managers. Its corporate structure also presupposes financial resources or credit by which the enterprise can wait out the period before production, and can obtain and maintain the necessary processing equipment.

Barbadian estates, like estates throughout the British West Indies, were financed originally by English merchants or merchant groups. Planters and Caribbean-based merchants participated in the marketing of sugar during the initial growth of the plantation economy. The Navigation Acts passed by the English parliament in the late seventeenth century, however, eliminated the trading freedoms Barbadians had experienced earlier and channeled trade and investment to London. By the eighteenth century the trading pattern was for planters to consign to London commission agents all of their sugar exports. These agents arranged for the sale of the sugar, forwarded capital and consumption goods to the planter on account, and invested residual profits. By the middle of the eighteenth century, West Indian plantations were largely run on credit from London commission houses that invested plantation profits only partly back into the West Indies. During this period, the West India Interest in Britain, which centered around absentee planters and the commission houses that served the West Indies, lobbied policies in Parliament that protected British West Indian sugar from competition from other sources of supply.

Plantations can operate profitably only when they control the production from relatively extensive areas, even when they enjoy a protected market. This means that plantations must control the production of large numbers of smallholders, or they must plant and harvest from large areas. The first option was not feasible during the initial period of settlement in the Caribbean, and to plant and harvest from large areas required a large, but not a skilled, labor force. To provide for the labor force meant that plantations had to provide for their own food and energy supplies, their own roads, perform their own construction, and provide their own housing, entertainments, and health care. Typically, only about half of a West Indian plantation was planted in cane; the other half had to be devoted to woodlands, housing areas, and grounds for growing food "provisions." Despite early efforts to produce their own food supplies, sugar production took precedence and West Indian estates soon were nearly wholly dependent on imports for their food and finished products.

Plantation labor was originally provided by English indentured servants, some who came voluntarily and others, perhaps the vast majority, who were kidnapped or forcibly deported from England. The English Civil War broke out soon after Barbados was settled and, during Cromwell's reign, it became policy to "barbadose" criminals and objectionable prisoners of war. Although the original group of Barbadian settlers brought with them 10 slaves captured from a Spanish vessel en route, by 1640 there were still less than 6,000 African slaves and slightly more than 37,000 whites on the island. The vast majority of whites were indentured servants, but this number also included 11,200 smallholders. By 1680, however, there were more than 40,000 African slaves. Servants had fled, or left the island after they had worked off their seven-year period of indenture. There was no unclaimed land they could work. Some smallholders were bought out by large planters. Others, who found that they could acquire no further land on Barbados, migrated to regions in which they could, such as Antigua, St. Kitts, Virginia, South Carolina, Surinam, Martinique, Guadeloupe, and Jamaica. Free, skilled craftsmen followed the small planters to other islands. The white population has continued its downward trajectory ever since.

Barbados and the Maturation of
the English Industrial Economy

By the end of the eighteenth century, the English economy had begun to industrialize and England had acquired a world empire the most important components of which were in Asia, and that did not depend on the use of slave labor. The protectionist legislation passed earlier in the century continued to protect West Indian planters, which now were only a backwater of the British Empire. Sugar was produced much more cheaply in the French West Indies and in British-controlled India and Mauritius. British-controlled territories could not produce all the sugar that British manufacturers needed, and they imported sugar from Brazil, Cuba, and the French territories.

However, import duties continued to keep prices high for British consumers and prevented the growth of the internal sugar market. The same duties forced up prices for the goods English manufacturers sought to sell overseas. British sugar refiners could not compete effectively with their French, German, and Dutch rivals. Protectionist policies began to be questioned on the basis of Adam Smith's radical notion that a nation's production could be maximized if both labor and trade were free, and the advantages that Caribbean planters had enjoyed were gradually reduced. The English Parliament abolished the slave trade in 1808 and emancipated slaves throughout its empire in 1834. Between 1846 and 1855, sugar duties were equalized, making it possible for all sugar to be imported into Britain at the same rate as West Indian sugar. Competition from other cane growing regions was significantly augmented by the emergence of sugar production from beets in the late 1800s. Within the Caribbean, Cuba became a major sugar producer and was responsible for about half of all the sugar produced in the region by the mid-nineteenth century. Cuba was responsible for three-quarters of all the sugar produced in the region, and for 30% of the world's supply, by the end of the century.

These events precipitated fundamental changes in Caribbean economies because they lowered sugar profits at the same time that they threatened to raise the costs of production. The abolition of the slave trade meant that planters would have to change the conditions of plantation life in ways that promoted the survival and reproduction of their labor forces. Emancipation meant that planters would have to attract a labor force with wages and better working conditions. The equalization of sugar duties meant that planters would have to improve their productivity. The advent of steam power crushers increased the amount of juice one could extract from cane by 25% or more. Vacuum pans made it possible to control the evaporation process more efficiently. Boiling could occur at lower temperatures and there was less danger of loss by overheating. Centrifugal driers made it possible to separate crystalline sugar from molasses more efficiently. But these technical innovations required a large capital outlay and a much larger volume of cane to justify that investment.

West Indian creditors became increasingly reluctant to extend or to expand planter indebtedness as the date for abolition and emancipation came nearer. After emancipation, planters throughout the West Indies found it difficult to obtain a reliable labor supply, and credit for capital improvements became almost impossible to obtain. The labor problem was not entirely resolved by the importation of large numbers of East Indian indentured workers over the last half of the nineteenth century. Planters throughout the West Indies went bankrupt or abandoned their estates. By the beginning of the twentieth century, sugar continued to dominate the economies of only four former British West Indian countries: St. Kitts-Nevis, Antigua, British Guiana (now, Guyana), and Barbados.

In England, by contrast, the growth in the size and competitiveness of the world market for sugar selected for mergers and consolidation that reduced domestic competition and that placed firms in a more competitive international position. At the beginning of the nineteenth century, there were several thousand West Indian plantations, each owned by individuals or by families. At the end of the nineteenth century, there remained only a fraction of the original number and most of these had become subsidiaries of growing multinational corporations. The maturation of England's industrial economy was marked by the emergence of vertically and horizontally integrated multinational corporations, and this was as true for sugar as it was for the other sectors of the economy.

Barbados remained aloof from the foreign corporate consolidation of its industry.[3] While sugar was declining elsewhere in the British West Indies, Barbadian sugar exports rose consistently. On Barbados, it was possible to operate estates profitably even in the face of reduced prices because the costs of production were so low. Barbadian planters, unlike planters on most other islands, were able to mesh an abundant and relatively cheap labor supply with a series of technical improvements in production and extraction. Crop rotations were introduced, manuring was increased, and better weeding and mulching practices were developed. The first steam factory on Barbados was established in 1841; there were 95 by 1890. Barbadians consolidated their own plantations. They were able to do so because of a fortuitous conjunction of political independence, an extraordinarily rapid growth in population, and an absence of local commercial or financial competition from English or North American firms.

First, Barbados enjoyed an unusual degree of political independence. The English Civil War, which provided Barbados further settlers, also provided an opportunity for the planters to assert their independence from England. Cromwell reestablished English control of the island, but only at the cost of granting the island a significant degree of parliamentary self-government. The Articles of Agreement that acknowledged English authority and Barbadian self-government were ratified by the English Parliament in 1651, and have provided the basis for Barbadians' claim that, outside England itself, they have the oldest continuing parliamentary democracy in the world—albeit one with a franchise extended until recently almost exclusively to propertied, white males. The small size of the island limited the size of the plantations that could be formed, and so limited the profits that could be realized. Consequently, it limited the number of planters who could establish themselves as absentee owners in England. The relatively large proportion of planters who were resident on the island used their powers of self-government to make nonresident ownership of Barbadian estates nearly impossible (see Karch, 1979: 142-156).

Second, the Barbadian population increased more than three-fold over the nineteenth century. Conditions of slavery were considerably ameliorated over the last years of the eighteenth and the first years of the nineteenth centuries. The Barbadian population increased from around 60,000 to nearly 200,000 solely on the basis of improved living conditions, and in the face of significant levels of emigration toward the end of this period (Lowenthal, 1957: 449). Barbadian planters did not face the significant labor shortages after Emancipation that plagued planters elsewhere in the West Indies. The increases in wages and large-scale importation of Asian labor that were used in other sugar-producing regions of the Caribbean were unnecessary on Barbados. The island's population density was easily the highest in the region.

The absence of unclaimed land onto which they might relocate meant that freed slaves had to remain on the plantations. The lure of higher wages and better working conditions elsewhere led some Barbadians to emigrate. But the Barbadian government placed constraints on this movement and these opportunities were eliminated once significant levels of Asian indentured laborers began to be imported to Trinidad and British Guiana. Moreover, the equalization of sugar duties was accompanied by a decline in wages throughout the region.

Although emigration was sharply curtailed until the end of the nineteenth century, wage competition among planters made it possible for workers to seek better working conditions and higher wages and led to labor supply uncertainties. The Masters and Servants Act of 1840 created what came to be known as the "located-laborer system" and stabilized plantation work forces. In return for an allotment of land on which to erect a house and grow food, workers paid a rent either in cash or labor and were required to work on the plantation for five days a week at a fixed wage below the market price.

Third, the withdrawal of British commission houses created a commercial and financial vacuum that was filled by Barbadian merchants, who could cater to the consumption needs of a population that grew at an annual rate of more than 1.2%. By the early twentieth century, the Barbadian commercial sector had come to be dominated by a small number of firms known, even today, as "The Big Six": Jones and Swan, Da Costa, Wilkinson and Haynes, R. and G. Challenor, Manning, and Gardiner Austin (see Karch, 1979: 156-184). These firms functioned as commission agents, importer-wholesalers, shipping operators, and as retailers. Profits made locally were reinvested throughout the West Indies, but particularly in Barbados and in Barbadian plantations. As Barbadian merchants financed and bought into Barbadian estates, they made possible the capital improvements necessary for the survival of an independent sugar industry. However, their growth and expansion also challenged the control exercised previously only by the heavily indebted "plantocracy."

The Big Six controlled the pricing and viability of all smaller distributors on the island because banks would lend money only to large commercial houses. Their import-export oligopoly thus could not be challenged by firms lower in the distribution hierarchy, which depended on them both for credit and supplies. Banks also would lend to large planters, who controlled and limited the growth of smallholders. But planters were dependent on the Big Six for the marketing of their production and for all of their supplies. The commercial firms had invested heavily in the production sector of the economy and, by virtue of their position in both production and distribution, dominated the economy. Plantations, Ltd. was formed in 1917 as a cooperative venture by planters to challenge the position of the Big Six. Plantations, Ltd. acted as a wholesale purchaser of supplies required by member estates, as a marketing agent that would purchase produce at market rates, and as a retailer. The Big Six formed Barbados Trading and Shipping in 1920 to counter the planter challenge. Together, these firms controlled all of the central sugar factories on the island and controlled all exports and imports. In 1934, Plantations, Ltd. and B.S.& T. joined together in the Barbados Produce Exporter's Association to form a monopoly controller of the island's economy.

Cecilia Karch (1979: 157-158) points out that the corporate consolidation of Barbadian estates was integral to the consolidation of production, distribution, and political power in the hands of a new agro-commercial elite. This oligopoly, like the plantocracy it superseded, functioned as a gatekeeper for all others on the island for all essential resources. A small professional, managerial, and white-collar middle class grew over the nineteenth century. It was mostly white, but it included an increasing number of black merchants and well-educated black professionals. Irrespective of color, the middle class depended on the elite and on the firms controlled by the elite for credit, clients, and job security. Barbadian society included a small number of poor whites, the Redlegs (Sheppard, 1977), who lived on the fringe of the white community. The vast majority of Barbadians, however, were poor blacks who were largely dependent on the plantations for employment. Such employment was available only seasonally, and was subject to all the vicissitudes of the sugar industry—hurricanes, drought, and market prices.

The agro-commercial elite on Barbados was not under significant external competitive pressure over the first half of the twentieth century. European and North American firms were not attracted to the island, Barbadian sugar exports rose significantly after 1920 and, after World War II cut off supplies of sugar from Asia and Europe, Barbados and other West Indian sugar producers enjoyed a protected market in the UK that lasted until 1951. The Barbadian oligopoly effectively stifled internal economic growth and development. As one would expect when resource access is highly centralized among a small number of inter-related gatekeepers (see Chapter 2), moreover, prices were high, wages and salaries were low, and employment and advancement were dependent on elite patronage. The conditions of living for the immense black lower class of laborers may have been the worst in the entire British West Indies. Infant mortality rates are widely recognized as one of the most sensitive indicators of material poverty. Barbadian infant mortality compared very unfavorably with the infant mortality rates in tropical Africa. Early in the century, one out of every four infants died before his or her first birthday. Infant mortality varied seasonally. It was low during crop time, when employment was most available. When plantation employment was not available, one out of every two children born died before age 1. As late as the 1950s, nearly 15% of all infants born alive died before their first birthdays.

Living conditions for most Barbadians worsened over the last portion of the nineteenth century and the first portion of the twentieth. Over the last half of the nineteenth century, as many as 50,000 Barbadians may have emigrated to Trinidad and British Guiana, and smaller numbers emigrated to Surinam and St. Croix (Marshall, 1982). Most of these migrants returned home, but many remained, and even today there is a trickle return migration by the children or grandchildren of these emigrants. From 1904 to 1914, as many as 60,000 Barbadians migrated to Panama to work on the Panama Canal (Newton, 1984: 93, 96). Of this number, 42,000 may not have returned to the island. The Great Depression eliminated these safety valves and so precipitated massive labor disturbances in Barbados as throughout the Caribbean. The size and extent of the unrest in the Caribbean led Britain to send a series of Commissions to investigate the conditions that had given rise to them. Their subsequent reports vividly documented the abysmal circumstances of the powerless lower classes.

These reports, especially the Moyne Commission Report, established grounds for fundamental political change. On Barbados, the Barbados Labor Party was formed and established a formal alliance between nonwhites in both the lower and middle classes. Its industrial branch formed into the Barbados Worker's Union in 1941 with assistance from British labor organizers. The franchise, that had begun to be extended in the late nineteenth century, was made universal in 1943. By the 1950s, blacks controlled the Barbadian Assembly and set in motion a series of actions that were to transform the island in fundamental ways.

RESOURCE STRUCTURE AND FAMILY RELATIONSHIPS

As of the 1950s, however, Barbadian resource structure was fundamentally unchanged. It was oligarchic and, thus paternalistic. It allocated opportunities largely on the basis of personal relationships, and these on basis of sex, class, and color.

This meant that most Barbadian men and women could optimize their resource control only if they exploited the weaknesses of the other. Men exploited women's economic dependence on them to gain sexual conquests, children, and unquestioned authority, attributes that enhanced men's reputations and thus their ability to find and maintain employment. Women exploited men's desire for children, men's absence from the home, the money men spent not on the family but at the rum shop and on other women, and men's failure to develop close relationships with their children to undermine both the authority and the emotional closeness children might feel for their fathers. In this way, women turned childbearing into a means for obtaining liens both on men's income and on the income of their mature children.

Women's Economic Dependence

The fact that women were economically dependent on men did not mean that women didn't work. On the contrary, 1946 census data reveal that female worker participation rates averaged close to 60% from age 15 through age 55, and female worker participation rates were probably higher in the 1950s than after 1960 (see Massiah, 1984: 86). Economic dependence stemmed simply from the fact that work available to women was almost solely restricted to menial employment at wages much lower than men's. Thus in 1946, 98.5% of all women workers were employed in "manufacturing" (meaning cottage industry, mostly seamstress work), "commerce" (meaning petty trade), and "services" (meaning domestic work; Massiah, 1984: 114). Women's situation had changed little by the mid-1950s. As one parent commented to Greenfield (1966), "You are lucky if a daughter can earn enough to help herself, let alone help you" (p. 105).

A young woman's resource access and thus her material welfare was conditional on liens she held on men's wages. She gained these liens through spousal relationships. Such relationships, however, were unstable. And even stable relationships required her subservience. Men exploited women's dependent position to obtain sex, children, and unquestioned authority, all of which contributed significantly to men's sense of self-esteem. A male, after all, was not a "man" unless—and to the extent to which—he could boast among peers of his sexual conquests, his sons, and his ability to provide a house and income for a woman to whom he was legally married.

Men's Economic Dependence

These accomplishments were important to men for two primary reasons. First, Barbadian resource structure generally denied men opportunities for any other source of control and freedom. Second, what little control a man exerted over the resources on which his well-being depended was obtained via personal relationships and his reputation among peers and superiors. Because the resource gatekeeper organizations monopolized employment opportunities on the island and were not subject to important competitive pressures themselves, personal relationships, rather than technical competence, were of critical importance (see Handwerker, 1987).

The instability of employment led in Barbados, as elsewhere in the Caribbean, to a pattern of occupational multiplicity. Thus Greenfield observed (1966: 68) that "steady employment at a given job, so normal to Western observers, is the exception rather than the rule. Most individuals in the lower and middle classes usually work at two or three jobs at a time, devoting more or less time to each job as circumstances require." One's ability to find consistent employment and one's ability to search out the few available opportunities for advancement were conditional on personal contacts and personal recommendations. As an older man observed to me:

> You had to live in circles, you had to keep societies where the white people were. If you wanted to get the big office job, the coloured had to get mix up, have a friend to tell the white man you don't have a job. That friend will tell his friend that he has a friend who needs a job, and you would get through.

Another man elaborated:

> It was important to know people in certain positions—not really for you to know them but for them to know you. Because without that they are no help to you. For instance, I was in the army and I wanted to go on the police force. My army officer and the police officer were friends and I only had to tell him I wanted to join. The police only have 7 or 8 positions and there were 700-800 people wanting those jobs. But for me, I had no problem of selection. My contacts were already made and my job was assured. I know people who took the exam for police work and who got in long after I did. It might not have been the best way, because qualifications had nothing to do with acceptance, but it was the general way you got ahead.

Richardson (1985) suggests, at least obliquely, that such paternalism began to decline with the emergence of contractual labor. My data indicate, to the contrary, that such paternalism was still strong in the 1950s. As Greenfield (1966: 71) observed, paternalism was even apparent in union activities: "The high wages and increased security [available to unionized sugar workers] appear to have resulted in a recent tendency for the factory Works Committee to have a strong say as to who is to be employed, and to the restriction of hiring to close relatives, specifically children of the older employees." The Barbados Ministry of Labor organized an employment bureau in the early 1950s. The 1957 annual report commented on the failure of the employment bureau because "of the reluctance of the larger employers of labour to use [the bureau]. Nearly all jobs are filled by personal contacts, and even the majority of employers of casual labour prefer to take their workers from an unsightly knot of men hanging around the site" (p. 7).

In the 1950s, the private sector was still very small and not subject to significant levels of competition. As one person commented: "Everybody knew everybody." If you wanted a good job, you turned to your connections in this large family. From the perspective of employers, hiring tended to be casual—one man in his late fifties described hiring practices the following way:

> Oh yes, that is the Jackson boy. I know his father. Tell him to come around tomorrow and we will see where we can fit him in.

In the upper and middle classes, as in the lower (see next), fathers accepted a responsibility to place their sons in good positions. They did so by consulting the boy and by contacting their friends and friends of friends who were engaged in work in which the boy expressed some interest. Once employed, it was almost unheard of for anyone to be fired even if they consistently performed poorly. One distinguished business executive observed that "One of the biggest crimes on Barbados is to fire someone." Employers, after all, knew the boy's parents—or knew of the boy's parents—and may have been close friends of the family. Because firms were not subject to significant levels of competition, incompetents did not constitute serious threats to their economic viability. Firing employees who performed less than fully satisfactorily would only, and unnecessarily, create ill-will among people whose good-will (and whose continuing purchases from the firm) could ease life in this island family.

Greenfield (1966: 73-75) emphasizes the importance on Barbados of the belief that anyone who works hard may achieve the goals he desires. This belief appears as strongly held in the 1980s as it was when Greenfield was in the field. Nonetheless, people outside this family had poor prospects. As an older man pointed out, "Blacks were not seen in banks then" (see Karch, 1981). The only way up was either by getting out or making connections. "Connections" were contingent on being known as a man with a "good character." *Character* was not defined in terms of skills, talent, or job performance. Instead, *character* was defined in terms of a man's (or his father's) reputation for honesty, deference to those in higher positions, ability to follow superiors' instructions, and ability to maintain his position as a man—that is, he should adequately support his family, maintain proper discipline of children, and demonstrate prowess with women.

The material importance of one's reputation selected for behavioral patterns which women, in turn, could exploit. To maximize their reputation and, thus their income potential, men sought positions of absolute authority within their homes, but spent their time at work and in the company of friends. The more successful men took advantage of the surplus of women to establish extramarital relationships.

MEN AND FAMILIES

Home Ownership

One cannot overestimate the importance of house ownership in Barbados. A house symbolized and legitimized an independence and authority that, outside the agro-commercial elite and the small middle class, was available to neither men nor women. Within his house, a man had nearly absolute say over anything that might concern him, assuming that his income also was sufficient. In fact, few young men ever were in a position to own their own homes. Greenfield (1966: 129) reports that only 18.5% of all houses were owned by men younger than 40 years of age. Since much of the pride men took in themselves, and much of the respect given them by others, was contingent on house ownership, this meant that a major goal in men's lives was to become owner of their own house.

Household authority was contingent on house ownership. If the house belonged to the man, he had undisputed say about decisions that affected the household. Both within the household and outside, for public consumption, men asserted their unquestioned authority. As one person noted, "If my father came home and he didn't like the food my mother cooked, he would throw it out the door—the food, the pot, the plates! He would say, 'If I don't like it, no one will eat it.'"

Many men appeared to believe that women simply were not sufficiently responsible to assume a position as a major household decision maker. As one man commented, "I am the one who made decisions for my household. I don't think a woman is sensible enough." Some women agreed and rationalized their position relative to men as being biblically grounded. Many men simply observed that "I am the boss!" Women who accepted their subservience to men believed that men appropriately fulfilled their familial duties when they brought in the income and made the household decisions.

This position of authority, of course, was not accompanied by men's participation in household affairs. "Minor" decisions concerning everyday household maintenance and such were clearly women's responsibilities. Nonetheless, a husband's position of authority was impressed upon children when, upon asking their mother if they could go out to play or to visit a friend, their mother sent them to their father for permission. It made no difference that fathers sent the children back to the mother. As one woman saw it, "That [earning money and making decisions] is what he is here for!"

The preceding comments do not mean that women uniformly accepted their subservient status. On the contrary, 78.5% of the women aged 55-64 (those aged 20-44 during the 1950s) reported that they expected their husband to treat them as equals. However, only 33.9% of these women reported that their spouses actually met these expectations. Some women, in short, were fortunate to find companionship in their spousal relationship(s). Most commonly, however, women described spouses as "not really part of my family" and described their spousal relationship in words best summarized by the comment of a 57-year-old woman: "He [my husband] just wanted a slave, not a companion."

Women's subservience to men, and men's attitudes toward women, were grounded proximately in their early household training. A 59-year-old woman explained that she had not expected her husband to help around the house: "That is something you have to learn from your mother's house and, as a man, he did not want to work in the house because he was not taught that housework was a man's job." All children began working when they were capable of helping. Girls learned early that their life's work was to bear children and serve a man. As early as age 5 or 6, girls began to sweep, dust, straighten, to wash, dry, and put dishes away, to fetch water, to put water on for tea, to look for eggs, feed the chickens, collect firewood, and to wash, dry, and iron clothes. Boys, too, were assigned small tasks at early ages. But women consistently reported that their brothers did not begin regularly helping around the house until they were significantly older—at ages 8 or 9. Moreover, the jobs boys were assigned followed a sexual division of responsibilities in which their tasks were primarily outside chores—boys took care of the stock and helped their fathers. Most important, boys' work was never as continuous as that of their sisters. Boys, consequently, had much more leisure time than did girls. As boys, men received the message that their proper place was outside the home. As girls, women received the message that their place was to marry and serve a man. The skills they learned were explicitly designed to facilitate these ends. One woman noted that her mother taught her that "if you want a man you need to cook. The first thing a man wants in a wife is a cook."

A woman's subservience to a man was reinforced when she lived in his house. The economic basis of female dependency was clearly understood by most women. When explaining why their spouses treated them as inferiors, women commonly reported that "he worked for more money and I lived at his house; therefore, I had to do what he wanted." If implicit economic sanctions were insufficient, men asserted their authority physically: "I couldn't say what I wanted; if I did I'd get my face beat up."

Given these circumstances, if a couple first lived in a house the woman owned, her spouse was given additional incentive to build his own house. Even if he was successful, however, the woman was highly unlikely to move into a house that was owned by her husband. Conversely, if a woman inherited a house, she was likely to move out of her husband's house. Women who owned their own houses were less subject to spousal demands. Women house owners possibly had the most congenial spousal relationships, for men who remained in a union with such a woman either had to circumscribe their overt authority or had developed a genuine affection and concern for the woman. More commonly, the underlying conflict between men and women was made explicit when women came to own a house, and led to the dissolution of the relationship.

Men: In Households and Out

Thus men's family responsibilities were minimal. They consisted primarily of providing a dwelling and financial support for his spouse and children. As Greenfield (1966) observed:

Most of [a man's] day is spent away from home at his place of employment. He has little contact with the other members of the household, but his consent is necessary for any major decisions affecting any members of his family. He usually gives his wife a fixed amount of money every week, holding the balance for himself. Her share is used to cover all expenses of managing the household [p. 102].

and:

> If the man works close to home, he will return for his food, usually eaten alone. When he is finished he will take care of odd jobs, leaving to return to work before the children are home from school. Only in rare instances will he have time to play with the younger children or to see the older ones on their return from school [p. 86].

Men would rarely cook, sweep floors, wash, or care for the children (cf. Greenfield, 1966: 103-104). Of the women 55-64 years of age in 1985—those who were aged 20-44 during the 1950s—only 27.7% reported that spouses helped cook; only 18.5% reported that spouses helped wash clothes; only 33.8% reported that spouses helped wash dishes; only 21.9% reported that spouses helped bathe the children; and only 60.9% reported that men helped care for the children—and then mainly in their capacity as disciplinarians.

Financial responsibility for sons was terminated when they were old enough to work on their own. After a boy had completed his formal schooling, his father helped him learn a trade. Once the boy was employed, however, fathers assumed no further support obligations. Fathers took for granted that daughters had poor economic prospects and supported them as long as they continued to live at home. Stepfathers, however, might resent having to support other men's daughters and might try in various ways to force such girls to find homes elsewhere. This contingency was especially likely if he was the house owner. Fathers (including stepfathers) also assumed the responsibility for protecting daughters from the unwanted attentions of young men, disciplining them if their relationships were not sufficiently discreet, and representing the interests of the girl and her mother when a young man wished to formalize his commitment to the girl and the pending child. To shorten the time that stepdaughters remained financially dependent on them, stepfathers were more likely to encourage the attentions of suitors.

Such concern for their daughters' (or their stepdaughters') respectability did not, of course, extend to other men's daughters. Greenfield (1966: 104) notes that "It is assumed that a man, especially if moderately successful, will have extramarital affairs":

> It is normal for a man to take most of his entertainment in the company of male friends. No activities are ever planned to which the husband and wife go as a couple. Excursions and dances may be attended by a group of men who will seek female companionship while at the social affair. A wide range of behavior may take place at such times, but a man is not guilty of improper conduct as long as his escapades are not committed within his

wife's presence. Infidelity is tolerated as long as it is not embarrassing to the wife.

Older men concurred with this assessment. As one man explained to me:

> A fellow felt he was a big man when he can walk into his house and into other women's houses and show that he is a man. That was the order of the day to have children all around. The man had his family to support and what he worked for had to support them. And what else he had he'd give the other women.

This pattern of extraresidential mating owes much to Barbados' low sex ratio. Women were rarely able to achieve even a moderate level of material well-being independent of men and the scarcity of men meant that some women could never become part of a monogamous consensual union or legal marriage. These circumstances created a significant level of competition among women for the available support from men.

Whereas young men may have recognized the advantage their relative scarcity gave them in their dealings with women, young women frequently did not perceive the converse. Their mothers led them to believe that respectable young women should have certain standards for behavior in a man and that they should look for men who met those standards. In the past, it is possible that many young women did not learn about the pattern wherein married men had girlfriends and outside children because men's visiting unions with other women frequently were kept as secrets open only to older women and men. One 32-year-old woman commented: "When I was young, I never knew men had girlfriends. I was such a silly girl!" Girlfriends were common, but much talked about only behind one's back—and men tried to keep their extramarital affairs secret. One woman cited an instance of a neighbor's mother who went to see who was at her door one day. Her husband slept at home every night and she had never had reason for thinking that the man had a girlfriend. A woman was at the door and asked to see her husband. The neighbor's mother was a bit affronted—it wasn't proper for other women to come to your home to ask for your husband—and she asked for an explanation. She was told that [one of the woman's sons] was sick. It turned out the man had four other children by this other woman—and they were teenagers! Another woman related an instance in which a woman discovered belatedly that her best friend had been her husband's girlfriend for years.

Young women today commonly recognize this pattern but learn about it most commonly through their friends, who talk about the affairs of other men, or when they read letters printed in the newspaper advice column. Mothers still married to a daughter's father have not shared with their daughters the problems they have had with their own husbands. Instead, they have substituted oblique aphorisms such as: "Don't look for a married man" or "Home drums beat first" or "Never live with a man until he marries you—why should he buy the cow when he can get the milk free!"

Be that as it may, the knowledge that men are likely to have extramarital affairs does not arouse noticeable levels of anxiety among younger women. One such woman, recently married, commented merely that "I hope it doesn't happen to me." But it appears that many young women do not perceive the pattern for married men to have girlfriends as real; it is something that happens to other women. Women who grow up in homes where the father has left, or women who discover spousal infidelity, gain personal experience of a kind that raises quite serious anxieties.

The shortage of men can become evident when a woman suddenly finds that her friends are married and that she is not. Alternatively, a married woman may find out that her spouse is seeing other women. Barbadian women seem to be as (un)willing to share their husbands as are women in North America, and discovery of significant infidelity may lead to the dissolution of the union. Other women try to stick it out "because of the children." Still other women reconcile themselves to the reality that their husbands see other women—so long as the girlfriend(s) does not constitute an important drain on income and his affairs do not become an obvious part of the local gossip mill. Most women appear to accommodate themselves to the availability of single women who themselves are looking for support and who are willing to accept a part-time spouse in the absence of a full-time man, at least partially. In competition with other women, women with husbands have an advantage. But they can keep that advantage only so long as they make concessions. Those concessions include granting men more household authority than their economic and emotional contributions might otherwise warrant.

MEN AND WOMEN

Thus in the 1950s a man who met all his socially accepted adult responsibilities was one who (1) worked long hours, usually at several jobs, (2) provided more than an adequate material base for his wife and children, (3) exercised absolute authority within his home, and (4) spent his free time either with men or with other women. These factors conspired to produce on the part of fathers a minimal emotional involvement with their families. Fathers' relationships both with their spouses and with their children were largely predicated on the material support they provided. If that support was substantial, fathers could dictate to them as he willed. If that support was minimal, the esteem in which their children held them diminished and their household authority was minimal. Even when a man's household authority was minimal, however, he remained responsible for enforcing household discipline. His activities as disciplinarian further alienated his children, especially in households in which he was otherwise viewed with little respect.

Conversely, even when a man's household authority was substantial the respect accorded him by his children was not necessarily matched by emotional commitment. As a young woman noted, even fathers who contributed to a relatively good home life were not necessarily a part of that life themselves.

> I've seen my father intervene in a fight that involved one of his friends, get stabbed in the arse with a knife and spend three months in the hospital. And when my father hears from a friend that his children have done such-and-such, and his children deny it—accurately—he doesn't believe them. Friends are more important than children.

Thus when a man met the highest standards by which men were judged, he was unlikely to have developed a companionate relationship with his wife and he was likely to have alienated his children. Few men can be expected actually to have met all their socially accepted adult responsibilities. Men who had not, of course, created still less satisfactory family relationships with their wives and children.

It is difficult to quantify the quality of spousal relationships, especially in a context in which few women experience a single long-term relationship with only one man. In an attempt to quantify at least one aspect of such relationships, women were asked to evaluate the relative importance of spouses and their parental family. I assumed that since women could obtain emotional support, but only the most meager financial assistance from mothers and siblings, those whose spousal relationships proved to be generally satisfactory on both a material and emotional basis would report that their spouses were more important to them than were their mothers and siblings. The replies were about evenly split among three major alternatives: 34% reported that their family relationships were more important, 37% reported that their spousal relationships were more important, and 29% reported that spousal and family relationships were equally important. These results suggest that about 60% of these women had experienced spousal relationships that were either severely deficient in important respects or only marginally satisfactory.

Women also were asked to evaluate the relative importance of spousal relationships and relationships with their children. Some 57% of the women reported that relationships with their children were more important than were their spousal relationships. Only 1.6% of the women ranked their spousal relationships higher than their relationships with children. These results suggest that the 60% of these women who found their spousal relationships severely deficient or only marginally satisfactory focused their attention on their children.

WOMEN AND CHILDREN

The options women faced prior to 1960 can be summarized as follows. The probability that a woman could adequately support herself through her own employment was close to zero; consequently, women had to establish liens on the income of men. So long as a woman remained in her father's house (assuming that her mother was, in fact, married or involved in a long-term consensual relationship with a man) she could expect some support. However, the primary support available from parents was likely to be in kind: a place to sleep, some clothes, food, and housing. To improve her material position significantly she would have to establish ties with other men.

The probability that one man would provide for her long-term support was also close to zero. To gain control over resources necessary for her material well-being, a woman had to compete for the attentions of the available men. Such competition was unlikely to be overt while she was young. Competition became overt only after the woman became aware that her support was threatened by the presence of other women. Consequently, a woman would became less demanding of her spousal relationship, (for instance, tolerating the existence of her spouse's extramarital affairs), or she accepted support from a man who was married or involved in a long-term consensual relationship with another woman.

However, childbearing was the primary means by which women competed with each other, for it was the primary means to establish a lien on a man's income. Children, of course, guaranteed neither marriage nor support. Indeed, young women overtly traded sex for financial support. Pregnancies and children occurred as mere by-products of that exchange. However, children provided the only socially sanctioned means by which a woman could legitimize her demand for financial support from a man. Moreover, in lieu of quality spousal relationships, women could look to their children for support. As Greenfield (1966: 109) observed, although children might be burdensome while they were young, older children could alleviate a woman's household responsibilities and mature children could be expected to provide women at least semi-independence from spouses—and perhaps make a woman fully independent of a spousal relationship.

Sons were taught to assume special responsibilities for their mothers. If a father beat his spouse, the son—perhaps even a *step*son of the mother—was and is expected to defend her, physically if necessary. The maturation of young men marked a crisis point in family relationships, as enshrined in the saying that "two men cannot live in the same house." Each will take the house to be his domain. Whereas the father believes he is the one with the rightful authority within the house, his son assumes increasing authority as a protector of his mother. The son, who chafes under his father's thumb, will be asked to leave, will be thrown out, or will move out by himself.

Whether sons or their fathers moved out, however, varied with the mother's spousal relationship and with the relative economic position of sons. In either event, however, sons did not abandon their maternal obligations. Indeed, mothers might pressure their sons, if not to move out of the house, at least to begin to work to provide them with important financial assistance. Daughters were not generally expected to do so, but under severe circumstances daughters, too, were pressured to work and to share their earnings with their mothers.

Children thus functioned as important resource access gatekeepers for their mothers. Consequently, women could optimize or improve their resource control only by unrestricted childbearing. Getting pregnant and bearing children tended to be viewed both as a woman's duty and as her goal, and mothers generally took the view that their children owed them support for bringing the children into the world.

These dimensions of moral economy were quantified in an additive index of two questions (see appendix). A woman who responded that she saw childbearing as her goal in life received a code of 2, a woman who responded that she sought to balance childbearing with independent career goals received a code of 1, and a woman who responded that she sought career goals over her childbearing received a code of 0. Similarly, a woman who responded that she believed her children owed her more than she owed her children received a code of 2, a woman who responded that the obligations of children and parents balanced received a code of 1, and a woman who responded that parental obligations to children outweighed children's obligations to parents received a code of 0. A range of scores from 0 to 4 was obtained by summing the codes for the two questions. Women who scored low expressed the view that childbearing is a consumption activity that one must balance with other options available to women; women who scored high expressed the view that childbearing is an investment activity that yields net material rewards. Women who ranged in age between 20-44 during the 1950s (women aged 50-64 in 1985) reported answers that averaged 3.045 on this moral economy index. More than 70% of these women scored at the highest levels of this index (a score of 3 or 4).

In short, in the 1950s women overwhelmingly viewed childbearing not as a consumption decision to be balanced by considerations of alternative uses for time, energy, and money, but as an investment that yielded the highest available money dividends. One younger woman remarked, "My mother wanted children to yield grandchildren! The more there were, the greater chance there was that some would grow up to be someone big—a doctor, or lawyer." Of course, if a child made it big, the woman would be very well taken care of in her old age; and in the meantime the woman would be assisted with regular monetary gifts that, depending on their amounts, would make her independent or semi-independent of a spousal relationship, which, most likely, was less than satisfactory.

Toward this end, mothers acted in ways "conditioning the child to pay her back" when they began to work; for example, saying things like "all the pain I went through to get this child . . .'" Mothers reinforced their words by doting on the children and giving them special presents. One woman recalled her activities as follows:

> I may be at the market with my last $20 and I need . . . and see oranges. Now oranges are out of season, but I say to myself "won't the children just love those!" and I get the oranges.

A young woman illustrated further:

> My father just loves blackeyes, but none of the children did. It has been *years* since we had blackeyes in our house.

Later, the mother reminded the children of her dedication and commitment to the children's welfare during their formative years.

> They would say they worked hard to get and spend money on them to send them to school, feed, and clothe them—"breaking my back" for you, as they would say. So, the children owe them every possible favor. They would recall having to work in the blazing sun on the sugar plantations for many days. The majority of women worked as domestic help. They don't

let the children forget that their chores were laborious, having to attend to the general ones of cooking, cleaning, and looking after their employer's children, but also in washing the loads of laundry (and the whites had to be spotless). Having done all that at someone else's house, they still had to go to their own homes and attend to chores there. These mothers don't forget these things. As a matter of fact, they remember to their death. Some even *demand* some sort of reward of gratitude.

The eldest daughter frequently was taken out of school to help care for the younger children. This process created daughters who were bitter because they had not been able to realize their own ambitions. These daughters understandably adopt the attitudes of their mothers toward their younger siblings, and they too will remind their juniors of all the time and attention they gave them, the real sacrifice they have made, especially if their juniors grow up to take on significant positions as doctors, lawyers, nurses, and teachers.

One woman expressed her view this way: "Parents go to the trouble to give children care and attention, and their children should give them proper respect and help." They should give them money and presents, especially money—to pay for food, the light bill, clothes, doctor, and so forth. These expectations apply to daughters as well as to sons. When daughters are not working or when they have only marginal spousal support, daughters are expected to help only in kind—they should visit, help to clean the house, and bring food. However, when daughters work or when daughters have substantial levels of spousal support, they, like sons, are expected to contribute to their mothers' welfare.

One woman remarked: "Your mother expects you to put the money in *her* hand." Another woman added: "And if you give her $10, you don't dare cut back! If you do you will never hear the end of it." If a daughter does not give money to her mother, at the very least the mother will be disappointed, and she may very well call the daughter to ask, "You forget about me? The money didn't come this month." A common complaint among the senior generation is that the young do not help as they should. Of emigrants, the women complain: "They don't remember me; they don't send me anything." Or, "Oh the years I spent with that boy. I give him [this]; I give him [that]. And he don't look at me now."

The survey responses surely reflect some adjustment of opinion over the years and many women one would expect to have viewed their childbearing activities as investment activities do not concede the point. Many such women do, in fact, feel that their children owe them support but they are not vocal about it. As one young woman remarked, "My mother doesn't say that she feels I owe her money support; but she expects it."

These obligations are specific to mothers and specifically exclude fathers. The money goes into the hand of the woman. If parents have been living together continuously as a couple, the children may think of themselves as contributing to their father and as fulfilling an obligation to their father. Yet, money is not put in his hand. Even when a father has been faithful to his wife and has supported the family well, the money goes to the mother. One person explained that "The obligations are the same [for both parents], provided your father actually raised you." The father receives support from the money if and only if he stays with the woman. If he has left but has given good support, he may receive some money, but not often. If he is living with another woman, even if he has provided good support, he doesn't get a cent. The children become incensed, hurt, and reject him. Women who have suffered beatings, embarrassment, and lack of support in spousal relationships use this information to coerce sympathy and assistance later. A young woman observed, "Mothers remind you how it was when she was younger. She ring it in your ear!"

Even in the best of circumstances, there is a widespread belief that "men can take care of themselves." Some fathers have, in fact, developed both a companionate relationship with their spouses and strong emotional bonds with their children. Such a man believes his behavior justifies the respect given the mother when assistance money is placed in her hand. Thus one woman pointed out:

My father wants the money to be put in his hand. But it never goes to him. He says "I'm working and saving my money because when I get old I know you're not going to give me a cent!" And then later he will say, "I'm working and saving my money and when I die all of it will be yours [his children's]."

Such men clearly want the respect they (rightly) believe is due them. The fact that the mother is the one who receives the money can hurt terribly.

UNRESTRICTED CHILDBEARING

Greenfield (1966: 108-109) writes of childbearing in the 1950s:

There appears to be a general belief that abstention from sexual activity is conducive to poor health. Birth control is not generally practiced, and there is a belief that a woman who fails to bear all the children she is capable of will suffer from high blood pressure and other diseases. Moreover, children are desired, particularly the first few. . . . When pregnancy is avoided for any reason, both abstention and contraception are rare; abortion is the more common practice.

As one might expect, older Barbadian women reported no rigid guidelines about when it was appropriate to begin childbearing or about when it was appropriate to cease. Most women felt that it was best to begin having children during one's twenties and to cease in one's forties. All women, however, pointed out that "pregnancies just happened" and "babies just came." As Greenfield (1966: 108-109) observed, most first pregnancies occurred because women were ignorant about basic sexual physiology. "Repeated admonitions about 'staying away from boys,' young women complained, never included a discussion of 'what to stay away from'" (Greenfield, 1966: 109) As one woman elaborated:

> Most [first pregnancies] happened out of ignorance. The oldest child had to stay home caring for the younger ones while the mother work on the farms and, so, many mothers never sat down to tell you things. In the country, the most people went to was to Church, school, and to the beach. And you go to Sunday School. Most times you had to walk and a mother might not go back to church in the evening if they were there in the morning. So a lot can happen on walking to church or even fetching water, which we had to fetch from far. If a man who is a friend of the family visits regularly, no one would think anything if he visits while the woman's parents were away. And that was when men and women got involved also.

Most women in their seventies and over reported that when they were young (in the mid-1930s and before) they had no knowledge of how to prevent conception and could not remember anyone having had an abortion. However, abortions were performed and women occasionally sought contraception, even if only rarely. Women reported home abortion remedies that included the use of bush teas (most commonly infusions of senna leaves), epsom salts, castor oil, or sea salts. There were also a small number of women who were known to perform effective abortions. Douches, and using castor oil to "clean you out" were cited as contraceptive measures. The only contraceptive measures that required the involvement of men were withdrawal and abstinence. Women claimed that both abortion and contraception were rarely attempted but that, of the two, abortions were more common. It appears that abortion was attempted primarily when a girl's mother was unduly embarrassed by her daughter's early pregnancy. One women who was forced to abort her first pregnancy, which she wanted very much, reported that she has never spoken to her mother since. Condoms and spermicides were reported to have come into use after World War II (also see Lowenthal, 1957).

Even in the 1950s, however, few women attempted to restrict their childbearing systematically. As one woman observed, "If you run from your husband tonight, you come back tomorrow night." Another woman explained, "You get a child to enjoy yourself!" Thus after the first, women bore children as their sexual involvements permitted: "In my time," a woman in her fifties summarized, "you have children until you can have no more."

SUMMARY

Prior to 1960, the Barbadian economy was characterized by an uncompetitive and oligopolist resource structure that allocated opportunities on the basis of personal relationships, and these on the basis of sex, class, and color. For the majority of the Barbadian population, this structure created a fundamental conflict between the interests of men and women in which the only way each could optimize their resource control was to exploit the weaknesses and dependencies of the other. The only means by which women could gain access to the resources on which their material welfare depended was their children, for children could function as resource channel gatekeepers. In a woman's youth, children legitimated her claims on income from men. In her middle age, children provided financial support that could make her independent of her prior dependency on men. In her old age, financial support from children meant the difference between abject poverty and a moderate, or even comfortable, level of living.

In the 1950s, a man could not win either with his spouse or with his children. A man was pressured to get a job to bring in money to help his mother. To get a steady job, to find additional work, or to get a better job, a man needed contacts with other men. To maintain those contacts, a man needed a good reputation. To gain and maintain a reputation meant that a man had to exploit the women with whom he became involved by demanding of them sexual and domestic services and children and by spending his time in the company of men and other women. As he responded rationally to the resource structure in which he was enmeshed, a man invited complaints and criticisms from his women and alienated his children. A man's only effective role in child care was as the disciplinarian, which in the absence of any other activities to offset the anger/hostility such a role generates in children guaranteed that children would be less inclined to help him later. A woman, in the meantime, not only drilled into her children how much she sacrificed and how hard she had to work to raise them properly, but that her labors were made only that much worse because she had no companion (a husband) to help her. Family hardships thus became perceived as owing to the fact that a child's father, and men generally, were simply irresponsible.

Thus women exploited men's weaknesses and dependencies in turn. A mothers' influence on her children was continuous: she bore the children, fed the children, clothed the children, washed the children, and otherwise cared for them. She avoided undue alienation by letting her spouse function as disciplinarian. Men were peripheral to the processes of family life and, "naturally," the children came "to cling" to their mothers. Because childbearing entailed only investment expenditures, a woman experienced fertility levels limited only by constraints on her fecundity and by constraints on her sexual activity implicit in the different forms of spousal unions in which she could be involved.

NOTES

1. Thus Stoffle (1972: 64) reported that 25%-35% of all divorces occurred only after 20 years of marriage—that is, after children had grown and had begun to make their mothers economically independent of their spouses.

2. More recently, it has become possible to convert *bagasse,* the fibrous residue of juice extraction, into the energy that fuels sugar factories and excess energy can be fed into the public grid. Bagasse can also be turned into a variety of other useful products, which it increasingly is (see Hagelberg, 1985 for a good review of sugar in the contemporary Caribbean).

3. See Cecilia Karch's excellent (1979) analysis of economic and social change on Barbados over the nineteenth and the early twentieth centuries. The following account relies heavily on Karch's study.

—4—

TO CHART MY OWN COURSE—SOCIAL REVOLUTION AND FERTILITY TRANSITION

BARBADIAN FAMILY RELATIONSHIPS IN THE 1980s

Barbadian women in the 1980s generally see themselves as being able to "chart their own course in life" in ways that were denied their mothers. This comment by a woman in her thirties perhaps best summarizes the changes in women's position in Barbadian society between the 1950s and the 1980s. This view also reflects family relationships that are radically different from those that prevailed prior to 1960. Women aged 20-34 in 1985 are only part way through the family life cycle. Nonetheless, it has become clear that conjugal bonds—if not actually stronger than those of their mothers' generation—are characterized by companionate qualities that mothers' relationships might take on only late in the life course, if ever. The young marriage cohort is likely to exhibit a relative absence of stable nuclear family units, but no more so than families in North America or Europe. The weak bonds between fathers and children appear to be in the process of replacement by bonds more nearly equal to the bonds between mothers and children. The bonds between mothers and children appear to be undergoing a qualitative change in emotional and intellectual content.

Both men and women continue to take part in a relatively large number of spousal relationships, but young women's expectations that their husbands will remain faithful to the relationship appear to be considerably stronger than were their mothers' expectations. Young women are not likely to be economically dependent on their men. Barbadian women in the 1980s are educated to levels equivalent to those of men. Although Barbadian women still suffer discrimination in the job market, women now have opportunities to work not only as seamstresses, hucksters, and field labor, but as technical specialists, secretaries, receptionists, business executives, university instructors, and lawyers. Thus Barbadian women in the 1980s tend to earn incomes far higher in real terms than their mothers and grandmothers could ever dream of.

Changes in the perspectives of women have been accompanied, although they have not been matched, by equivalent changes in the perspectives of men. Indeed, the transition of Barbados' family relationships from the 1950s to the 1980s is fairly described as a process of liberation for both men and women—liberation specifically from the mutually exploitative relationships that characterized Barbadian family relationships in the 1950s. Young men, like young women, have been able to take advantage of educational and economic opportunities denied their fathers and grandfathers. The existence of these opportunities has meant that young men, unlike their fathers and grandfathers, have *not* been placed in a position in which they must exploit the women with whom they become involved in order to respond rationally to the resource structure in which they find themselves. Sexual exploitation still occurs, of course. However, it no longer is the order of the day.

RESOURCE STRUCTURE AND SOCIAL RELATIONSHIPS

These changes in family relationships coincided with a sharp discontinuity in Barbadian economic history. Between the mid-1950s and the mid-1960s, the Barbadian economy experienced the decline of sugar and the ascendancy of industrial manufacturing and tourism. This economic change was part of a much broader historical process in which the scale of world trade increased enormously. On Barbados, it was set in motion after the agro-commercial elite had lost direct control over the Barbadian assembly. These changes meant that the economic well-being of the Barbadian elite was increasingly subject to selection on the basis of quality and cost factors set in international markets. New firms were established on the island. Some of these have been extensions of multinational corporations, some have been extensions of Barbados Shipping and Trading, some have been established by new emigrants to Barbados, and others have been established on the basis of indigenous, nonelite (and nonwhite) entrepreneurship. The establishment of these firms created new resource access opportunities for the Barbadian population and, consequently, undermined the gatekeeper position of the agro-commercial elite. An island with an immense lower class was transformed into an island with an immense middle class.

Sugar

The United Kingdom ceased acting as a clearing house for West Indian sugar in 1951. Barbadian producers could export fixed quantities of sugar to the UK after that date, but prices had to be negotiated annually and production over the agreed limits had to be sold at highly volatile market rates. Barbados sugar producers had some security under this arrangement, but, as Hagelberg (1985: 105) noted, not such as to "invite complacent disregard of changing political, economic, and technical circumstances." Barbadian producers thus found themselves under competitive pressure by world markets. Over the course of the 1950s, Barbadian planters responded by mechanizing production. Technological change was accompanied by major structural changes within the industry. The units of production declined from 34 factories in 1950 to 8 in 1980. As the productive technology changed, so did the skills necessary to operate it efficiently. The demand for unskilled labor declined and a demand for skilled labor emerged.

Haynes (1980) points out that in 1946

> sugar accounted for almost 40% of Barbados' gross domestic output and almost all of visible foreign exchange earnings. . . . Moreover, though sugar workers were accorded very low status, limited employment opportunities elsewhere left many with little alternative to working in the industry, and the sector provided jobs for almost one-third of the working population [p. 82].

By 1980, the sugar industry contributed only about 6% of domestic output, less than 10% of employment, and 10% of foreign exchange earnings. These changes in the sugar industry over the 1950s were accompanied by initially slow but increasingly rapid growth in manufacturing and tourism. In contrast with sugar, in 1980 manufacturing and tourism contributed respectively about 11% and 12% of domestic output and about 18% and 41% of foreign exchange earnings.

Industrial Manufacturing

By the 1960s Barbadian labor was drawn increasingly to the new opportunities for employment in industrial manufacturing, tourism, and in residential sectors supporting these new sectors. Growth in manufacturing was built, like the Puerto Rican "Operation Bootstrap," on the basis of protective tariffs and incentive legislation (Cox, 1982:

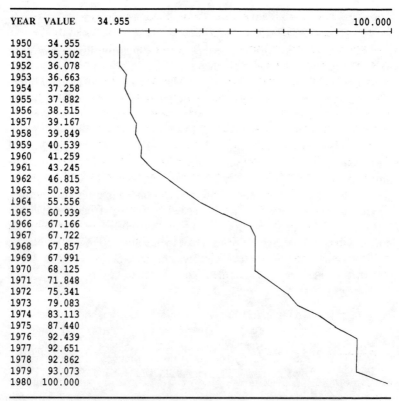

YEAR	VALUE
1950	34.955
1951	35.502
1952	36.078
1953	36.663
1954	37.258
1955	37.882
1956	38.515
1957	39.167
1958	39.849
1959	40.539
1960	41.259
1961	43.245
1962	46.815
1963	50.893
1964	55.556
1965	60.939
1966	67.166
1967	67.722
1968	67.857
1969	67.991
1970	68.125
1971	71.848
1972	75.341
1973	79.083
1974	83.113
1975	87.440
1976	92.439
1977	92.651
1978	92.862
1979	93.073
1980	100.000

Figure 4.1:   Growth of industrial manufacturing employment on Barbados, 1950-1980,
as measured by an index of the size of the labor force employed in this sector
(1980 = 100).

47), and was called "Operation Beehive" to emphasize the similarity.
Figure 4.1 traces the growth in industrial manufacturing employment
over the period 1950-1980 (data from Worrell, 1982; see Chapter 8 for a
detailed description of this variable). With the exception of two
slowdowns, one in the late 1960s and the other in the late 1970s,
industrial manufacturing employment grew exponentially.

In the post-World War II period, manufacturing activity was largely
restricted to the food processing industry. By the late 1950s and the early
1960s, manufactured goods began to include intermediate inputs for
other sectors, the Barbadian garment industry was established, and the
manufacturing sector grew to include furniture, ceramics, phar-
maceuticals, phonograph records, wood processing, paints, structural
parts of concrete and steel and asphalt roofing materials for the

construction sector, and the production of industrial gases and lead acid batteries. In the 1970s, the manufacturing sector expanded further to include petroleum refining, paper products, data processing and electronics components assembly.

Growth in manufacturing did not change the female work participation rate. However, it radically changed the work opportunities available for women. Whereas in 1946 female employment in manufacturing was 14.4% of the labor force (and even then it was employment only in cottage industry crafts), by the late 1970s women held more than 50% of the jobs in the manufacturing sector, primarily in the garment industry and in metal products and electronic component assembly (Cox, 1982: 63). Despite improved opportunities, however, women continued to hold positions that paid less than the positions held by men. In every industrial subsector, women have earned less than men on average. In 1975, the average wage of women employed in the manufacturing sector was only half that paid to men (Cox, 1982: 65-66).[1]

Tourism

Figure 4.2 traces the growth of tourism in Barbados over the period 1950-1980 (data from Worrell, 1982; see Chapter 8 for a detailed description of this variable). Figure 4.1 illustrates growth in the Barbadian manufacturing sector by direct employment, and Figure 4.2 illustrates the impact of the growth in tourism by an index of tourist spending (in 1980 dollars). Tourism is a notoriously ambiguous sector because tourists spend only a part of their money on accommodations. The actual number of people employed in the "tourist sector" necessarily is very low. However, a sizable portion of the tourist dollar is spent on services and goods Barbadians themselves use extensively. Tourism's impact on the Barbadian economy thus is best summarized by tourist spending. With the exception of a reversal following the OPEC oil embargo-influenced rise in inflation, and a world recession after 1972, tourist spending, like employment in the manufacturing sector, grew exponentially.

Barbados has hosted people on trips who were combining business and pleasure since the 1600s (Phillips, 1982: 107). However, travel for pleasure did not become economically important until the advent of the steamship in the 1800s. Although there were limited, private attempts to encourage the growth of Barbadian tourism in the early twentieth century, Barbados did not experience the growth of an important tourist

YEAR	VALUE
1950	2.393
1951	3.356
1952	4.370
1953	5.401
1954	6.448
1955	7.546
1956	7.594
1957	10.153
1958	10.622
1959	12.883
1960	15.144
1961	18.474
1962	21.856
1963	21.943
1964	26.193
1965	28.621
1966	30.356
1967	34.432
1968	52.125
1969	60.624
1970	69.991
1971	83.174
1972	86.123
1973	84.302
1974	68.777
1975	61.145
1976	60.104
1977	75.195
1978	84.302
1979	93.669
1980	100.000

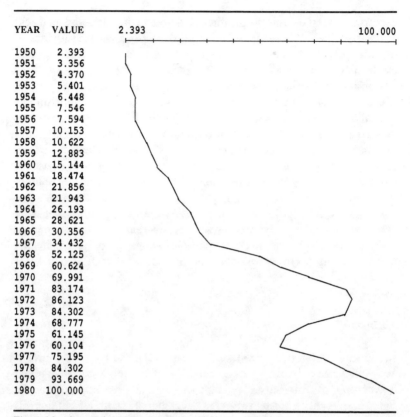

Figure 4.2.   Growth in tourist spending on Barbados, 1950-1980, as measured by index
values (1980 = 100).

industry until the 1950s when the government actively worked to
encourage its growth by the use of fiscal incentives and the establishment
of a tourist board.

Because the sector is so ambiguous, the employment impact of
tourism cannot be documented easily.[2] Outside of employment in places
of accommodation and restaurants, tourist spending surely has greatly
increased the level of employment in services and has contributed to
growth of public sector employment. Perhaps the most significant
impact of tourism, however, has been a qualitative change in the class
distribution of employment. Industrial manufacturing employment
gives rise predominantly to a class of skilled blue collar workers.
Tourism also contributes to employment for blue collar workers:
waiters, maids, groundskeepers, and so forth. However, tourist spending

has also and more importantly added significantly to employment in white collar, professional, and managerial occupational classes.

Structural Change

Because of the slow rates of growth in manufacturing and tourism during the early 1950s, it is likely that employment in these sectors alleviated economic inadequacies that stemmed from the sugar monopoly. Ironically, mechanization of the sugar industry meant that this sector may have been the first to emphasize the importance of skills and performance. After 1960, however, increases in manufacturing and tourism would be expected to be reflected in subsequent change in other economic sectors, both in opening up new employment opportunities and in changing the conditions of employment from paternalism to performance. This opening and diversification of resource structure meant employment and advancement opportunities that had never before been available to women and that had rarely before been available to men.

The economic well-being of Barbadian manufacturing and tourist sectors was subject to selection on the basis of quality and cost factors set in international markets. Consequently, employment and upward mobility in these new employment sectors came to be subject to selection on the basis of qualifications and performance rather than personal relationships with employers. The opening of new and competitive resource access channels thus was accompanied by a shift in the means by which both men and women could best optimize resource control. "Godfathers" were no longer necessary for well-paying employment.

Impact on Social Relationships

Patronage and the importance of personal relationships with prospective employers have not disappeared, of course. Despite the increased opportunities implicit in the growth of manufacturing and tourism, unemployment levels on Barbados remained largely unchanged (at around 10%-15%) from 1949 through the early 1980s (Mascoll, 1985). Indeed, especially when the economy contracts, such relationships continue to be instrumental in obtaining jobs that, outside agriculture, have been scarce relative to people seeking positions. A well-placed executive remarked, "The Old Boy system on Barbados still operates very efficiently. If you have a job available, chances are you can think of half a dozen friends and, perhaps, some relatives that can fill the position."

The terms of employment have changed radically, however. Because the employing firms themselves have come under increasing selective pressure from international markets, employment and advancement now require high levels of formal education and performance. Figures 4.3 and 4.4 trace out changes in (1) the mean years of formal schooling women had completed and (2) the proportion of women who had completed a secondary level of education over the period 1950-1980. Each datum constitutes an estimate of the respective variable for succeeding cohorts of women aged 20-24. These data were estimated from the sample of women described in the appendix by assigning cohort means to the years 1950, 1955, and so forth. Missing points in the resulting series were estimated on the assumption of constant growth rates between existing points. Both figures reveal massive increases in womens' participation in the Barbadian educational system. Although there appears to have been a brief period of slow growth during the early 1960s, the average level of educational attainment rose fairly consistently throughout the 31-year period from 1950-1980. The proportion of women who actually completed secondary school, however, rose imperceptibly over the first part of the 1950s. In the late 1950s, the proportion of women who completed secondary school rose dramatically and increased steadily thereafter, albeit at slower rates during the early 1960s and the early 1970s.

Young people who enter the job market today, both men and women, must exhibit, in the words of one older man, "a higher level of performance to perform satisfactorily" than had applied in the past. Common ways to express the changes that have occurred over this period include "things move at a much faster pace today," or "things are much more sophisticated than they were in my day [the 1950s]." Consequently, to remain viable, firms must actively compete for business. Lawyers who thought nothing about maintaining offices with books and documents piled here and there on old and well-worn furniture in the 1950s, now take pains to present their clients with very well-appointed surroundings in which to conduct business. Retail firms, whose business increasingly is dependent on tourist spending, take pains to maintain cleanliness, to have cleanly dressed, friendly, and efficient staff, and to offer an increasing array of articles for sale. As Barbadian's tastes have changed, even the neighborhood store has found that sales increase when they can improve the variety of goods they offer and can offer surroundings that appeal to their prospective customers. Thus, whereas formerly there was only a small shop, run from someone's home

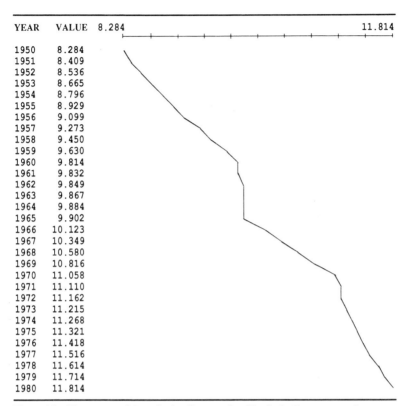

YEAR	VALUE
1950	8.284
1951	8.409
1952	8.536
1953	8.665
1954	8.796
1955	8.929
1956	9.099
1957	9.273
1958	9.450
1959	9.630
1960	9.814
1961	9.832
1962	9.849
1963	9.867
1964	9.884
1965	9.902
1966	10.123
1967	10.349
1968	10.580
1969	10.816
1970	11.058
1971	11.110
1972	11.162
1973	11.215
1974	11.268
1975	11.321
1976	11.418
1977	11.516
1978	11.614
1979	11.714
1980	11.814

Figure 4.3. Mean years of formal schooling completed by Barbadian women who were aged 20-24 at year t.

and offering for sale sundries and rum, "mini-marts" have sprung up all over the island.

A large number of small, family-run retail firms has emerged. Because these firms depend on volume rather than margins, they have been able to undercut severely the large commercial houses that dominated the Barbadian economy in the 1950s and before. Farmers have responded to changes in consumer tastes by significantly diversifying their production. Even small-scale agriculture can be lucrative, and a significant number of young people have begun to farm. New firms that supply inputs for farmers have emerged, and older firms have found it necessary to compete for the available market. Firms that supply agricultural inputs have come to compete with each other not only in price, but in services offered. Such firms conduct on-farm research with new products and provide regular extension assistance. One such firm has actively sought out the market of small farmers.

YEAR	VALUE
1950	0.030
1951	0.033
1952	0.036
1953	0.039
1954	0.044
1955	0.048
1956	0.063
1957	0.082
1958	0.108
1959	0.142
1960	0.186
1961	0.188
1962	0.190
1963	0.192
1964	0.194
1965	0.196
1966	0.216
1967	0.239
1968	0.264
1969	0.291
1970	0.321
1971	0.323
1972	0.326
1973	0.328
1974	0.330
1975	0.333
1976	0.364
1977	0.398
1978	0.435
1979	0.476
1980	0.520

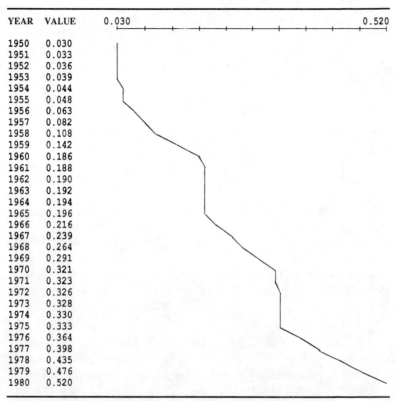

Figure 4.4.   Proportion of Barbadian women aged 20-24 who had completed secondary school by year t.

As industrial manufacturing, but especially tourist-related employment, came to dominate the Barbadian economy, increases in the demand for labor have meant increases in the demand for special skills and abilities. Mascoll (1985) has shown that, although real wages have not quite kept pace with the major increases in productivity that characterized the Barbadian economy after 1960, increases in the demand for labor have been accompanied by increases in real wages. Such increases have been used to attract people with the skills, qualifications, and education to enable firms to perform at increasingly higher levels.

Thus the character of competition for the available employment has also changed. Generally, Barbadian employers have maintained a competitive advantage over job seekers. Because employers have experienced increased competitive pressures, however, they have increasingly sought out the best available help—hiring women as well as men, without regard to skin color, for positions that never before were attainable by men with black skins or by women whose skins were whatever shade of brown. Moreover, employers are, as one executive noted, "less reluctant" today, compared with the 1950s, to fire staff who do not perform satisfactorily. One large employer estimated that blue collar employees were perhaps twice as likely to be terminated for poor performance than were white collar employees. Nonetheless, employees generally recognize that performance standards have risen significantly, that intra-island competition has meant that firm survival has come to depend increasingly on both employer and employee productivity, and that, if they do not perform well, there are many people with equal or better qualifications who are waiting to take their places.

A further effect of this increased competition has been a general depersonalization of social relationships. Older people recall that during the 1950s hardly anyone locked his or her door and that neighbors looked after one another. If a woman was out and it began to rain, a neighbor would take in the laundry hanging on the line. A woman in her sixties expressed the view of nearly all the older people I spoke with when she observed that

> in the old days people lived good. If you had a friend and you did not have anything to cook for yourself or the children and that friend had something, you could be sure that you could get food for that day and the next. People today have become selfish. People who have anything want more and are not willing to share.

Older people, especially, are likely to reflect sadly on the changes they have seen and to wonder why "there is so little love in the world today." Today, hardly anyone does *not* lock their door and strong interhousehold ties have become increasingly rare. A man aged 64 summed up his view of young people: "They too hard, mon, too hard."

As implicit in the introductory section of this chapter, however, such a characterization is only partly accurate. When in the 1950s and previously, interhousehold ties were strong, those ties helped off-set the emotional and material poverty of intrahousehold social relationships. The 1980s appear to be characterized by the converse: relatively weak interhousehold relationships balanced by intrahousehold relationships that display a new emotional richness and material abundance.

Elsewhere in the Caribbean, where agriculture remains undeveloped and industrial employment minimal and/or protected, occupational multiplicity and personal relationships remain important avenues both for employment and promotion. The minimal (or even nonexistent) competition among firms means that employers have the power to coerce sexual favors from women who seek employment or a raise, and it gives politicians scope to exercise patronage based on family membership, voting record, political party support, and past favors given. Thus the Brana-Shutes (Brana-Shute and Brana-Shute, 1980: 77) observed in St. Vincent in the late 1970s what older informants remembered for Barbados in the 1950s:

> Many young people who are either unemployed or in such unremunerative and low status occupations as unskilled laborers, estate workers, porters, and errand runners regularly point out that access to even a minor position requires the intervention and endorsement of a patron who will "arrange matters."

Increased levels of competition do not make such practices—or discrimination on the basis of either skin tone or sex—entirely disappear. But increased levels of competition do greatly moderate their incidence because performance criteria become more important determinants of the economic viability of firms. Thus by contrast, the Brana-Shutes (1980: 9) point out that

> Barbados tends to function more as a meritocracy at most levels than do the [other] societies of the LDCs. Consequently, one finds a sense of optimistic ambition and sense of achievement motivation more prominent in Barbados. This is coupled with the fact that Barbados is a more individualistic society wherein people see activities, commitments, and associations spread over a wide range of personnel and institutions rather than, for example, rooted in their family or village or place in life.

They go on to note that Barbados in 1980 is very different from Barbados in 1960. Whereas contemporary observers—islanders and researchers alike—consistently remark about the "privatized" social relationships on Barbados, this phenomenon is a novelty that has emerged only over the last 30 years.

THE FAMILY LIFE COURSE IN THE 1980s

Table 4.1 illustrates continuities and changes in the early part of the family life course by comparing yearly union durations for the youngest and oldest age cohorts. Overall, there is little numerical difference between these cohorts. Young women continue to become involved in visiting relationships with young men over the course of their late teens and early twenties, visiting relationships tend to be transformed into

TABLE 4.1
The Mean Proportion of a Year Barbadian Women Spend
in Different Forms of Spousal Unions:
Contrasts Between
Women Aged 20-34 (n = 164) and 50-64 (n = 109) in 1985

Union Type	15-19	20-24	25-29
Legal			
cohort aged 20-34	.009	.085	.263
cohort aged 50-64	.039	.207	.417
t-statistic	2.159	3.348	2.526
probability	.032	.001	.012
Consensual			
cohort aged 20-34	.038	.131	.265
cohort aged 50-64	.042	.154	.222
t-statistic	.246	.627	.795
probability	.806	.531	.428
Visiting			
cohort aged 20-34	.430	.569	.396
cohort aged 50-64	.382	.459	.270
t-statistic	1.144	2.177	2.230
probability	.254	.030	.027
Out of Union			
cohort aged 20-24	.523	.215	.076
cohort aged 50-64	.538	.180	.092
t-statistic	.317	.848	.427
probability	.751	.397	.669

consensual unions when women pass through their twenties, and consensual unions tend to be transformed into legal marriages, particularly toward age 30. It is reasonable to expect that the time young women will spend in visiting unions will display the consistent declines that were apparent for their mothers' and grandmothers' generations. Similarly, it is reasonable to expect that the time young women will spend in consensual unions will increase into their thirties and decline thereafter as the probability of legal marriage increases.

Although the "types" of union and the duration trends for different forms of spousal union remain unchanged, the context in which unions are created and function has changed radically. The content and meaning of unions have changed as well. Thus for instance, parents continue to try to thwart the undesirable interests of young men. However, young women no longer face the constraints on meeting young men that existed for their mothers or grandmothers. Since the early 1970s, when secondary schools became coeducational, the sexes have mixed freely—at school, at dances, in the streets. Long telephone conversations have become a common nuisance for parents with teenagers.

The probability values in Table 4.1 do not constitute tests of specific hypotheses and thus cannot be relied upon to identify empirically real cohort differences. Properly, we should correct alpha; I have done so here, and in subsequent analyses, with the Bonferroni procedure. Since there are 12 comparisons in Table 4.1, alpha should equal 0.05/12, or about 0.004. Only one probability value falls below this adjusted alpha level. There are several probability values that are relatively low and that may, albeit ambiguously, indicate a patterned generational difference. This patterned difference is a reduction in the amount of time women spend in legal marriages and a concordant increase in the amount of time such women spend in visiting relationships.

If this pattern is empirically real, it surely reflects the increased length of time that women (and men) spend in school. Because of increases in educational facilities and job opportunities, boys no longer have to depend on their fathers to arrange for training in a trade to escape the drudgery of field labor; girls no longer have to depend on children and men simply for an adequate level of material support. Parents continue to assume financial responsibility for adult children who remain at home. Most likely, the increased prevalence and tenure of formal schooling has increased the proportion of older children who continue to live with their parents. But both sons and daughters tend to be pressured to work so that they can assist with household expenses. Young people on Barbados, like young people in North America, tend to look for employment at levels appropriate to their education and training. They avoid field labor at low wages. A common complaint in 1985 among older Barbadian parents is that many young people refuse to find work. They seem to express the concerns of North American parents who grew up with experience of the Depression and find it disconcerting that young people do not accept jobs indiscriminately, merely for the sake of being employed.

However, higher levels of education and the ability to find employment with skills developed in school have meant that young people can be "on their own" far earlier than in the past. Owning a home continues to be important, but house ownership is a far different matter than it was in the 1950s. As did their fathers and mothers, young people tend to chafe under parental restrictions. Parents still become furious with young women who get pregnant early and may throw them out of the house. Now, however, such women may choose not to return and young working couples may form consensual relationships without having to live with the girl's family. They seek privacy and they want to avoid the interference of mothers-in-law. A rented apartment adequately serves the purpose of independence and, increasingly, young people establish independent households early in their lives. Consensual unions for such couples, or for couples who have attained higher levels of education, have taken on new meanings and have become reinterpreted as "trendy" North American "trial marriages." As women have acquired greater economic independence from men, the importance of marriage itself has waned. Older people tend to see a "breakdown in family life." One younger woman pointed out that she and many of her peers felt that parents were to blame: parents try to control too much; parents try to coerce assistance that the youngsters do not think proper. An older woman offered a rebuttal: "Then they have children and then they remember the parents"—as babysitters.

MEN AND FAMILIES

The most significant change in men's relationships with their families seems to be the prevalence with which young men view their spousal relationships and families less as things to be administered and exploited than as people to interact with and enjoy. Younger couples and their children, especially, actually share entertainment time. They may go to the beach, have a family picnic on Sunday in Queen's Park in Bridgetown or at Farley Hill up in the Parish of St. Peter, they visit the "tourist" attractions like the Flower Forest or Harrison's Cave, they take holidays together. The more affluent (and increasing numbers of Barbadians fall into this category) visit Disney World, Miami, New York, Antigua, St. Lucia, Caracas, London, or Rio.

The young men of the late 1970s and early 1980s tend to enter spousal relationships with skills and perspectives very different from their fathers': They have learned to be independent of the services of their mothers and, thus independent of services traditionally provided by wives. A woman in her early twenties remarked, "My brother says he doesn't want a wife. He can cook and wash for himself."

Similarly, whereas in the past men expected to be the sole household breadwinner, such expectations are far less likely today. Some men continue to view their household role in this way and continue to give their spouses an allowance to be used for household expenses. Men, more likely, expect that their wives will work and will contribute an equal share to household expenses. Some men (albeit only a few) even expect wives to work and to use pay from such work to provide for all household expenses.

Similarly, few young men expect to assume a position as autocratic household decision maker. Even if a man does make such an assumption, women are much more likely than in the 1950s to participate forcefully in household decision making. Men in their thirties and older tend to chafe when their spouses assume an independent role in household decision making. For public consumption and, occasionally, even within the household, such men continue (as did their fathers) to declare "I am the boss of this household!" Their spouses, however, are likely to observe, "But we [women] know better. We just let him talk on and go our own way." Such strategies, of course, are not novel with young women. However, the ability consistently to influence household decisions based on mutual discussion is.

Table 4.2 documents some of these changes in perspective. Women were asked if they expected their spouses to help cook, wash clothes, wash dishes, bathe the children, take the children places, or care for the children. The proportion of women in younger cohorts who answered these questions positively exhibits increases that are both consistent and dramatic.

As indicated in Chapter 3, women generally assumed full responsibility both for the household chores and for the children in the 1950s. Women found their identity and self-esteem in their children, in how they kept their houses, and (when possible) in how they treated their husbands. They were attuned specifically to their neighbor's standards and suffered in respect and self-esteem to the extent that they could not meet such standards. Whereas in the past men did little in the home—other than when it interested them—to direct what would and would not be done, today men participate much more both in household affairs and child care. A woman in her fifties commented: "You never used to see a man walking with a child." Now you see men carrying their children; taking them to the clinic, to school, and to the beach; dressing them, washing them, taking complete care of them if the woman is elsewhere; cooking, food shopping, doing the laundry, and pressing clothes.

These remarks should not be construed to mean that Barbadian women experience true sexual equality in household affairs. Barbadian men are at least as apt as North American men (and perhaps more) to avoid housework and child care. Similarly, Barbadian men are at least as apt as North American men (and perhaps more) to suspect that women are not really the equal of men and to act in ways that assume male precedence over women.

TABLE 4.2

**The Proportion of Women in Different Age Cohorts
Who Reported that Their Spouses Assumed
Selected Household Responsibilities**

		Household Resp nsibilities				
Cohort	Cooking	Wash clothes	Wash dishes	Bathe children	Transport children	Supervise children
Aged 20-24	0.974	0.816	0.947	0.974	0.974	0.974
Aged 30-34	0.768	0.661	0.857	0.927	1.000	1.000
Aged 35-39	0.710	0.609	0.768	0.725	0.855	0.870
Aged 40-44	0.760	0.640	0.800	0.720	0.900	0.920
Aged 45-49	0.571	0.476	0.619	0.667	0.952	0.952
Aged 50-54	0.488	0.341	0.561	0.512	0.805	0.829
Aged 55-64	0.277	0.185	0.338	0.219	0.625	0.609
F-test probability	.000	.000	.000	.000	.000	.000

This attitude is particularly and, to women, most offensively evident in men's possessiveness. Most young Barbadian men continue to act on the assumption that women are to be won and lost in competition with other men, that women are a weaker sex whom other men can seduce merely with a more appealing line or appearance. The possibility that women evaluate their relationships with men on other grounds—for instance, on the respect and sharing they experience with a particular man—is not often seriously considered. Hence, for many men, a woman cannot truly be trusted. On the contrary, in this regard she is not really a person; she is a thing to be seduced and, if continually desirable, then continually guarded against the predatory advances of other men. When a man wants to go out he assumes the freedom to do so: "I comin' back now" and he leaves without indicating exactly when he is "comin' back"; "I goin' down the road" and he leaves without indicating exactly where "down the road" he is going. A woman's request for more specific information about where he is going or when he plans to return tends to be treated as illegitimate. A woman's whereabouts, however, are to be closely monitored. The offense a woman may feel at being so obviously distrusted and closely questioned leads to spousal arguments and, occasionally, wife beatings.

The generational differences in perspective and behavior between young and older men are marked nonetheless. It is common to hear young women remark of their spouses: "Yes, he helps around the house. He likes to cook and he loves his children." Rather than leaving early for work, coming home, eating and (when appropriate) disciplining the children, and then leaving to be with either men or women elsewhere, today men spend time with their families. Couples may drive to work together and wives may pick up their husbands after work. Household division of labor tends to be arranged on the basis of spousal employment schedules (see Stoffle, 1972: 174-180). I never encountered the equivalent to a North American "househusband," but men unemployed temporarily function similarly for they take responsibility for domestic duties while their wives work. By contrast, unemployed men avoided domestic responsibilities in the 1950s. Domestic responsibilities properly belonged only to women's domain.

About a quarter of the young women sampled were unemployed. Some of these women were unemployed because they were still in school. Women who are unemployed and not still in school—that is, women who are housewives—tend, like their mothers and grandmothers, to assume primary responsibility for household affairs. But they still expect their spouses to help with domestic chores. More significantly, and unlike their mothers and grandmothers, young women commonly can make real, voluntary, choices to be, or not to be, housewives.

WOMEN, EDUCATION, AND WORK

These changes in men's behavior and expectations relate in large part to changes in women's behavior and expectations. As one woman (aged 21) commented:

> The question of equality don't really come in. It is taken for granted that we [women] are human beings. We not goin' to be havin' a heart attack or somethin' if we have to open a car door. A young man today, he assumes you open the door for yourself. If you don't, he drive off and don't even know you aren't there!

She elaborated by pointing out that:

> part of it is how you carry yourself. We don't act as if we are weak; we can take care of ourselves; we not dependin' on you [men] at all.

Women's expectations are grounded in an ideology of equality that they consistently identify as deriving from their experiences in school and with media influences from North America. Women have generalized this egalitarian ethic, and expectations of egalitarian behavior, to all social relationships. Thus as one young woman (aged 22) explained of her relationships with men: "I want to be treated like a person, not like an animal, not like a possession." Women take the view that they, like all people, are unique; that their perspectives may be different from one another, and different from the men with whom they become involved, but that their perspectives, like the perspectives of men, are valid simply because they are people. Because women, like men, have legitimate points of view, it follows that it is wrong for men to impose their will on women.

Women's behavior is grounded in their new-found economic independence. The generational differences in economic independence are implicit in the changes in women's occupational placement as documented in Table 4.3. Women were unlikely to find other than menial employment prior to 1960. Table 4.3 reveals that few women in the oldest cohort have been able to take advantage of the employment opportunities opened to their daughters. In 1985, 90% of these women were either unemployed or employed only in the lowest paying positions. Subsequent cohorts, by contrast, have found increasing employment in jobs where working conditions and pay are markedly higher. As indicated earlier, women still tend to receive lower pay than do men and still there are relatively few women in professional and managerial positions. Nonetheless, the proportion of younger women employed at this level has increased by 250%-400%. The proportion of younger women employed in skilled technical positions or as white collar workers has increased even more dramatically.

Such employment provides young women with power that was denied to their mothers. Moreover, young women enjoy changes in men's expectations that stem from the different living conditions those men experienced. Men in their twenties, especially, are likely to have been raised in a home in which their own mothers were working regularly in positions that paid well and that provided a basis for gaining self-esteem other than from her family. Such women have tended to expect their sons, like their daughters, to participate in housework. Men raised in such a context are those whose family training predisposes them to treat their wives with an equality foreign to the generation of their fathers.

Spousal relationships continue to experience strains that were documented by Greenfield (1966) in the 1950s. Mothers-in-law continue to interfere in a son's choice of spouse, especially when it means depriving them of material support they believe to be rightly theirs. Similarly, men who find themselves living with their in-laws continue to be frustrated by a lack of independence. The number of couples who experience such strains, however, appears to be much smaller than in the 1950s.

TABLE 4.3
Occupational Class by Cohort

Occupational Class	Cohort			
	20-34	35-49	50-64	Total
Professional	3.68	1.85	.00	2.07
Managerial	4.29	6.79	2.75	4.84
White collar	23.93	23.46	3.67	18.66
Skilled labor	17.79	13.58	4.59	12.90
Laborer	18.40	23.46	22.02	21.20
Hawker	.00	1.85	12.84	3.92
Cottage industry crafts	1.23	.62	4.59	1.84
Farmer	.61	1.85	2.75	1.61
Unemployed	30.06	26.54	46.79	32.95
TOTAL	100.00	100.00	100.00	100.00
n =	164	163	109	436

Test statistic	VALUE	DF	PROB
Likelihood ratio chi-square	88.267	16	.000
Coefficient	value	asymptotic std. error	
Goodman-Kruskal gamma	.2831	.05144	

A new source of strain stemming from women's increased levels of education and income is of greater significance among younger couples. When men and women used to quarrel, as one woman pointed out, "They still had to live with one another and there was no TV or video or extra bedrooms to retreat to." House structure and women's dependence on men facilitated agreement and, perhaps, wife beatings. Today, however, when women argue with their spouses they can throw out "I got my own . . ." and can either retreat to another bedroom or separate themselves by watching the television or a video tape. Women who seek to assert control over their own lives can overdo it, deny their spouses the respect they seek for themselves, and create tensions that simply did not exist for their mothers.

Moreover, and primarily since the late 1970s and early 1980s, the affluence of contemporary Barbadian households has been accompanied by the phenomenon of parents who assume responsibility for household chores and children who assume little or none. In the 1950s, most families experienced a situation in which everyone had to help in one way or another if the family was to live comfortably. You had to fetch water, sweep the house, wash dishes and clothes by hand, and tend the animals. In the 1980s, virtually every Barbadian household has running water and electricity. "Labor-saving" appliances have reduced the need for unskilled household labor. Parents generally neither find alternative employments for their children nor demand that their children assist around the house in serious ways. Children have come to expect their leisure and to complain when their parents ask them to work. As likely as not, children of the 1980s come home from school and immediately turn on the television or watch a video tape. More than one exasperated mother (ages ranged from the late twenties through the thirties) exclaimed, "They [the kids] think it [TV, video] has always been here!" and "Young people today don't like to do anything but lay around!"

RESTRICTED CHILDBEARING

The ethnographic data reviewed in Chapter 3 suggest that, because childbearing entailed only investment expenditures, women experienced fertility levels limited only by constraints on their fecundity and by constraints on their sexual activity implicit in their spousal unions. The ethnographic data reviewed in this chapter indicate that younger women bear children in a material context in which children can no longer function effectively as resource channel gatekeepers. The cohort age-specific fertility ratios presented in the appendix reveal that age-specific fertility has fallen consistently for all cohorts beyond the oldest. The fertility at ages 15-19 and 20-24 for women in the youngest cohorts is only 50%-60% of the comparable fertility of the oldest cohort. The fertility of cohorts beyond the youngest exhibits equivalent reductions when compared with the fertility of women aged 50-64 in 1985, the women who constituted the bulk of the childbearing women of the 1950s.

These fertility declines have been matched by changes in women's view of the moral economy of childbearing and parent-child relationships. Whereas in the 1950s, women generally looked upon childbearing as an investment activity, in the 1980s, women generally look upon childbearing as a consumption activity that must be balanced by their desire to pursue a career outside the home and by their (and their spouse's) alternative uses of time, energy, and money. Women in the 1950s overwhelmingly believed both that childbearing took precedence over alternative activities and that children *owed* them support because they gave their children life. How should children fulfill those maternal obligations? Simply, as one older woman pointed out, "by bringing me money every month!"

These differences in the moral economy of childbearing and parent-child relationships were measured by a simple index constructed as the sum of the scores from two questions (see appendix for a fuller description): (1) Do you think that children *owe* their parents more than their parents owe them, or that parents owe their children more than their children owe their parents? and (2) Should getting pregnant and having children take precedence over personal goals (having children *is* my personal goal), or should reaching personal goals (e.g., a career) take precedence over having children? Both questions were scored on a three-point scale: 0 if the response indicated that children constituted a net economic loss to parents, 2 if the response indicated that children constituted a net economic gain to parents, and 1 if the response indicated a balance between these options. The moral economy index thus could attain values of 4, 3, 2, 1, and 0. High values (e.g., 4 or 3) indicate that childbearing is viewed as an investment activity. Low values (e.g., 1 or 0) indicate that childbearing is viewed as a consumption activity.

Figure 4.5 traces this change in women's perspective over the period 1950-1980 by plotting the proportion of women aged 20-24 during a given year who scored a 3 or 4 on the moral economy index and can thus fairly be described as women who view childbearing as an investment activity. As in the case of the education time series, these proportions were estimated from the sample of women by computing cohort means and assigning missing points on the assumption of constant rates of decline between cohort means. The proportion of women who view childbearing as investment activity fell slowly throughout the 1950s. After 1960, however, this proportion fell dramatically and consistently to a low of about 17% in 1980.

Conversely, of course, the trends in Figure 4.5 also reveal an increase, especially after 1960, in the proportion of women who view childbearing as a consumption activity. In concrete terms, this means that women have come (1) to believe that parental obligations to children balance with or supersede children's obligations to parents and (2) to see their desire for a career take precedence over the bearing of children. The rationale behind both views is clearly understood.

Intergenerational Obligations

The vast majority of younger Barbadian women explicitly disavow that they "owe" their parents anything, occasionally with some vehemence. While they disavow that they owe their parents, younger women do tend to acknowledge that they have obligations to their parents. Their views contrast with those of their mothers or grandmothers in that they believe that parents should have equal or, most likely, greater obligations to their children. The means by which young women justify their position is intriguing. In West Africa, the single most regularly

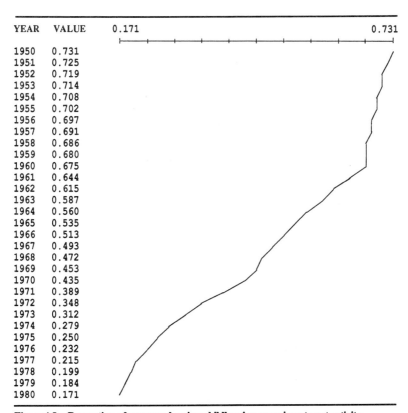

YEAR	VALUE
1950	0.731
1951	0.725
1952	0.719
1953	0.714
1954	0.708
1955	0.702
1956	0.697
1957	0.691
1958	0.686
1959	0.680
1960	0.675
1961	0.644
1962	0.615
1963	0.587
1964	0.560
1965	0.535
1966	0.513
1967	0.493
1968	0.472
1969	0.453
1970	0.435
1971	0.389
1972	0.348
1973	0.312
1974	0.279
1975	0.250
1976	0.232
1977	0.215
1978	0.199
1979	0.184
1980	0.171

Figure 4.5. Proportion of women who view childbearing as an investment activity.

cited reason children give for acknowledging that they owe support to their parents is that "They born me"—that is, their parents gave them life. Until recently, Barbadians concurred with this view. In the Barbados of the 1980s, however, this moral precept has been turned on its head to become the single most frequently cited justification of the view that children *do not owe their parents* and of the view that *parents owe their children.* When young Barbadians are pressured to provide maternal support, they respond, "I did not ask to be born!"

Why? Young women believe that it is wrong for people to use social relationships to engage in explicit, balanced material reciprocities. This, the very foundation (one could argue) of all human societies, is perceived to contradict directly a principle of egalitarianism. Corollaries to this principle are that everyone has the right to be independent of others and, conversely, that no one has the right to impose his or her will on others. When mothers try to justify support they believe is rightfully theirs, their daughters are likely to perceive their mothers as the ones who have provided material care for (immoral) ulterior motives and who are trying to impose their will on another unjustifiably.

A very common view among young women is that the obligations between parents and children should balance one another. Both mothers and daughters should help each other when each needs the help. The relative obligations vary over time. Children should receive the most help when they are young and mothers should receive more help when they are old.

But young people tend to believe that assistance provided among adults should be contingent on the relative economic position of mother and children. Significantly, young women conceptualize "relative economic position" in terms of their own wants and desires. If we use the criteria of working conditions and real income, Barbadians are far better off today than they were in the 1950s. In terms of the perceptions of younger people, however, the expenses of living make such criteria meaningless. Thus as one woman (aged 27) observed and rationalized, "My parents had harder working conditions, but I think I do a lot more for my children with education being so costly today."

Many younger people have thus come to look upon caring for an older mother as an illegitimate constraint on their own activities. Consequently, children are increasingly less likely to help their mothers and, when they do, they appear to give mothers smaller proportions of their income. One woman noted that a daughter may finally begin to help her mother, but only "when she sees her sisters and brothers not doing anything." The maternal obligations that used to be taken for granted— "giving was like breathing" an older woman observed—now is a source of conflict among adult siblings.

Childbearing as a Consumption Activity

Thus younger Barbadians take the position that their plans and dreams should take precedence over the wishes of others—their mothers included. In this sense, bonds between mothers and children have weakened considerably. However, this weakening has been accompanied by a change in the character of those relationships, at least between mothers and their daughters. The parental distance that characterized such relationships in the 1950s and that led to daughters being warned about keeping away from young men without being told what to keep away from has been replaced by an emotional closeness that has permitted greater intellectual sharing, and more direct information about men and sex.

Young women's beliefs that their plans and dreams should take precedence over the wishes of their mothers are consistently applied to their own children, for they see their obligations to their children as superseding their children's maternal obligations. Yet, as a man in his early thirties pointed out, "There is the water bill, the light bill, the grocery bill, and school fees." Children cost money. If you ask almost any Barbadian why young people don't have more children, they respond, "They cannot afford them!"

Of course, this proximate motivation to reduce age-specific fertility and to truncate reproductive careers sharply cannot explain the Barbadian fertility transition. If you ask a West African the same question, he or she will give you the same answer. The difference is that Barbadians "can't afford" more than one or two children and West Africans "can't afford" more than six or seven.

These responses appear to tap an important dimension of fertility change, nonetheless: When economic conditions improve, fertility is likely to increase; when economic conditions worsen, fertility is likely to decline. It is thus crucial to differentiate fertility declines that result from fluctuations in economic conditions from fertility declines that result from the social conditions that precipitate fertility transition. The former stems from short-term fluctuations in economic conditions.[3] The latter stems, this study argues, from a fundamental change in the position children occupy in resource structure. Both can exist jointly: Increasing prosperity can reduce the rate at which fertility transition proceeds and decreasing prosperity can increase the rate at which transition proceeds. Fertility declines that stem from depressed economic conditions do not constitute fertility transition. In Chapter 8, I examine the effect of this macro-level phenomenon, differentiate fertility fluctuations resulting from economic fluctuations rather than fertility transition, and show that increases in real income have, in fact, led to increases in fertility. Here, I simply observe that when young Barbadians claim that they "cannot afford" to have more than one or two children, they directly contradict the massive increases in material affluence Barbados has experienced over the last 30 years.

If the sharply restricted childbearing of young Barbadian women cannot be explained by reference to the objective costs of bearing and raising children, then what does explain it? It is plausible that the Barbadian fertility transition has been a simple function of "modernization" and all that it entails: increased levels of urbanization;

increases, both directly (because more Barbadians visit and have kin residing off the island than ever before) and indirectly (because of major increases in the level of media consumption) in the impact of values imported from the developed countries of North America and Western Europe; massive increases in the level of education women experience and all that those increases entail for the widening of perspectives and for the inculcation of values that emphasize egalitarian family relationships; and massive increases in material wealth. An older physician with wide-ranging experience in public health and family planning observed that the Barbadian fertility transition was a simple function of changes in how people use their time: In the 1950s and previously, copulation was the predominant form of entertainment; in the 1980s, men and women have more and better things to do in their leisure time and don't want the burden and costs of children to interfere with those activities.

I believe his observation is correct, in part. However, a person who has been with the Barbados Family Planning Association since its inception makes the point more directly: "People today have prospects in life, hopes they want to realize." As indicated earlier in this chapter, the mothers and fathers of women in the youngest cohorts view the behavior of their sons and daughters with some trepidation. They variously observe that

   young people do not respect their elders;

   young people are materialistic;

   families are breaking down;

   young people have less concern for what their parents say and want, and for
      what others say and want, than in the past; and young people simply are
      disrespectful.

I believe that what older Barbadians observe is merely that young people "have prospects in life, hopes they want to realize." Surely older Barbadians had their own dreams when they were younger. The prospects available to older Barbadians, of course, were in fact highly constrained. Changes in the Barbadian resource structure have lifted many of those constraints. Young people can, with substantial justification, look forward to realizing dreams denied to their fathers and mothers.

The presence of constraints associated with the Barbadian resource structure prior to 1960 meant that, especially for women, children functioned as crucial resource channel gatekeepers. Children cannot serve as gatekeepers in the presence of competitive employing organizations that, consequently, increasingly emphasize owner and employee productivity. Children thus become consumer durables—very special ones, of course; consumer durables that one can love and that can love in return; but consumer durables nonetheless. Bearing children thus becomes a consumption decision in which children must be selected like television sets or videos. Parents have special obligations to their children—once they are born. Children can and do take precedence over many if not all other consumer choices they make. Hence, it becomes wrong that *bearing* children itself take precedence over a woman's personal goals and dreams.

Therefore, I believe that the Barbadian fertility transition reflects, on the micro level, a change in way in which women conceptualize themselves. In the 1950s, women were, as described by a woman aged 49, "trapped"— subordinated to men in a resource structure they could not influence. Most Barbadian women could improve or optimize their resource access only by bearing children. In the 1980s, women are becoming—indeed, younger women have in large part already become—agents who can chart their own course in life. However, these micro-level changes in women's view—both of themselves, and in the moral economy of childbearing and parent-child relationships that follows from that view—can be realized only because of the macro-level changes in the Barbadian resource structure reviewed at the beginning of this chapter.

Of course, women's experience in school (on the micro level) and the increasing proportions of women who have completed ever higher levels of formal educational training (on the macro level), may have had a profound influence on women's perceptions of moral economy: of relationships between men and women as well as of relationships between parents and children. Women themselves tend to identify such influences as having had direct bearing on how they view themselves. I believe, however, (1) that ideologies stemming from formal educational training provide post hoc justification for women's beliefs; (2) that education itself is not necessary for the emergence of such beliefs; (3) that the presence of real opportunities for improving one's material well-being independently of social relationships is both necessary and sufficient for acting on such beliefs; and (4) that the opening of new and competitive resource access channels provides those opportunities. At the micro level, I believe that the Barbadian fertility transition has been a simple function of increasing proportions of women who view childbearing as entailing consumption expenditures. The increasing proportion of women who view childbearing as entailing consumption expenditures has been a simple function of the opening of new and competitive resource access channels. Hence, at the macro level, the

Barbadian fertility transition has been a simple function of the opening of new and competitive resource access channels.

Of course, both these claims and the view that the Barbadian fertility transition has been a simple function of all that "modernization" or "westernization" entails are empirical issues that ethnographic data and analysis can evaluate only ambiguously. Subsequent chapters subject these contrasting views of the Barbadian fertility transition to explicit and systematic statistical tests.

NOTES

1. Stoffle (1972: 138) documents the sexual discrimination in hiring practices that were being practiced in the late 1960s and early 1970s.

2. With some justification, tourism is also a much maligned development strategy. Karch (1979: 271-278ff) nicely summarizes the criticisms that apply to the role of tourism in development, as well as the problems that attend "industrialization by invitation," although she misjudges many of their effects at the micro level.

3. See Easterlin (1978) for one theoretical foundation of this claim. Wrigley and Schofield (1981) document fluctuations in fertility with economic conditions for historical English data; Hum and Basilevski (1978) demonstrate economic fluctuations in fertility for Jamaica.

CHILDREN'S IMPACT ON WOMEN'S INCOME

WERE CHILDREN REALLY INCOME PRODUCERS?

The ethnographic data reviewed in Chapter 3 revealed that, prior to 1960, children functioned as resource channel gatekeepers for their mothers. In a woman's youth, children legitimated her claims on income from men. In her middle age, children provided financial support that could make her independent of her prior dependency on men. In her old age, financial support from children meant the difference between abject poverty and a moderate, or even comfortable, level of living. These data also revealed that women believed that it was right for children to provide them support and they geared their lives to producing and raising them. But is there anything other than anecdotal evidence to support these claims? The following analyses reveal that these expectations and the moral economy on which they were based were solidly grounded in material reality.

Two of the analyses reported in this chapter use retrospective estimates of income levels as dependent variables. As indicated in the appendix, these variables are *not* based on retrospective reports of the income flows from specific individuals. Such reports would contain far too much error to be useful. In lieu of accurate data on particular income flows, I collected information on *sources* of income at different ages. These data appear to be readily and accurately recalled. I also collected data on estimates of weekly income levels for sequential five-year periods at the beginning of the reproductive period. Estimates for five-year periods capture error from many sources (income rises and falls, sources change, income flows from particular sources change) and thus tend to randomize it, albeit with noticeable error variance. Women who felt uncertain about previous income levels were recorded as not providing information. With few exceptions, the reported income estimates followed expected patterns. The exceptions were identified statistically and were recoded as missing data. The remaining income estimates surely contain error, but the error variance appears to be small and randomized. Parameter estimates will be unbiased and consistent and all statistical tests will apply. Hence, measurement error that attaches to the retrospective income variables will not distort the conclusions of the following analysis.

This analysis is divided into two segments. The first segment addresses the relative dependence of young women's material welfare on themselves and on spouses. The second segment addresses the relative dependence of older women's material welfare on themselves and on others, especially their children.

HAS YOUNG WOMEN'S MATERIAL WELFARE BEEN DEPENDENT ON SPOUSAL SUPPORT?

In the absence of historical data on wealth flows through particular channels, we can ask: What components of women's weekly incomes can be accounted for by different sources? If a source consistently contributes relatively large proportions of women's weekly incomes, that source will be closely correlated with income level after we control for the effects of other potential sources, and it can be identified by its associated t statistic. If children functioned as resource channel gatekeepers prior to 1960 and not afterward, we would expect that

(1) prior to 1960, women's contributions to her own weekly income would be negligible compared with spousal contributions, and

(2) after 1960, women's contributions to her own weekly income would equal or supersede spousal contributions.

This hypothesis can be modeled in the following way:

$$Y = \beta_0 + \beta_1 X_1 + \beta_2 X_2 + \beta_3 (D*X_2) + \epsilon$$

Where Y = real weekly income (adjusted for inflation; see the appendix)

X_1 = Spousal contributions, indicated by 1 if a current mate contributes to a woman's income and 0 otherwise

X_2 = women's contributions, indicated by 1 if they are employed and 0 otherwise

D = a dummy variable equal to 1 if the time period is prior to 1960 and 0 otherwise

Spousal contributions to women's incomes both prior to and after 1960 are estimated by the regression coefficient β_1. Women's contributions to their own income from employment are estimated in two ways. After 1960, women's contributions are estimated by the regression coefficient β_2. Prior to 1960, women's contributions are estimated by: $\beta_2 + \beta_3$.

Figure 5.1 traces normal probability plots of real weekly incomes both for ages 15-19 and ages 20-24. As one would expect with income data, these plots reveal sharp skews. Such a sharply skewed distribution presents a real problem for model estimation in the absence of independent variables that can capture an exponential series. However, the distribution of both variables is smoothed considerably when we transform them by taking their natural logarithm (see Figure 5.2). The distribution of incomes for ages 15-19 still displays marked non-normality at its lower end. This discontinuity reflects an unusually large number of women aged 15-19 who reported no income. This poses a problem for estimation, but the large proportion of women reporting no incomes for these ages appears to be an empirically real phenomenon. The discontinuity can be eliminated, but adjustments to the data base do not alter conclusions based on the existing set of measurements and (see next) no further adjustment of the data were undertaken.

Table 5.1 presents correlation matrices that include as potential independent variables all recorded sources of women's income for ages 15-19 and 20-24. Exploratory multiple regression models of income that used all sources of income as independent variables confirm the results of even a cursory examination of these matrices. Both matrices reveal (1) that sources of income are so diverse and occur in such diverse combinations that there is virtually no multicollinearity in these data, and (2) that the only variables that display a close relationship with levels of real income are spouses' and women's own employment. The absence of multicollinearity makes interpretation of the following models clear: During their early reproductive period, the only individual sources that regularly contribute to weekly incomes in significant ways are spouses and women themselves, through their own employment. The constants in the models appear to capture the effects of the other sources of income, which contribute in various combinations but (on average) in relatively small and equivalent quantities.

Table 5.2 presents the solution for the model that embodies the hypothesis already developed. The normal probability plot of residuals in Figure 5.3 reveals that, with the exception of the large proportion of women who reported no income for the ages 15-19, the residuals are normally distributed. The skew for Model 1 can be eliminated if we eliminate women who reported no income. Regression results are substantively unchanged, however. Elimination of these women seems unwarranted because the only effect of their inclusion is to make

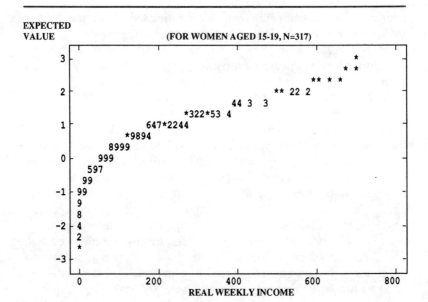

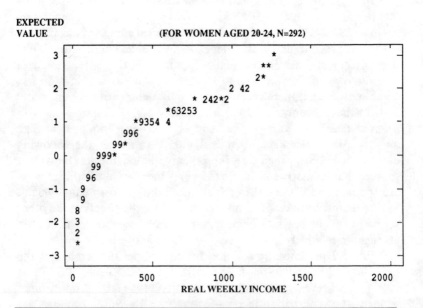

Figure 5.1.   Normal probability plots of real weekly income.

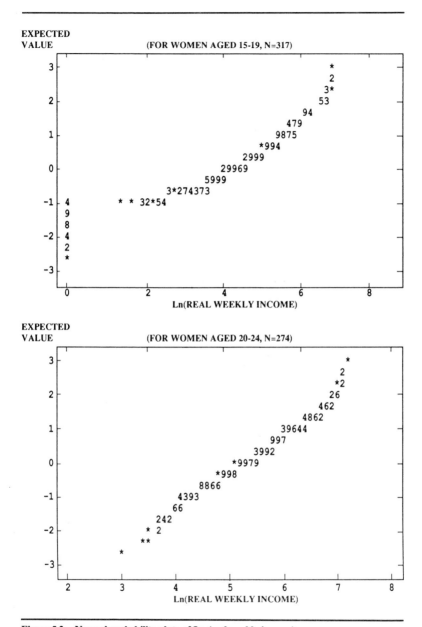

Figure 5.2. Normal probability plots of Ln (real weekly income).

TABLE 5.1
Intercorrelations Among Sources of Young Women's
Real Weekly Income

	M	F	B	Z	GP
Women aged 15-19 (N = 317)					
Mother	1.000				
Father	0.146	1.000			
Brother	-0.050	0.055	1.000		
Sister	0.036	-0.046	0.115	1.000	
Grandparent	-0.014	-0.057	-0.051	-0.027	1.000
Other	-0.142	-0.090	-0.002	-0.037	-0.062
Former mate	0.002	0.020	-0.034	0.132	-0.033
Remittance	0.010	0.035	0.153	0.307	-0.009
Spouse	-0.043	-0.090	-0.029	-0.018	-0.067
Job	-0.164	-0.135	-0.015	0.048	-0.191
Ln (income)	-0.129	-0.103	0.040	0.128	-0.197

	O	FM	REM	H	J
Other	1.000				
Former mate	-0.036	1.000			
Remittance	0.261	0.223	1.000		
Spouse	-0.095	0.006	-0.046	1.000	
Job	0.006	0.034	-0.036	0.052	1.000
Ln (income)	0.033	0.045	0.080	0.337	0.510

	M	F	B	Z	GP
Women aged 20-24 (N = 292)					
Mother	1.000				
Father	0.416	1.000			
Brother	-0.049	0.020	1.000		
Sister	-0.096	-0.072	0.050	1.000	
Grandparent	0.116	0.080	-0.043	-0.045	1.000
Other	-0.057	-0.067	-0.003	-0.009	-0.070
Former mate	-0.034	0.037	-0.055	0.009	0.004
Remittance	0.027	0.060	0.093	0.395	-0.102
Spouse	0.007	-0.050	-0.124	-0.068	-0.015
Job	-0.124	0.018	0.096	0.057	-0.148
Ln (income)	-0.013	-0.041	-0.044	0.046	-0.048

	O	FM	REM	H	J
Other	1.000				
Former mate	-0.046	1.000			
Remittance	0.329	0.075	1.000		
Spouse	-0.010	0.074	0.016	1.000	
Job	-0.019	0.001	0.004	-0.180	1.000
Ln (income)	-0.061	-0.002	0.056	0.170	0.218

TABLE 5.2
Spousal Contributions to Young Women's Weekly Income

Dependent Variable: Ln (Real Weekly Income)
Model 1: Ages 15-19 (N = 317)
R²: .382 Adjusted R²: .376   Standard Error of Estimate: 1.367

Variable	Coefficient	STD. Error	STD. Coef.	T	P (2 Tail)
Constant	2.816	0.118	0.000	23.944	0.008
Spouse	1.239	0.168	0.330	7.357	0.000
Woman's job	1.848	0.159	0.535	11.627	0.000
Pre-1960s job	-1.183	0.337	-0.163	-3.511	0.001

Analysis of Variance

Source	Sum-of-Squares	DF	Mean-Square	F-ratio	P
Regression	361.041	3	120.347	64.367	0.000
Residual	585.218	313	1.870		

Model 2: Ages 20-24 (N = 294)
R²: .117 Adjusted R²: .108   Standard Error of Estimate: 0.898

Variable	Coefficient	STD. Error	STD. Coef.	T	P (2 Tail)
Constant	4.558	0.175	0.000	26.102	0.000
Spouse	0.503	0.134	0.212	3.752	0.000
Woman's job	0.658	0.139	0.272	4.728	0.000
Pre-1960s job	-0.608	0.151	-0.229	-4.022	0.001

Analysis of Variance

Source	Sum-of-Squares	DF	Mean-Square	F-ratio	P
Regression	30.880	3	10.293	12.767	0.000
Residual	233.815	290	0.806		

estimates of the very lowest incomes less reliable. The plots of studentized residuals by the estimates of these models, in Figure 5.4, reveal that residuals are uniformly distributed for both models.

The results presented in Table 5.2 do not change when other sources of income are added to the equation, either singly or in combination. Likewise, these results do not change when we test for a change in the level of men's contributions prior to 1960. Model 1 accounts for nearly 40% of the variance in weekly incomes for women aged 15-19. Model 2 accounts only for about 10% of the variance in weekly incomes for women aged 20-24. This discrepancy almost certainly reflects the increasing importance of occupational class position at older ages (see the following analysis). The incomes of the youngest women reflect

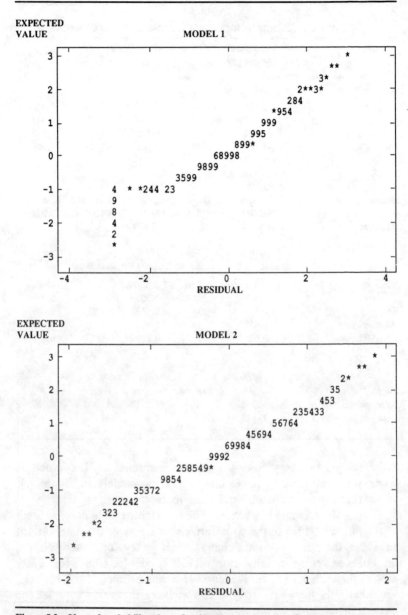

Figure 5.3.   Normal probability plots of residuals.

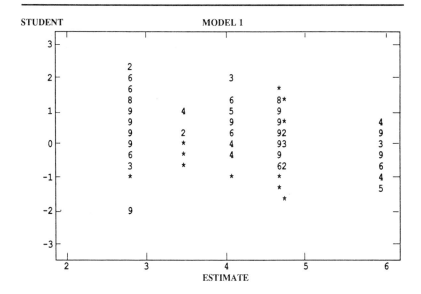

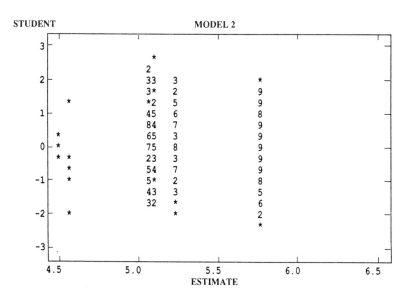

Figure 5.4.   Studentized residuals by the estimate.

relatively little variance in class position either for spouses or for the women themselves. Income at these ages commonly stemmed from low-level working-class positions, only infrequently from the white-collar class, and almost never from managerial or professional classes. Employment in occupations that yielded markedly higher incomes becomes prevalent only during women's early twenties.

The results for the 15-19 age period and the 20-24 age period are equivalent and unambiguous. Prior to 1960, women's earning power was negligible to very low relative to men's. Spousal contributions sharply increased women's income. Thus, during the 1950s, 15- to 19-year-old women who did not work and who were supported only by the kinship sources identified previously could expect weekly incomes of only about BDS\$16.71. Such women could double their income by working—working 15- to 19-year-old women without a spouse could expect weekly incomes of: $\beta_0 + \beta_2 + \beta_3$, or about BDS\$32.50. However, spousal support increased expected weekly incomes nearly three and one-half times—to $\beta_0 + \beta_1 + \beta_2 + \beta_3$, or about BDS\$112.17. The income discrepancies for women in their eary twenties are less marked, but sharp nonetheless. Thus 20- to 24-year-old women who did not work and who were supported only by the kinship sources identified previously could expect weekly incomes of about BDS\$95.39. Such women could add to their expected weekly income only incrementally (to about BDS\$100.28) by working. However, spousal support increased expected weekly incomes by 65%, to about BDS\$165.84.

After 1960, however, women's ability to support themselves—and thus their ability to control their own lives—increased dramatically. Thus, after 1960, 15- to 19-year-old working women could expect weekly real incomes of about \$106.06, or more than three and a quarter times their expected weekly incomes prior to this time; 20- to 24-year-old working women could expect weekly real incomes of about \$184.20, or nearly 84% more than their expected weekly incomes prior to this time. Spousal contributions continued to add significantly to women's incomes. Nevertheless, women's increased ability to support themselves independently of men marked a major change in Barbadian family relationships.

HAS OLDER WOMEN'S MATERIAL WELFARE BEEN DEPENDENT ON SUPPORT FROM CHILDREN?

We can evaluate the claim that older women's material welfare has been dependent on support from their children with better measures of both independent and dependent variables. These measures are better because they are measured for a current period (1985). These current data bear on an hypothesis concerning 1950s behavior for several reasons. First, the young women who contributed most heavily to high 1950s fertility did so partly under the assumption of long-run support for children. Second, the women who were young in the 1950s have become dependent on support from their children only recently. Because employment opportunities for women have expanded tremendously since 1960, and since most young women (and young men) reject the obligations of support expected by their mothers, the fact that these data bear on 1985 behavior should actually make it more difficult to demonstrate older women's dependence on support from children than if we had used data for the 1950s on women who were old then. The only children who could honor obligations to elderly mothers in 1985 were women in their late thirties and forties whose principal childbearing occurred at the beginning of Barbados' fertility transition. Of course, this group includes many who radically changed their view of the moral economy of parent-child relationships. Had these women not been subject to the changes in perspective that accompanied fertility transition, we could expect their level of maternal support to be higher than it actually has been.

As in the previous tests, the dependent variable is weekly income. Income at all ages should be a function of whether or not a woman is employed and, if she is, her occupational class. The empirical examination of income and class presented in the appendix suggests that class bears a close relationship with income, but that the income levels of some classes cannot be differentiated. I used distinctions that emerged in that analysis to rank women's classes as follows: 1 if unemployed, 2 if working class (farmer, petty trader or cottage industry producer, or laborer with varying degrees of skill), 3 if white-collar employment, and 4 if managerial or professional. The box-plot of income by class in Figure 5.5 reveals a good fit.

Figure 5.5 also suggests two further modifications: (1) that class bears an exponential relationship to income and (2) that levels within the managerial/professional class need to be differentiated. I adjusted for differentiation within the managerial/professional class by returning to the original data and assigning a new rank 5 to the highest levels of that class. An exponential series was created by squaring the class rank. Figure 5.6 reveals that there is an excellent fit between a woman's occupational class and her weekly income level after these adjustments are made.

The analyses presented in Table 5.2 revealed that, even in 1985, young women's income continued to be partly dependent on spousal contri-

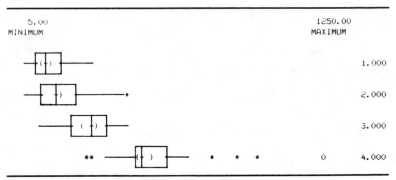

Figure 5.5.   Box-plot of current income by occupational class.

butions. An older woman's income also plausibly depends, at least partly, on spousal contributions and, thus on spousal class position. Evaluation of a box-plot of spousal class and income did not reveal an exponential relationship. Moreover, white collar contributions to women's income could not be discriminated from contributions by professional or managerial level spouses. Accordingly, spousal class was coded as follows: 1 if there was no spouse or if he was unemployed, 2 if he was working class, and 3 if he were employed in either white-collar, professional, or managerial occupations.

Current incomes are also likely to reflect the structural break in the Barbadian economy that occurred around 1960. The occupations that offered the best incomes and chances for advancement opened up after 1960 and few women over age 50 could have taken advantage of those positions. We might expect that class advantages would result in the same income slope irrespective of structural break, but that women over age 50 would have a lower origin.

Income should also reflect such variables as length of time on the job, the competitiveness of the firm for which the employee works (and thus its salary schedule), the sector of employment, and the woman's special skills and abilities. Variables such as these could not be measured in this research and must be excluded from the model.

Most important for purposes of this study, however, the income of older women should be dependent on contributions from their children. If pretransition fertility reflected a resource structure in which older women's material welfare was dependent on the number of children she bore, we should be able to show that the weekly income of older women increases with the number of children who contribute income. (In individual cases, income may also reflect sources other than the woman,

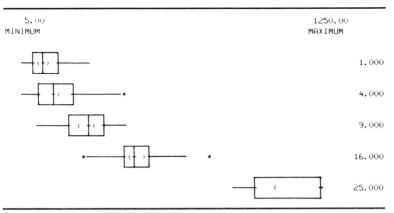

Figure 5.6. Box-plot of income by occupational class adjusted for differentiation within the managerial/professional class.

her spouse, and her children, but sources of income other than these were not generally significant.)

Table 5.3 presents data on the weekly income contributions of children for the cross-section of cohorts used in this study. These data suggest that children first begin to contribute maternal support when their mothers are in their late thirties. Both the proportion of women who are supported by children and the mean number of sons and daughters who contribute support increase regularly up to age 50. After age 50, the mean number of children who contribute support to their mothers increases, but the proportion of women who are supported by their children remains reasonably stable at over 80% of all women aged 50 years or over. The evidence reviewed suggests that sons should provide important levels of income in their late teens and early twenties and may contribute important levels of support to women in the late thirties and early forties. However, as sons move into their late twenties and beyond, the probability that they will contract legal marriages or establish consensual unions increases sharply. The level of support sons can provide mothers should decline sharply. Daughters, however, should not be subject to such restrictions. Indeed, the income daughters would have available to support their mothers should actually increase as they marry legally or contract consensual unions. Hence, if children do constitute net income producers by the end of a woman's life, we would expect that it will be the contributions from daughters that function this way.

TABLE 5.3
Resource Flows From Children to Their Mothers

Income Contributors	Age of Mother				
	35-39	40-44	45-49	50-54	55+
Mean number of sons	.029	.216	.488	.976	1.328
Mean number of daughters	.029	.255	.558	.857	1.119
Proportion of mothers who receive support from children	.058	.294	.535	.810	.821

The reasoning just outlined can be modeled in the following way:

$$Y = \beta_0 + \beta_1 X_1 + \beta_2 X_2 + \beta_3 X_3 + \beta_4 D + \epsilon$$

Where: Y = current income in BDS$
X_1 = spousal class position
X_2 = class position of woman
X_3 = the number of daughters who contribute support to women aged 50 and over.
D = a dummy variable equal to 1 if the woman is aged 50 or over and 0 otherwise.

The income of posttransition women is estimated by: β_2* the woman's class position. The income of pretransition women is estimated by: β_2* the woman's class position + β_3* the number of daughters who contribute material support + β_4.

The solution presented in Table 5.4 reveals that this model accounts for nearly 70% of the variance in women's current reported weekly incomes. As in the case of the incomes for young women, the independent variables have very low intercorrelations and the model is not subject to multicollinearity problems. The regression coefficients do not change significantly when the model includes control variables (e.g., contributions from remittances and other sources of income entered either individually or in combination) or when alternative model specifications are used (e.g., testing the possibility that the slopes of the class variables change for older women), and no additional variable adds significantly to our ability to account for variance in current income. The t statistic for the older women variable is relatively low, but this model stipulates 1-tailed tests and the associated probability easily falls within conventional alpha rejection regions.

Figure 5.7 reveals (1) that the residuals are distributed approximately normally and (2) that there may be some outliers. Three outliers show up

TABLE 5.4
Daughter's Contributions to
Elderly Women's Weekly Income

Dependent Variable: Current (1985) Income　　N: 344　　*Squared Multiple R: .678*
Adjusted Squared Multiple R: .674　　*Standard Error of Estimate: 100.164*

Variable	Coefficient	STD. Error	STD. Coef.	T	P (2 Tail)
Constant	-18.230	18.215	0.000	-1.001	0.318
Spousal class	48.265	8.568	0.175	5.633	0.000
Woman's class	28.405	1.151	0.779	24.688	0.000
Older women	-35.558	18.583	-0.075	-1.913	0.057
Number of D's	27.180	10.761	0.099	2.526	0.012

	Analysis of Variance				
	Sum-of-		Mean-		
Source	Squares	DF	Square	F-ratio	P
Regression	7151634.241	4	1787908.560	178.207	0.000
Residual	3401103.873	339	10032.755		

in Figure 5.8. The plot of studentized residuals by the estimate reveals that residuals are distributed uniformly. The three outliers apparent in these plots indicate that the model significantly underestimates the highest weekly income levels. Reexamination of the original data indicate that these income points are not errors. Had we been able to include other pertinent independent variables (mentioned previously), these outliers almost certainly would not exist. In the absence of these variables, the outliers must remain.

With the minor qualification that the model of current incomes underestimates the highest incomes, this analysis confirms the hypothesis just developed and reveals that the material well-being of older Barbadian women is significantly improved by maternal support provided by daughters. In general, as the number of daughters who contribute maternal support increases, so does maternal weekly income.

Of course, not all daughters contribute maternal support, especially in 1985. To judge from the concerns of West African women, however, fear that some children may "turn out bad" and not honor their maternal support obligations makes it especially important to follow a risk aversion strategy of high fertility (Handwerker, 1986c). Such women believe that additional children offset the ungrateful offspring who do not honor maternal support obligations and lead to increased material support in old age. Figure 5.9 reveals that there is only a weak (r = .391) positive association between Barbadian women's completed fertility and the number of their daughters who contribute to their

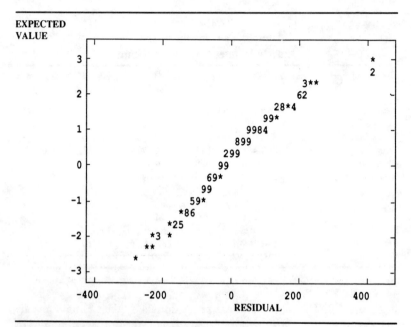

Figure 5.7. Normal probability plot of residuals.

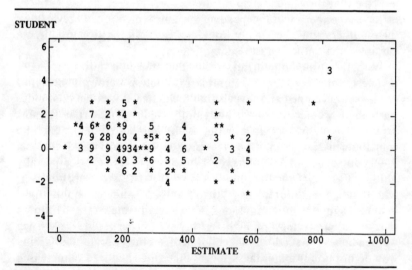

Figure 5.8. Studentized residuals by the estimate.

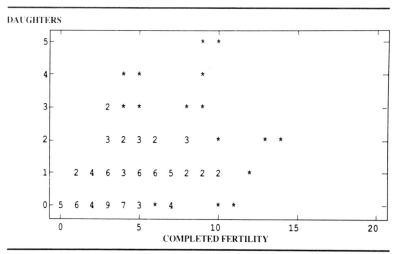

Figure 5.9. **Plot of the number of daughters who contributed financial support to their mothers by their mothers' completed fertility (women 50 years of age and older).**

financial support. The relationship between completed fertility and the number of sons who contribute financial support is slightly weaker (r = .336). Although the number of sources of financial assistance in old age tends to increase with family size, Barbadian women in the 1950s, like West African women in the 1980s, found it far safer to have too many children than to have too few.

Older women enjoy substantive income advantages if they have children who honor material support obligations. These advantages are most clearly revealed by the coefficients in Table 5.5. The regression results in Table 5.4 revealed that the intercept term could not be distinguished from the origin. If we recompute the model through the origin, we obtain the coefficients of Table 5.5. Comparison of the standard error of the estimates in Tables 5.4 and 5.5 reveals that the coefficients model the same relationship. I do not report R^2 for Table 5.5 because, in the absence of a constant, its value is inflated and does not measure the quantity we normally associate with this coefficient.

Examination of the coefficients in Table 5.5 reveals that post-transition women can expect weekly incomes estimated as: β_2*economic class. Thus working-class posttransition women can expect weekly incomes of 28.09*4, or about BDS$112.36, independent of spousal

TABLE 5.5
Daughter's Contributions to
Elderly Women's Weekly Income
(regression through the origin)

Dependent Variable: Current (1985) Income			Standard Error of Estimate: 100.164		
Variable	Coefficient	STD. Error	STD. Coef.	T	P (2 Tail)
Spousal class	40.826	4.262	0.285	9.579	0.000
Woman's class	28.089	1.106	0.711	25.387	0.000
Older women	-38.430	18.360	-0.054	-2.093	0.037
Number of D's	27.588	10.754	0.062	2.565	0.011

	Analysis of Variance				
Source	Sum-of-Squares	DF	Mean-Square	F-ratio	P
Regression	.259968E+08	4	6499210.482	647.796	0.000
Residual	3411153.071	340	10032.803		

contributions. Lower-level professional/managerial-class posttransition women can expect weekly incomes of 28.09*16, or about BDS$449.44, independent of spousal contributions.

By contrast, pretransition women can expect income levels estimated as: β_2*economic class + β_3 + β_4*number of daughters contributing support. In general, pretransition women can expect a weekly income about BDS$38.43 *lower* than their pretransition counterparts—*unless they have daughters who can make up the deficit.* Thus pretransition working-class women without children can expect a weekly income of only about BDS$73.93. However, if three daughters contribute maternal support, such women can expect weekly incomes more than twice as high: BDS$73.93 + 3*27.59, or about BDS$156.70.

SUMMARY

The analyses presented in this chapter constitute strong evidence for the claim that children constituted crucial sources of income for women prior to the beginning of fertility transition around 1960. The income-generating capacity of children was predicated on their position as resource channel gatekeepers. In the absence of employment oppor-tunities that rewarded women's individual skills and abilities, women could access resources by investing in children. In a woman's youth, children legitimated her claims on income from men. In her middle age,

children provided financial support that could make her independent of
her prior dependency on men. In her old age, financial support from
children meant the difference between abject poverty and a moderate, or
even comfortable, level of living.

—6—

CHANGES IN THE MORAL ECONOMY OF CHILDBEARING AND PARENT-CHILD RELATIONSHIPS

Between 1950 and 1980, Barbadian family relationships experienced substantial change marked by a growing power of women to control their own lives and a concomitant growing ideology of (and, to some extent, behavioral) equality between men and women. The blossoming of an equality between men and women has been manifested in an increasing emotional commitment of men to their families that, as the current young cohorts mature, is likely to be accompanied by an increasing emotional bond between fathers and their children, and by an increasing emotional bond between spouses. There is, as yet, no perceptible change in the way women view men: young women continue to report, in approximately the same proportion as did their mothers and grandmothers, that their tie to their own mothers is stronger than their tie to their spouses. Men are still perceived as potentially, if not actually, unreliable. Men actively contribute to this view by continuing to act on the assumption that women are possessions that must be defended from the predatory behavior of other men, and by justifying their own infidelities on the grounds that women themselves cannot be trusted. Greater experience with the young cohort of men may bring about a change in women's views of men. More likely, however, the skewed sex ratio that continues (albeit less intensely) to characterize Barbados will continue to offer young men unusually good opportunities for extra-marital affairs, young men will unduly alienate their spouses by failing to grant them the respect and emotional sharing they want, and change in women's view of men will be slow.

Between 1950 and 1980, the relationships between Barbadian mothers and their children were also transformed. For the most part, women in the younger cohorts have come to believe that, as parents, their responsibilities to their children supersede their children's reciprocal obligations. These beliefs constitute a generalization to their children of the views they have already adopted toward their mothers. Thus the greater freedom young women have been able to realize has led to a weakening of the bonds between mothers and children.

More specifically, Barbadian women have reoriented their emotional commitments. Women in the 1950s were part of an intergenerational continuum traced along maternal lines. Women invested heavily of their time, energy, and emotions in the raising of their children and saw in their children a continuity of obligations they accepted and felt for their own mothers. Women in the 1980s invest less heavily in their children and have created a discontinuity in intergenerational obligations. These comments are not meant to imply that younger women do not, in fact, continue to help their mothers. Many young women do, some in substantial ways. However, young women's investment of time and energy in their own mothers has been sharply reduced over previous generations. Women's own goals and dreams, which include plans for the few children they now have, take precedence over their inter-generational obligations.

CONTRASTING THEORETICAL EXPECTATIONS

These changes in family relationships are not inconsistent with expectations one might have from the viewpoint of standard demographic transition theory. Modernization, after all, should be characterized by a growing ability of women to make independent choices and a decreased subordination of women to men. Likewise, modernization is expected to be accompanied by the breakdown of the extended family and the increased importance of the nuclear family. Considering the historical patterns of Caribbean family organization, one might anticipate that a nuclear family organization would not emerge full-blown in the early stages of modernization, but the data can be used to argue that preconditions for the emergence of a nuclear family pattern have been established on Barbados.

Similarly, these changes in the moral economy of childbearing and parent-child relationships are not inconsistent with expectations one might have from the viewpoint of standard demographic transition theory. Modernization, after all, should be characterized by a growing awareness that unrestricted childbearing may severely constrain the ability of a woman (or a couple) to take advantage of opportunities offered by societal-wide increases in the standard of living. Similarly, since modernization can be expected to be accompanied by the breakdown of the extended family and the increased importance of the nuclear family, one might also expect that such families will come to emphasize the rearing of "higher quality" children—ones who are prepared for the changes in economy and life-style that are part of the modernization process. Parents who have large families cannot afford to provide their children with the schooling and other amenities that might best prepare those children for the future.

If the modernization hypothesis best fits the data, we should be able to show that multicollinearity problems make it difficult to demonstrate the existence of important determinants of the change in the moral economy of childbearing and parent-child relationships. However, if it is possible to identify a clear determinant of changes in moral economy, one might suspect that it would be infant mortality or an index of the rising standards of living that accompany modernization. By contrast, if wealth flows theory correctly interprets fertility transition we should be able to show that change in the moral economy of childbearing and parent-child relationships has been unambiguously and strongly determined by variables that measure the onset of mass, Westernized education. By contrast, if predictions from the resource access hypothesis best fit the data, we should be able to show that change in moral economy has been unambiguously and strongly determined neither by educational variables nor by an index of rising standards of living or declining infant mortality but by variables that measure the creation of new and competitive resource access channels.

This chapter tests these contrasting expectations by exploring both micro- and macro-level determinants of the moral economy of childbearing and parent-child relationships. We shall be concerned with two principal questions. First, can these changes be considered merely as one component of broad social changes that accompany modernization, or do these changes have clearly identifiable determinants? Second, can these changes be best explained by (1) the rising standards of living that modernization theory posits as central to fertility transition, (2) the educational variables that wealth flows theory posits as central to fertility transition, or (3) the growth of employment in industrial manufacturing and tourism, which, on Barbados, constitute indexes of the emergence of new and competitive resource access channels that the resource access hypothesis posits as central to fertility transition?

THE VARIABLES

Dependent Variables

The measure of moral economy used in subsequent analyses is described in the Appendix and has been examined closely in Chapters 5 and 6. This variable consists of an index that measures the extent to which women conceptualize childbearing as an investment or as a consumption activity. This variable is the sum of two questions and can attain values of 4, 3, 2, 1, and 0. High values indicate that childbearing is viewed as an investment activity. Low values indicate that childbearing is viewed as a consumption activity. Regression analysis of this variable that used responses to the two questions from which it was constructed as independent variables revealed that neither original question contributed disproportionately to the final summed score. The micro-level dependent variable is a woman's moral economy index score. The macro-level dependent variable is the proportion of women (aged 20-24) whose score revealed that they clearly viewed childbearing as an investment activity. This variable was described and its historical time-series was plotted in Chapter 4.

Independent Variables

The principal micro-level independent variables are (1) educational attainment, (2) occupational class, and (3) cohort. Educational attainment is expected to capture any effects of the westernization processes that wealth flows theory emphasizes. Occupational class might be thought of as a proxy for the emergence of new and competitive resource access channels. This possibility is not theoretically grounded, however, because this research conceptualizes the effect of new, competitive resource access channels solely as a macro-level phenomenon. Occupational class is expected to capture such effects only marginally. The pertinent macro-level effects are likely to be captured by the constant term and the cohort variable. Cohort is expected to capture the expectations and opportunities that women of (approximately) the same age share with each other. I anticipate that these expectations will reflect macro-level changes in opportunities women perceive, whatever the source of these influences, (e.g., rising standards of living, education,

or changes in resource structure). The question of whether these macro-
level effects stem from rising standards of living, education, the opening
of new and competitive resource access channels, or some combination
of these influences, is the subject of macro-level analysis. In the
following analysis, cohort is measured by women's placement in the
series of five-year cohorts, from 1 (age 20-24) through 8 (age 55-64), as
described in the appendix.

Macro-level variables include measures of (1) educational attainment,
(2) educational prevalence, (3) the level of employment in industrial
manufacturing, and (4) the level of tourist spending, all of which have
been previously described and plotted. Because the modernization
interpretation of fertility transition places such importance on increases
in the standard of living, however, the following analyses will also
examine two further macro-level independent variables: an index of real
wages and infant mortality levels.

Because rising standards of living mean that consumers can purchase
more goods and services per monetary equivalent earned, increases in a
population's material well-being perhaps are best measured by an index
of real wages. This variable, which is described in detail in Chapter 8, is
plotted in Figure 6.1. Real wages tended to fall during the early 1950s
but rose dramatically over the course of the 1960s. The OPEC oil
embargo in the early 1970s adversely affected the cost of living on
Barbados as it did throughout the world. Nonetheless, real wages in
1980 were nearly twice as high as they had been during the early 1950s.
If, as standard demographic transition theory posits, rising standards of
living are accompanied by changes in a population's perspective on
childbearing that lead them to reduce their fertility, we should find that
the increases in real wages Barbados has experienced should lead to
reductions in the proportion of women who view childbearing as an
investment activity.

Of course, Chapter 4 raised another possibility—rising standards of
living may increase the income flows from children. If increases in real
wages have this effect, increases in the index of real wages should lead to
increases in the proportion of women who view childbearing as an
investment activity.

Infant mortality is a sensitive indicator of a region's poverty and, thus
also constitutes an index of a population's material well-being. Infant
mortality on Barbados from 1950 to 1980 is plotted in Figure 6.2. This
variable has been constructed from data provided by census reports and
by various numbers of the archived Barbados Annual Report of the
Director of Medical Services.

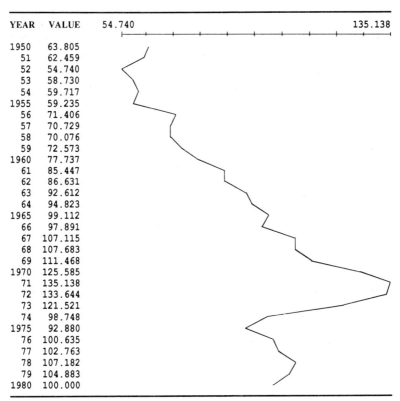

YEAR	VALUE
1950	63.805
51	62.459
52	54.740
53	58.730
54	59.717
1955	59.235
56	71.406
57	70.729
58	70.076
59	72.573
1960	77.737
61	85.447
62	86.631
63	92.612
64	94.823
1965	99.112
66	97.891
67	107.115
68	107.683
69	111.468
1970	125.585
71	135.138
72	133.644
73	121.521
74	98.748
1975	92.880
76	100.635
77	102.763
78	107.182
79	104.883
1980	100.000

Figure 6.1. Index of real wages on Barbados (1980 = 100), 1950-1980.

Infant mortality on Barbados has been notoriously high, as was indicated in Chapter 3. In the early part of this century, infant mortality averaged around 250 deaths for every 1,000 children born. Figure 6.2 reveals that infant mortality was well over 100 as late as the 1950s, long after infant mortality on other islands had fallen well below that level. After 1955, however, improvements in public health care and in the material living conditions of the Barbadian population dramatically reduced infant mortality levels. Comparison of the time series for real wages and infant mortality reveals, as one might suspect, that infant mortality levels began falling precisely when real wages began a dramatic rise in the late 1950s. Overall, the time series correlate inversely very closely ($r = -.858$).

Infant mortality may affect women's perspective of the moral economy of childbearing and parent-child relationships independently

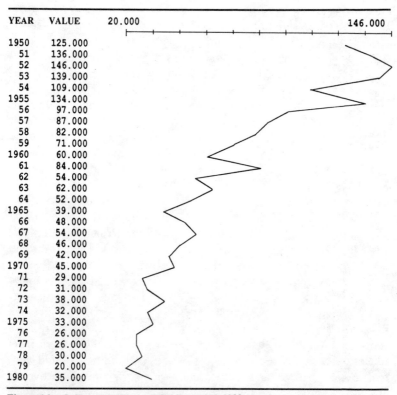

YEAR	VALUE
1950	125.000
51	136.000
52	146.000
53	139.000
54	109.000
1955	134.000
56	97.000
57	87.000
58	82.000
59	71.000
1960	60.000
61	84.000
62	54.000
63	62.000
64	52.000
1965	39.000
66	48.000
67	54.000
68	46.000
69	42.000
1970	45.000
71	29.000
72	31.000
73	38.000
74	32.000
1975	33.000
76	26.000
77	26.000
78	30.000
79	20.000
1980	35.000

Figure 6.2.   Infant mortality on Barbados, 1950-1980.

of its effect as an index of material poverty. If, as standard transition theory posits, populations have high levels of fertility to offset losses from high levels of infant mortality, reductions in infant mortality should lead to reductions in the proportion of Barbadian women who view childbearing as an investment activity. If, as the resource access hypothesis claims, infant mortality becomes dissociated from fertility for women who take the view that childbearing is a consumption activity, there should be no relationship between the level of infant mortality and the proportion of women who view childbearing as an investment activity (see Handwerker, 1986a).

MICRO-LEVEL INFLUENCES ON MORAL ECONOMY

Examination of the micro-level influences on moral economy cannot be carried out with ordinary least squares procedures because two key variables, education and moral economy, may influence each other. Increasing levels of education plausibly affect women's conceptualization of the moral economy of childbearing and parent-child relationships through two paths. First, education may widen the horizons of young women, allow them to recognize new possibilities for personal achievement and freedom, and thus lead them to become dissatisfied with their dependent position relative to men and their children. Second, education may provide women the egalitarian principles that both legitimize women's rights independent of men, children, and mothers, and so constitute a foundation for reconceptualizing their relationships with men, their children, and their mothers. Of course, these paths are not altogether distinct. Moreover, education might influence moral economy through other paths. However, if a woman's education significantly influences her view of moral economy, we can expect a measure of educational attainment to exhibit a clear impact on moral economy, through whatever path it does so.

There remains the possibility, raised by the resource access hypothesis, that ideology will be subject to a selection effect. If women cannot realize egalitarian principles or potential career goals—if, like the women of the 1950s, they have little if any chance of escaping a dependence on men and children—then ideological influences from educational institutions can have little effect. Selection should concentrate conceptual and behavioral innovations that improve or optimize resource access. Consequently, women should reinterpret their view of moral economy to permit it to jibe with their material experience. In the absence of the emergence of new and competitive resource access channels, moral economy should remain largely unchanged by ideology.

Moreover, if such channels come into being—as they have in Barbados, with major increases in employment in industrial manufacturing and in sectors supported by tourist-spending—children will no longer be able to serve effectively as resource channel gatekeepers and women will change their view of the moral economy of childbearing and parent-child relationships *independently* of ideological influences. Because educational qualifications have become of increasing importance in career trajectories, women who seek a career will remain in school longer, on average, than will women who have no future goals beyond finding a mate and bearing children. The women who seek a career, who have future goals beyond finding a mate and bearing children, should be the women who have come to believe that childbearing is a consumption rather than an investment activity. In short, a woman's view of the moral economy of childbearing and parent-child relationships should influence her level of educational attainment.

These possibilities lead to the following set of simultaneous equations:

$$Y_1 = \alpha_0 + \quad\quad\quad + \alpha_2 Y_2 + \alpha_3 Z_1 + \quad\quad + \epsilon_1$$
$$Y_2 = \beta_0 + \beta_1 Y_1 + \quad\quad\quad\quad\quad + \beta_4 Z_2 + \epsilon_2$$

Where: Y_1 = a woman's moral economy index score
$\quad\quad\quad$ Y_2 = a woman's completed level of formal schooling
$\quad\quad\quad$ Z_1 = a woman's economic class
$\quad\quad\quad$ Z_2 = a woman's cohort

The first equation tests the micro-level hypothesis that a woman's moral economy index score is a function of (1) the level of formal schooling she has completed and (2) her awareness of new and competitive resource access channels. The occupational class variable, of course, captures this macro-level effect highly imperfectly. The constant term in the equation should capture the principal macro-level effects. The second equation tests the micro-level hypothesis that a woman's completed level of formal schooling is a function of (1) her view of childbearing as a consumption rather than as an investment activity and (2) a cohort effect. These equations were solved using two-stage least squares and instruments that were weighted averages of the two predetermined variables in the model. Table 6.1 presents the results.

The first set of estimates in Table 6.1 reveal that educational level and, by implication, educationally acquired ideologies of egalitarianism and opportunity, have had weak, but empirically real effects on Barbadian women's view of the moral economy of childbearing and parent-child relationships. Occupational class does not appear to have real empirical effects on moral economy. The weak relationship between moral economy and education, however, indicates that the major determinant of changes in Barbadian women's view of childbearing have been macro-level influences that are probably captured by the highly significant constant term. As indicated earlier, the following section assesses the questions of whether these influences are (1) increased levels of schooling (as wealth flow theory claims), (2) increases in standards of living (as modernization theory claims), or (3) growth in industrial manufacturing and tourist spending (as the resource access hypothesis claims).

Of greater importance in the present context, however, is that the model coefficients indicate that it takes a considerable number of years of

TABLE 6.1

**Solution for the Micro-Level Structural Equations
for the Mutual Effects of Moral Economy and
Educational Attainment**

Dependent Variable: Moral Economy Index   *Squared Multiple R: .157*
Adjusted Squared Multiple R: .153   *Standard Error of Estimate: 1.221*

Variable	Coefficient	STD. Error	STD. Coef.	T	P (2 Tail)
Constant	6.155	.488	.000	12.601	.000
Education	-.370	.049	-.363	-7.610	.000
Class	-.075	.049	-.073	-1.525	.128

Analysis of Variance

Source	Sum-of-Squares	DF	Mean-Square	F-ratio	P
Regression	119.083	2	59.542	39.940	0.000
Residual	641.032	430	1.491		

Dependent Variable: Educational Attainment   *Squared Multiple R: .321*
Adjusted Squared Multiple R: .317   *Standard Error of Estimate: 1.894*

Variable	Coefficient	STD. Error	STD. Coef.	T	P (2 Tail)
Constant	14.306	.686	.000	20.844	.000
Moral economy index	-1.120	.538	-.256	-2.079	.038
Cohort	-.320	.124	-.317	-2.573	.010

Analysis of Variance

Source	Sum-of-Squares	DF	Mean-Square	F-ratio	P
Regression	727.657	2	363.829	101.456	0.000
Residual	1542.019	430	3.586		

education before women change their view of childbearing from an investment to a consumption activity. Thus if women complete 10 years of schooling, the model estimate of the moral economy index is still very high: 2.455. Indeed, even if women complete secondary school the model estimate of their moral economy index will still be 1.715, which is (roughly) at the middle point of the index. Thus even a relatively high level of education would still be expected to leave a woman only ambiguously committed to the view that childbearing is a consumption activity.

The second set of estimates in Table 6.1 reveal that women's view of moral economy has been a significant determinant of how far they progress through school. Indeed, women's view of moral economy appears to have a greater substantive impact on their subsequent education than their education has on their view of moral economy.

Thus women of the youngest cohort who had taken the view that childbearing was a consumption activity could be expected not only to have completed secondary school, but to have gone on to further technical training or to university. Women of the youngest cohort who persist, like their mothers, with the view that childbearing is an investment activity, can be expected to acquire only an incomplete secondary school education. For older cohorts, for whom educational facilities were less available and for whom secondary education was not free, these effects have been much more pronounced. Thus women of the oldest cohort who took the view that childbearing was an investment activity (moral economy index score of 4) can be expected to have acquired only an incomplete primary school education. By contrast, women of the oldest cohort who took the view that childbearing was a consumption activity (moral economy index score of 0) still can be expected to have completed a secondary school education.

Examination of the standardized coefficients reveals (1) that the cohort variable exhibits approximately the same effect on schooling as does the moral economy index, and (2) that cohort effects are distinct from effects of the moral economy index. As indicated earlier, however, the cohort variable is only an imperfect measure of macro-level effects. Although we will not subsequently examine macro-level determinants of women's participation in the Barbadian educational system, the micro-level findings reviewed here suggest that women's participation has been subject to at least two major influences: (1) the cost and physical availability of schooling, and (2) the job opportunities that make going to school worthwhile.

MACRO-LEVEL INFLUENCES ON MORAL ECONOMY

Although micro-level findings are most consistent with the expectations of the resource access hypothesis, those findings also provide some support for the expectations of wealth flows theory. However, macro-level analyses summarized in Table 6.2 reveal that women's increasing participation in the Barbadian economic system has been instrumental in bringing about a decline in the proportion of women who specifically view childbearing as an investment activity, *not* their increasing participation in its educational system.

The results presented in Table 6.2 derive from a test of the hypothesis that historical declines in the proportion of Barbadian women who view childbearing as an investment activity has been a function of the opening

TABLE 6.2

Macro-Level Determinants of Moral Economy

Dependent Variable: Moral Economy Index			Squared Multiple R: .991		
Adjusted Squared Multiple R: .990			*Standard Error of Estimate: .019*		

Variable	Coefficient	STD. Error	STD. Coef.	T	P (2 Tail)
Constant	1.002	.017	.000	58.511	.000
Manufacturing	-.008	.000	-.841	-16.666	.000
Tourism	-.001	.000	-.164	-3.243	.003

Analysis of Variance

Source	Sum-of-Squares	DF	Mean-Square	F-ratio	P
Regression	1.131	2	0.566	1507.252	0.000
Residual	0.011	28	0.000		
Durbin-Watson D statistic:	*.451*				
First order autocorrelation:	*.749*				

Control Variables

Variable	STD. Coef.	T	P (2 Tail)
Level of education	-.011	-0.153	.880
Completed secondary education	.011	0.143	.887
Infant mortality	-.036	-1.061	.298
Index of real wages	.097	3.226	.003

of new, competitive resource access channels, *not* the increasing educational attainment of Barbadian women, *not* the increasing prevalence of education among Barbadian women, *not* decreases in the level of infant mortality, and *not* increases in real wages. This test relied on the following model specification:

$$Y = \beta_0 + \beta_1 X_1 + \beta_2 X_2 + \beta_3 X_3 + \epsilon$$

Where: Y = the proportion of women who view childbearing as an investment activity

X_1 = the level of employment in industrial manufacturing

X_2 = the level of tourist spending

X_3 = the mean level of education of Barbadian women aged 20-24 or the proportion of Barbadian women aged 20-24 who had completed secondary schooling or the level of infant mortality or the level of real wages

The results for the control variables presented in Table 6.2 are those that obtained when each variable was added individually to a model that contained only X_1 and X_2. These results do not change if we add the control variables jointly or in various combinations. Further, we do not find multicollinearity disturbances of the model coefficients when we add control variables to the equation.

Table 6.2 reveals that the industrial manufacturing and tourism variables account for 99% of the variance in the proportion of women who view childbearing as an investment activity. The t-statistics for both education variables and the infant mortality variable reveal that their effects can best be explained as random sampling fluctuation. The t-statistic associated with the index of real wages, however, indicates that real wages have exhibited a real empirical relationship with the moral economy variable. However, contrary to the suppositions of standard demographic transition theory, increases in real wages have led to *increases* in the proportion of women who view childbearing as an investment activity. This finding suggests that Barbadian women have tended to interpret increases in real income as increasing the income flows from children.

Both because the effect of real wages is negligible (R^2 increases by 0.002) and because my intention in this chapter is to test hypotheses rather than to build a model, I take historical reductions in the proportion of Barbadian women who view childbearing as an investment activity to be fully explained by the opening of new and competitive resource access channels measured by the indexes of employment in industrial manufacturing and tourist spending. The normal probability plot of residuals in Figure 6.3 reveals no unusual departures from normality. Although the Durbin-Watson statistic indicates a high level of autocorrelation, the existing autocorrelation does not significantly distort the model's ability to accurately recreate the historical series when we compare the historical time-series of the proportion of women who viewed childbearing as an investment activity (Figure 6.5) with the plot of the model estimates (Figure 6.4).

Nonetheless, I took first differences and recomputed the model solution (Table 6.3). Examination of an autocorrelation plot of residuals from the recomputed model (Figure 6.5) reveals that there remained no statistically significant autocorrelation. Comparison of the original model solution with the first-differences solution reveals that corrections for autocorrelation create little difference in the model coefficients.

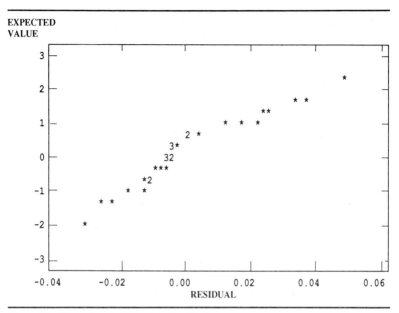

Figure 6.3. **Normal probability plot of residuals.**

SUMMARY

This chapter tested three contrasting views of the changes in women's view of the moral economy of childbearing and parent-child relationships that Barbadians have experienced since 1950. Standard demographic transition theory interprets these changes as the result of modernization, a macro-level process that involves highly interdependent change in many variables. Wealth flows theory interprets these changes as the result of a macro-level process of Westernization, which is accomplished by the assimilation of an ideology of equality through participation in formal educational systems. The resource access hypothesis posits that women will come to look at childbearing as a consumption activity in the presence of macro-level economic changes that create new and competitive resource access channels.

These contrasts in theoretical expectations permit us to construct specific hypotheses with which to test the adequacy of each formulation. If the modernization hypothesis best fits the data, we should be able to show that macro-level multicollinearity problems make it difficult if not impossible to demonstrate that these changes stem from a small, clearly

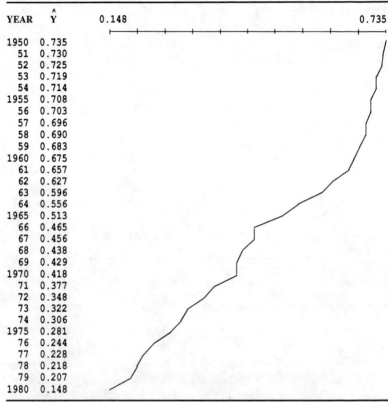

YEAR	$\hat{Y}$
1950	0.735
51	0.730
52	0.725
53	0.719
54	0.714
1955	0.708
56	0.703
57	0.696
58	0.690
59	0.683
1960	0.675
61	0.657
62	0.627
63	0.596
64	0.556
1965	0.513
66	0.465
67	0.456
68	0.438
69	0.429
1970	0.418
71	0.377
72	0.348
73	0.322
74	0.306
1975	0.281
76	0.244
77	0.228
78	0.218
79	0.207
1980	0.148

Figure 6.4.   Model estimates of the proportion of women who view childbearing as an investment activity.

TABLE 6.3
First Differences Solution

Variable	Coefficient	STD. Error	STD. Coef.	T	P (2 Tail)
Constant	1.030				
Manufacturing	-.006	.001	-.788	-7.314	.000
Tourism	-.001	.000	-.291	-3.023	.005

	Analysis of Variance				
	Sum-of-		Mean-		
Source	Squares	DF	Square	F-ratio	P
Regression	.011	2	0.005	40.949	0.000
Residual	0.004	28	0.000		

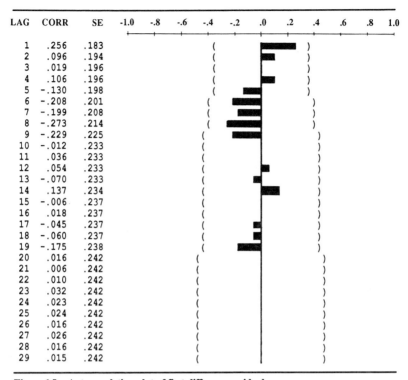

LAG	CORR	SE
1	.256	.183
2	.096	.194
3	.019	.196
4	.106	.196
5	-.130	.198
6	-.208	.201
7	-.199	.208
8	-.273	.214
9	-.229	.225
10	-.012	.233
11	.036	.233
12	.054	.233
13	-.070	.233
14	.137	.234
15	-.006	.237
16	.018	.237
17	-.045	.237
18	-.060	.237
19	-.175	.238
20	.016	.242
21	.006	.242
22	.010	.242
23	.032	.242
24	.023	.242
25	.024	.242
26	.016	.242
27	.026	.242
28	.016	.242
29	.015	.242

Figure 6.5. Autocorrelation plot of first-difference residuals.

identifiable, set of determinants. If it is possible to identify clear determinants of the moral economy of childbearing and parent-child relationships, however, those determinants should be indexes that measure rising standards of living. If wealth flows theory best fits the data, we should be able to show that change in the moral economy of childbearing and parent-child relationships has been unambiguously determined by educational variables. Finally, if the resource access hypothesis best fits the data, we should be able to show that moral economy has been unambiguously determined by the growth of employment opportunities in industrial manufacturing and tourist-related sectors.

These hypotheses were tested on both the micro and macro levels. In each case, test results revealed unambiguous determinants for both dependent variables. I infer that conventional modernization theory fundamentally misinterprets the processes of historical change on Barbados.

On the micro level, test results revealed that education clearly (albeit weakly) affected moral economy. As the level of women's completed education rose, they were increasingly less likely to view childbearing as an investment activity. Conversely, however, women who took the view that childbearing was a consumption activity went farther in school than women who took the view that childbearing was an investment activity. Model estimates suggested that moral economy effects on women's education were substantively more important than were educational effects on moral economy. Whereas even completed secondary schooling still left women of even the youngest cohorts only ambiguously committed to the view that childbearing is a consumption activity, if women took the view that childbearing is an investment activity their expected level of completed education was below the level of a completed secondary school education. Such effects were even more pronounced for older cohorts. Thus if women of the oldest cohorts took the view that childbearing was an investment activity, they could be expected to have acquired only an incomplete primary school education. Conversely, if such women took the view that childbearing was a consumption activity, they still could be expected to have completed a secondary school education.

On the macro level, however, the only important determinants of historical reductions in the proportion of Barbadian women who viewed childbearing as an investment activity were the level of employment in industrial manufacturing and the level of tourist spending, variables that measure the opening of new and competitive resource access channels on the island. The proportion of Barbadian women who viewed childbearing as an investment activity increased with rising real wages. I infer that the rate at which the historical reductions in the proportion of women who took this view took place was reduced by historical increases in real wages.

A MICRO-LEVEL MODEL OF BARBADIAN FERTILITY TRANSITION

THE MODEL

The ethnographic and historical data reviewed in Chapters 3 and 4 indicate that only three factors have borne centrally on the fertility of Barbadian women: (1) the type of spousal union they participated in and the length of time they spent in different types of union, (2) the degree to which they conceptualized children as capital or as a consumption item, and (3) biological constraints on fecundity. If major biological constraints on fecundity (e.g., early sterility) exist, of course, they would block the operation of the other factors.

The type of spousal union seems to affect fertility primarily by changing the average coital frequency. Union type corresponds roughly with union stability and also, especially in the case of visiting unions, with partner accessibility. Demographic literature on the Caribbean commonly remarks on a positive relationship between fertility and union stability as indicated by the visiting-consensual-legal classification of spousal relationships (e.g., Roberts, 1955, 1957; Blake, 1961; Stycos and Back, 1964; Marino, 1970). Thus we would expect that each type of union should provide distinct trajectories for fertility histories and that fertility should increase regularly with the length of time spent in any one form of spousal union.

Factor 2 is theoretically significant. Within constraints imposed by biological fecundity and time spent in one or another form of spousal relationship, birth trajectories should be altered by the extent to which women perceive children as capital or as consumption expenditure. Birth trajectories should be higher when childbearing is viewed as an investment activity and lower when childbearing is viewed as a consumption activity. This difference in birth trajectory based on a change in the moral economy of childbearing and parent-child relationships, should be, as Caldwell (1982) has suggested and as argued here, the major grounding for the Barbadian fertility transition over the last 30 years.

MODEL SPECIFICATION

This hypothesis can be modeled in the following way:

$$Y = \beta_0 + \beta_1(X_1 {}^* X_4 {}^* D) + \beta_2(X_2 {}^* X_4 {}^* D) + \beta_3(X_3 {}^* X_4 {}^* D) + \epsilon$$

Where: Y = total or cumulated fertility to age a
X_1 = cumulated years over the pertinent reproductive period spent in legal marriages
X_2 = cumulated years over the pertinent reproductive period spent in consensual unions
X_3 = cumulated years over the pertinent reproductive period spent in visiting unions
X_4 = an index of moral economy measuring the extent to which children are viewed as capital investments or as consumption expenditures
D = a dummy variable equal to 1 if there was no reported early onset of sterility and 0 otherwise

Thus after controlling for the early onset of sterility, Barbadian birth trajectories are modeled as simple functions of union durations interacting with the moral economy of childbearing and parent-child relationships. The birth trajectories of women who were involved in different forms of spousal union are estimated as: $\beta_0 + \beta_1$ (duration of legal marriages*a moral economy index measuring the degree to which women view children as consumption or investment expenditure) β_2 (duration of consensual unions*moral economy index) β_3 (duration of visiting unions*moral economy index). The birth trajectories of women who were involved in less than all three forms of spousal union are estimated simply by deleting the appropriate term or terms from the equation. The constant in the equation may be meaningless (and the equation can be re-estimated through the origin), or it may capture residual fertility from women who experienced an early onset of sterility.

THE VARIABLES

The Dependent Variable

All variables were measured during the survey of women undertaken in 1985 (see appendix). The dependent variable is women's individual

TABLE 7.1
Cumulated Fertility to Age 30

	Births									
	0	*1*	*2*	*3*	*4*	*5*	*6*	*7*	*8*	*9*	
Frequency	82	94	96	59	43	29	19	7	6	1	436
Percentage	18.8	21.6	22.0	13.5	9.9	6.7	4.4	1.6	1.4	0.2	100

cumulative number of live births experienced before exact age 30. As I show in the appendix, this variable is an excellent predictor of individual total fertility and, hence, is more than adequate as a measure of historical fertility trends in Barbados. On average, Barbadian women bear 66.2% of their children prior to age 30 and 84.3% of their children prior to age 35. Cumulative fertility to age 35 is an even better predictor of total fertility than is cumulative fertility to age 30. However, the results of the analysis presented next do not change when cumulative fertility to age 35 is substituted for cumulative fertility to age 30. Indeed, the results do not change if we use total fertility as the dependent variable and thus restrict the analysis only to the women who had completed their childbearing by 1985. However, such restrictions significantly reduce the sample size. More important, such restrictions make extension of the analysis to women of younger ages ambiguous or impossible. Use of cumulative fertility to age 30 as the dependent variable makes it possible to test the claim that all Barbadian cohorts (from age 20-64) have been subject to the same fertility processes.

Cumulative fertility to age 30 ranged between 0 and 9 live births and averaged 2.294 (SD = 1.930) (see Table 7.1).

Components of the Independent Variables

The number of years spent in legal, consensual, and visiting unions were recorded for five-year periods over the course of the reproductive span (e.g., 15-19, 20-24). The cumulative totals used in the following analysis are simple sums of the number of years individual women spent in different forms of spousal union during the 15-year span from age 15 to age 30. Some women were never legally married over this period and others were legally married for the full 15-year span. Some women were never involved in a consensual union over this period and others were involved in a consensual union for the full 15-year span. Likewise, some women were never involved in a visiting union and others were involved in visiting unions for the full 15-year span. Women spent an average of 2.229 years in legal unions (SD = 3.363), an average of 1.858 years in consensual unions (SD = 3.082), and an average of 5.943 years in visiting unions (SD = 3.946).

Time spent in marital unions can have no impact, or its impact will be much reduced, if there are major biological constraints on fecundity. A few women volunteered that they had experienced an early onset of sterility (see appendix). I controlled for this constraint by multiplying each of the union duration variables by a dummy variable equal to 0 if there were reported major biological constraints on fecundity, and 1 if there were no such reported constraints.

As Figure 7.1 reveals, fertility varies significantly with the index of the moral economy of reproduction and parent-child relations discussed in previous chapters. This is the case whether we examine this relationship only for women who had completed the reproductive span or for the entire sample. Because the lowest three values of the index cannot be differentiated by fertility, Figure 7.1 also suggests the presence of a structural break. To eliminate this nonlinearity in the following analysis I recoded the index as follows: former values of 0, 1, and 2 were assigned the value 1, former values 3 and 4, indicating successive degrees to which women viewed childbearing and parent-child relationships as capital investments, were coded 2 and 3 respectively. To test the claim that women's view of the moral economy of childbearing and parent-child relationships should alter the slope of the union duration variables, I multiplied each union duration variable by the moral economy index.

MODEL SOLUTION

Table 7.2 reveals that the model specified here accounts for more than 60% of the variance in the cumulated fertility of these women. The normal probability plot of residuals in Figure 7.2 reveals that there are no significant outliers and that estimates display no unusual departures from normality. The plot of studentized residuals by the estimate in Figure 7.3 reveals a minor tendency for overestimates of very low levels of fertility to display declining error levels. Overall, however, the plot reveals a homogeneous distribution of residuals. The approximately 38% of the variance in fertility that remains unexplained is probably to be expected from the random source of much fertility (e.g., individually unique spousal relationships), from the use of spousal union types to measure coital frequencies relative to ovulation, and from a number of unmeasured variables (e.g., individual levels of fecundity, variance in fecundity, and different modes used by women to increase or reduce the

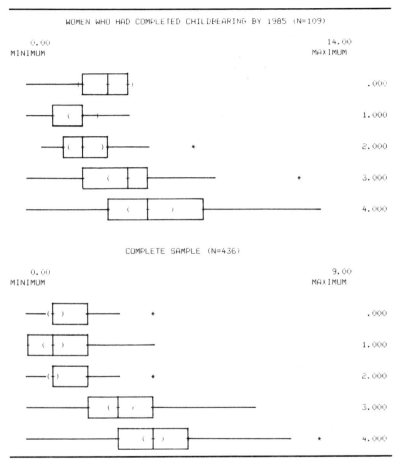

Figure 7.1. **Box-plots of total fertility and cumulative fertility to age 30 by the index of moral economy.**

number of live births, the number of partners). In sum, I infer that the specified model provides a parsimonious and very accurate summary of the variance in Barbadian fertility over the period 1950-1980.

FINDINGS

The solution presented in Table 7.2 reveals that the fertility of Barbadian women who belonged to age cohorts 20-24 through 55-64 in 1985 has been largely determined by interaction between (1) the

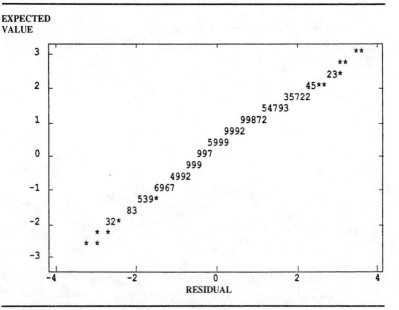

Figure 7.2. Normal probability plot of model residuals.

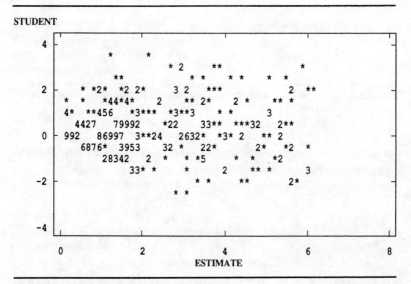

Figure 7.3. Studentized residuals by the estimate.

TABLE 7.2
Micro-Level Determinants of Barbadian Fertility, 1950-1980

Dependent Variable: Total Fertility to Age 30   *Squared Multiple R: .619*
Adjusted Squared Multiple R: .597   *Standard Error of Estimate: 1.196*

Variable	Coefficient	STD. Error	STD. Coef.	T	P (2 Tail)
Constant	0.229	0.098	0.000	2.333	0.020
Legal	0.133	0.008	0.500	16.623	0.000
Consensual	0.132	0.009	0.447	14.888	0.000
Visiting	0.112	0.006	0.524	17.604	0.000

Analysis of Variance

Source	Sum-of-Squares	DF	Mean-Square	F-ratio	P
Regression	1003.426	3	334.475	234.188	0.000
Residual	616.996	432	1.428		

duration of different forms of spousal union, and (2) women's view of
the moral economy of childbearing and parent-child relationships, once
we control for the early onset of sterility. The slope coefficients and their
standard errors reveal that birth trajectories tend to increase with union
stability. Birth trajectories are highest for legal marriage and consensual
relationships and the two trajectories cannot be discriminated with these
data. Birth trajectory falls significantly, however, for visiting unions.
Examination of the standardized coefficients reveals, conversely, that
visiting unions produce the greatest overall impact on fertility. Legal
marriage and consensual unions produce lower overall effects that
cannot be statistically distinguished. Visiting unions have a greater
overall impact on cumulative fertility than do legal or consensual unions
despite the fact that visiting union birth trajectories are lower than are
the birth trajectories of legal marriage and consensual unions. Visiting
unions have this effect because women spend more time in such unions
during their highest reproductive years.

The slope coefficients in Table 7.2 also estimate the extent to which
the slope of each of the union duration variables changes with different
degrees to which women view children and childbearing activities either
as capital investments or as consumption expenditures. We can clarify
the fertility effect of these differences in moral economy when we
examine their effects among women who spent the first 15 years of their
reproductive careers legally married. Cumulative fertility for such

women is estimated by: $\beta_0 + \beta_1$ (15 years*moral economy index value). When we substitute appropriate values for the moral economy index, we find that women who were legally married from age 15 to exact age 30 and who looked at children as consumption expenditures (Moral Economy Index = 1) had only about 2 children, on average, before they were age 30. Such women who looked at children as capital investments (Moral Economy Index = 3) had 5 or 6 children on average over the same time span.

This dramatic difference in fertility corresponds to the dramatic decline from total fertility rates of around 5 in the 1950s to total fertility rates of around 2 in the early 1980s. These results thus substantiate the claim that, at the micro level, the Barbadian fertility transition merely reflects a change in birth trajectories that came about because increasing numbers of women found that children could no longer function effectively as resource channel gatekeepers (see Chapters 6 and 8).

CONTROL VARIABLES

Of course, it is one thing to demonstrate that a specified model provides a good fit to a set of data. It is quite another to demonstrate that those relationships remain unaltered in the face of challenges from alternative hypotheses. The model results in Table 7.2 may change radically if we merely test for the main effects of the components of the interaction terms that comprise that model. Some of the women who reported an early onset of sterility bore a child, for instance, and it is possible that union duration variables uncontrolled for this factor, and uncontrolled for effects of the moral economy index, might reveal important effects. Similarly, it is possible that both the biological constraint variable and the moral economy variable have strong effects independently of the union duration variables, and have only weak (or absent) interactive effects.

Even if a test for main effects reveals that the model results do not change, perhaps the model variables operate differently with different cohorts? The results in Table 7.2 are based on analysis of the entire sample, including women younger than age 30. I believe this procedure is justified because the use of the cumulative totals spent in different forms of spousal union controls for effects stemming from the inclusion of women with truncated reproductive spans. However, I might be wrong. If the model variables operated differently for different cohorts, the inclusion of women under age 30 in the sample on which the solution was based will have biased the results. Further, even if the inclusion of such women does not bias the overall results, there may be historical trends that the model does not capture.

Finally, these results run counter to the conventional paradigm that views fertility transition as one component of a broader modernization or Westernization of society. The standard view is that we can expect fertility transition—on Barbados or anywhere else—when a society has experienced rising standards of living, increased levels of urbanization, declining infant mortality, rising levels of schooling, and the increased availability of family planning services, although different individuals emphasize different factors. This view from the macro level can be evaluated only partially with micro-level data. A macro-level model based on the resource access hypothesis (Chapter 2) is developed in Chapter 8. Pertinent macro-level control variables will be considered there. Here, however, we can examine the effects of several control variables that have figured prominently in alternative interpetations of fertility transition and that one might expect to alter significantly the conclusions drawn here.

Some variables that could be inserted as controls do not function effectively in the Barbadian context, however. One such variable is the mean duration of lactation. As the mean duration of lactation increases, one would expect a reduction of fecundability and lower fertility. As indicated in the appendix, the mean period of breast feeding is only about seven months (and only slightly higher for women over 50 years of age). Consequently, breast feeding is too short to have significant effects on fecundability (see Bongaarts, 1982). A test of its effects reveal that there is a significant *positive* relationship between the mean period of breast feeding and fertility (either total fertility, for women who have completed their reproductive span, or cumulative fertility to age 30): standardized coefficient = .106, t = 3.409, p = .001. I infer that mean breast feeding duration is acting as a proxy for biological fecundity. Probably, it captures a wealth effect: the greater the relative wealth, the better the nutrition and the greater the fecundity (see, e.g., Wilmsen, 1986). I discount the significance of this variable for this analysis both because the interpretation of its effects is ambiguous, and because addition of the variable adds negligibly to our ability to account for fertility (R^2 increases by only 1% and the standard error of the estimate declines by only .014).

Theoretically important control variables that can be usefully examined at the micro level include measures of the importance of family planning services, exposure to urban influences and values, exposure to the influences and values of the developed nations of the world, and exposure to modernizing influences through schools. If the standard version of fertility transition theory is correct, we would expect that fertility will decline with measures of each or any of these variables.

The following discussion is divided into four sections. The first section treats the basic methodological questions identified above. The second section examines the effects of some variables that figure prominently in alternative theories of fertility transition. Plainly, the tests reported in these sections were carried out as part of a fishing expedition: I tried to think of additional variables that might display significant effects on fertility or that might invalidate the model; I examined a total of 27 such possibilities. Of course, one cannot trust probability levels generated in this way. Consequently, I adjusted test probabilities with the Bonferroni procedure by dividing a standard alpha value of .05 by 27. Probabilities that fall at or below the result (.002) can be confidently used to reject the Null Hypothesis. Only one such probability was obtained, and the variable with which it is associated is marked (on Table 7.4). The third section evaluates the adequacy of the model in light of tests of control factors. The fourth section evaluates the impact of family planning services on fertility control and fertility decline.

METHODOLOGICAL QUESTIONS

Table 7.3 summarizes the results of tests that bear on the issues of (1) possible main effects for the components of the interaction terms used in the model, (2) the inclusion of women under 30 in the data base analyzed, and (3) the existence of historical trends not tapped by the model. Table 7.3 presents for each control variable the standardized coefficient, the t-statistic, the probability that the effect is present because of random sampling fluctuations, and the change in R^2. These results derive from solutions in which all variables (the model variables and the control variable or variables) were entered into the equation simultaneously. I do not present the coefficients for the model variables because they never changed significantly (there were no multicollinearity effects) and it would be unduly repetitious to include them. However, potential changes in these coefficients can be assessed in Table 7.5.

Test for Main Effects

Since the variables that comprised the interaction terms of the model were described earlier, the test results for main effects are directly interpretable. The biological constraint and the moral economy index

TABLE 7.3
Methodological Question Summary Statistics

Variable	STD. Coef.	T	P (2 Tail)	R² Change
Bonferroni Adjustment for Alpha: .05/27 = .002				
Tests for Main Effects				
biological constraint	-.043	-1.426	.155	+.002
moral economy index	-.001	-0.029	.977	.000
legal marriage duration	.049	0.770	.442	
consensual union duration	.135	1.968	.050	
visiting union duration	-.022	-0.430	.667	+.004
Test for Effects of Including Women Under Age 30				
legal *young women dummy	-.013	-.434	.664	
consensual *young women dummy	.029	.934	.351	
visiting *young women dummy	-.043	-1.357	.175	+.003
Test for Uncaptured Historical Trends				
legal *age	.196	1.229	.220	
consensual *age	-.094	-0.747	.455	
visiting *age	.073	0.579	.563	
age	.069	1.406	.160	+.009

variables were entered individually; the union duration variables were entered as a set. Tests for main effects revealed that the interaction terms completely captured the effects of biological constraints on fecundity, the moral economy index, and union durations. The consensual union duration variable exhibits a marginal t-statistic and probability level. However, the t-statistic for the constant term falls to 0.915 (p = .360). I infer that the consensual union duration variable picks up the low fertility of the women with an early onset of sterility who bore a child that was otherwise captured by the constant term.

Test for Effects of Young Women

To evaluate the effects of including women under age 30, I tested the model variables against a set of controls that differed from the model variables only in that they applied solely to women under age 30. The hypothesis that the processes captured by the model variables differed among younger women would be accepted if any one or the set of controlled variables exhibited a low probability. The control variables were created by multiplying each of the model variables by a dummy variable equal to 1 if the woman was under age 30 and 0 otherwise. Table 7.3 reveals that the hypothesis that young women's fertility responds to the model variables differently from older women can be rejected confidently. I infer that including younger women in the data base has not distorted model results.

Test for Uncaptured Historical Trends

To evaluate the hypothesis that the model variables do not capture important historical trends or cohort effects, I tested model variables against an age variable and a set of union duration variables that controlled for age. The hypothesis that the processes captured by the model variables miss important historical trends would be accepted if the age variable displayed a low probability. The hypothesis that the processes captured by the model variables miss important cohort differences would be accepted if union duration variables controlled by age exhibit low probability values. The control union duration variables were created by multiplying each model variable by the woman's age. Table 7.3 reveals that both hypotheses can be rejected confidently. I infer that the model does not miss important historical trends and that the processes captured by the model variables have not differed in significant ways from one age cohort to another.

THEORETICALLY SIGNIFICANT CONTROL VARIABLES

Table 7.4 summarizes the results of tests that bear on the hypotheses that fertility transition reflects the influence of values and perspectives (1) unique to urban living, (2) experience in the developed countries of North America and Europe, or (3) imparted by experience in formal schooling systems, especially one heavily influenced by Western values. Table 7.4 presents for each control variable the standardized coefficient, the t-statistic, the probability that the effect is present because of random sampling fluctuations, and the change in R^2. These results derive from solutions in which all variables (the model variables and the control variable or variables) were entered into the equation simultaneously. I do not present the coefficients for the model variables because they never changed significantly (there were no multicollinearity

TABLE 7.4
Summary Statistics for
Theoretically Significant Control Variables

Variable	STD. Coef.	T	P (2 Tail)	R² Change
Bonferroni Adjustment for Alpha: .05/27 = .002				
Tests for Effects of Urban Living				
years prior to age 20	-.041	-1.349	.178	+.002
years between ages 20-24	-.046	-1.526	.128	+.002
years between ages 25-29	-.034	-1.123	.262	+.001
years prior to age 25	-.042	-1.401	.162	+.002
years prior to age 30	-.042	-1.387	.166	+.002
Tests for Effects of Experience in North America and Europe				
years prior to age 20	-.035	-1.176	.240	+.001
years between ages 20-24	-.002	-0.052	.959	.000
years between ages 25-29	-.005	-0.178	.859	.000
years prior to age 25	-.026	-0.876	.382	+.001
years prior to age 30	-.023	-0.764	.445	+.001
Tests for Effects of Educational Experiences				
*years of formal schooling	-.095	-3.059	.002	+.008
years beyond secondary level	-.090	-2.847	.005	+.007
Tests for Educational Effects on Birth Trajectories				
legal *years of schooling	.071	1.214	.226	
consensual *years of schooling	.068	1.041	.298	
visiting *years of schooling	-.046	-0.933	.351	
years of formal schooling	-.098	-2.705	.007	+.011

effects) and it would be unduly repetitious to include them. Potential changes in these coefficients can be assessed in Table 7.5.

International and Urban Influences

If fertility transition was an effect of the Westernizing influences of exposure to values and behavior unique to the developed nations of North America and Europe or to urban living, I reasoned that measures of the length of time a person was directly exposed to such influences should tap these effects. I asked women to report how many years they had resided either in a more developed country (primarily the United Kingdom, Canada, and the United States) or in the urban agglomeration around Bridgetown on Barbados: (1) prior to age 20, (2) from age 20 through age 24, and (3) from age 25 through age 30. Some women lived in or around Bridgetown for the full 30-year period and some women lived in North America or Europe for a substantial period of time (18 of 30 years). On average, women reported having lived in or around Bridgetown for 13.9 years of this 30-year period (SD = 15.8). On average, women reported having lived in North America or Europe for .264 years (SD = 1.227), a low level that reflects the small number of women who actually lived abroad during their first 30 years. Each measure of both urban and international influence, plus measures that cumulated exposure years up to ages 25 and 30, was tested individually against the model variables. The results in Table 7.4 reveal that none of these variables revealed any independent effect on Barbadian fertility. I infer that the decline of fertility on Barbados over the past 30 years has reflected neither (1) women's exposure to the Westernizing influences of the developed countries of North America and Europe, nor (2) women's exposure to urban life-styles and values on Barbados itself.

The Influence of Education

There are a host of possible avenues through which schooling may bear on fertility (see Chapter 1). From the perspective of standard transition theory, there is something about the amount, the quality, and/or the content of schooling that may yield reductions in fertility. From the perspective of wealth flows theory, education changes women's view of family relationships and obligations. At the macro level, schooling has become much more available over the past 30 years, especially to women. Chapter 4 showed that increasing numbers of women complete their secondary education, and that women are going further in school than they have in the past. As of 1985, the average level of education among Barbadian women (aged 20-24) was more than 12 years, a level that does not differ substantially from the average level of education in the more developed countries of North America and Europe. The following chapter examines the fertility effects of the macro-level influences of increasing educational levels and of increasing educational prevalence.

At the micro level, the quality of education has been high throughout the period under review and the content has heavily reflected the influence of the United Kingdom. The quality and the content of schooling may bear on studies that compare Barbados with other islands or other world regions, but neither constitutes a variable for Barbados itself. The most plausible educational influence on fertility at the micro level is the amount of educational experience, which I measured by asking women how many years of formal schooling they had completed.

Examination of a scatterplot of cumulative fertility to age 30 and number of years of formal schooling suggested, like some previous studies (e.g., de Albuquerque, Mader, and Stinner, 1976; Powell, Hewitt, and Wooming, 1978, Caldwell, 1980) that schooling may lead to fertility reductions only after a threshold level has been passed (also see Chapter 8). To capture such an effect, I created a threshold education variable that measured individual women's schooling against the threshold of completed secondary schooling: 0 if they had not passed the threshold, and sequentially greater numbers (1, 2, 3, and so on) for each year of formal schooling they had completed beyond the secondary level.

Both measures of educational influence were entered individually (and simultaneously) with the model variables. The results presented in Table 7.4 indicate that both tests yielded nearly identical educational effects. I tested the possibility that these measures of educational influence were capturing different effects on fertility. The result (not presented in Table 7.4) was a multicollinearity problem: no model variable coefficients changed significantly, but both education variables had low t-statistics and high probabilities. I infer that both variables measure the same educational influence on fertility.

The slope coefficients of these variables (−.089 for the number of years of completed formal schooling, and −.107 for each year of completed formal schooling beyond the secondary level) also suggest that these variables have equivalent effects. Thus women who had completed college (and 15-16 years of education, depending on the exact route through school) can expect to have about one child less than do other women who have the same union durations and view of the moral economy of childbearing and parent-child relationships. Women who have gone on for a master's level degree, or who have extensive postcollege training, can expect to have as many as two children fewer than do other women with the same union durations and view of moral economy.

These estimates are revealing—they suggest that the effect of education on fertility is owing merely to delayed childbearing while women are in school. If education has the effects posited by standard transition theory and wealth flows theory, however, educational levels must change the *trajectory* of births.

To test the hypothesis that educational levels change the trajectory of births, I multiplied union duration variables by the completed level of formal schooling. I then estimated a model that included (1) the original model variables that controlled for the trajectory effects of variation in moral economy, (2) union duration variables uncontrolled for moral economy but controlled for the trajectory effects of variations in the level of formal schooling, and (3) the level of formal schooling variable. Evidence that standard theory correctly interprets the role of education in fertility transition would consist of high t-statistics and low probabilities associated with the union duration variables controlled for the trajectory effects of education.

The test results presented in Table 7.4 reveal that standard transition theory *misinterpets* the role of education in reducing fertility. An educational influence on fertility remains, but that influence consists solely of the main effects of the education variable. I infer that there is a real empirical relationship between educational levels and fertility by age 30, but that the decline in fertility associated with increasing levels of education stems merely from the fact that women delay childbearing while they are in school.

ARE REVISIONS TO THE MODEL WARRANTED?

The results of analyses summarized in Tables 7.3 and 7.4 reveal that we might improve the model developed at the beginning of this chapter if we included a measure of the fertility depressing effects of education. Table 7.5 presents the solution to a model of Barbadian fertility that was modified in this way.

A comparison of Table 7.2 with Table 7.5 reveals that the model variable coefficients and statistics are substantively unchanged. On the other hand, the substantive effects of the education variable are negligible. Taking into consideration the fertility reductions that occur because women spend time in school increases R^2 by only 0.008 (.8%) and reduces the standard error of the estimate by only 0.012. Examination of plots of residuals (not included) continues to reveal normality, no significant outliers, and the absence of heteroscedasticity. I infer that adding this variable to the model yields no real improvement in fit.

By contrast, union duration variables taken by themselves account for only about 30% of the variance in fertility. When we create the model interaction terms, we double the proportion of explained variance and reduce the standard error of the estimate by one-third (from 1.602 to

TABLE 7.5
**An Alternative Micro-Level Model of
Barbadian Fertility Transition**

Dependent Variable: Total Fertility to Age 30			Squared Multiple R: .627	
Adjusted Squared Multiple R: .618			*Standard Error of Estimate: 1.184*	
Variable	Coefficient	STD. Error	STD. Coef.	T	P (2 Tail)
Constant	1.284	0.358	0.000	3.584	0.000
	Model Variables				
Legal	0.131	0.008	0.491	16.399	0.000
Consensual	0.126	0.009	0.426	13.946	0.000
Visiting	0.107	0.006	0.501	16.493	0.000
	New Variable				
Formal schooling	-0.089	0.029	-0.095	-3.059	0.002
	Analysis of Variance				
	Sum-of-		Mean-		
Source	Squares	DF	Square	F-ratio	P
Regression	1016.535	4	254.134	181.378	0.000
Residual	603.887	431	1.401		

1.196). The addition of the education variable does express an increased understanding of factors that have borne on Barbadian fertility over the past 30 years or so. But the overall fertility effects of even advanced postgraduate work (which reduce the equation constant by 1-2 children) cannot account for the differences in fertility on Barbados between the 1950s and the 1980s. If we add that variable to the model, we do not affect the variables that are germane to the theory this research tests. The effects of education do not suggest that the resource access hypothesis in any way misinterprets the Barbadian fertility transition. Finally, the new variable contributes little substance to our model. One could use either model to estimate Barbadian fertility; the differences are negligible.

FAMILY PLANNING VARIABLES

I take it for granted that fertility transition cannot come about unless and until women effectively limit their births by contraception, abortion, or some combination of the two. For my purposes it is not important how they achieve low fertility, only that they do so.

The importance and effects of family planning services are distinct issues. If family planning services on Barbados have been responsible for reducing fertility, their effects would not necessarily show up in micro-level analyses. The potential macro-level effect of family planning services is treated in the following chapter. The most convincing evidence for micro-level effects of family planning services would be (1) reductions in births owing to intentional birth spacing, (2) reductions in births owing to the intentional termination of reproductive careers, and (3) a curvilinear relationship between completed fertility and the number of planned births that reveals a positive correlation at small numbers of actual and planned births (which indicates that women who planned small families successfully reached their goal) and an inverse relationship between actual and planned births as completed fertility rises (which indicates that high fertility occurred only because effective birth planning services were not available). To assess potential family planning effects on fertility reduction, I asked women: (1) if they intentionally spaced any of their children (women who responded positively normally indicated that, after a surprising and unplanned first pregnancy, they spaced most of their children), (2) if they intentionally terminated their reproductive careers, and (3) how many of their children they planned.

The model results presented in Table 7.2 apply to all women, both before and after 1960, and to women who have and who have not completed their reproductive careers. To test for possible effects of family planning variables, however, it is best to focus specifically on women who were at the end of their reproductive period or who had completed it by 1985. The bulk of the reproductive careers of even these women were spent after 1960 and one would expect that the effects of spacing and the early and intentional termination of reproductive careers would be clearest for the oldest cohorts. Inclusion of women who were younger might introduce an inordinate number of women who had planned to terminate childbearing early, but who had not yet chosen to do so.

Figure 7.4 reveals that neither the spacing variable nor the intentional termination of reproductive careers variable taps any systematic effect on fertility. Women who did not intentionally terminate childbearing early (n = 106) bore an average of 4.830 (SD = 3.016) children. Women who did intentionally terminate childbearing early (n = 44) bore an average of 4.432 children (SD = 2.645). A t-test of the difference yields a probability of 0.422, which indicates that this difference is best explained as sampling error. Women who did not space children (n = 102) bore an average of 4.216 children (SD = 2.480). Women who did

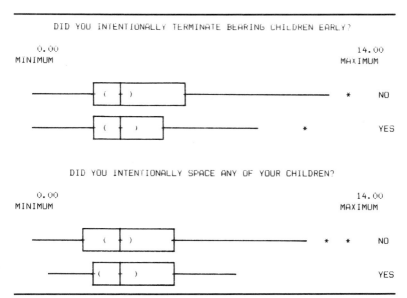

Figure 7.4. **Box-plots of total fertility by family planning measures (women aged 45 and over in 1985).**

space children (n = 39) bore an average of 4.641 children (SD = 2.206). A t-test of the difference yields a probability value of 0.325, which indicates that this difference also is best explained as sampling error.

It is possible, of course, that these measures simply are not sufficiently sensitive to family planning effects. This argument should not apply, however, to the question of birth planning. If family planning services permit women to better control their reproductive careers *and if they also reduce fertility*, (1) women who plan their births should have few children and the correlation between the number of births planned and low levels of completed fertility should be positive, and (2) women who do not plan their births (or who planned few or no births) should display high levels of fertility and there should be an inverse relationship between the number of planned births and actual levels of fertility.

As Figure 7.5 reveals, however, the relationship between total fertility and the number of births intentionally planned does not exhibit these characteristics. On the contrary, Barbadian women in the oldest cohorts reported planning most of their children. The number of children planned and total fertility covary 94% of the time (r^2 = .884). Figure 7.5 reveals some notable exceptions, but the regression solution (t-statistics in parentheses) reveals that older Barbadian women have had relatively

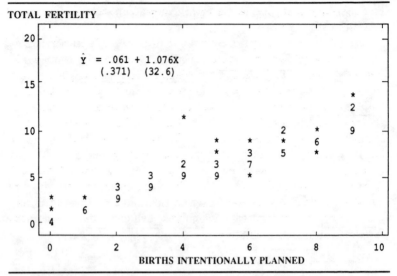

Figure 7.5.   Plot of total fertility by total births intentionally planned (women 45 and over
in 1985).

few unplanned births over the past 30 years. The standard error of the
estimate is only .940.

Surely, these data at least partially reflect a happy tendency for
people to match planning retrospectively with actual experience. On the
other hand, Figure 7.5 reveals a potentially broad range of studentized
residuals and the outliers one would expect from accurately reported
human (thus far from perfect) birth planning. Moreover, the ethnographic data together with the model results presented earlier lead to the
conclusion that there should be at least a reasonable fit between
intentionally planned births and actual fertility.

This conjunction of ethnographic and statistical evidence makes it
perverse to argue that family planning services have actually led to
reductions in births. On the contrary, these data clearly reveal that
means have been available for women to control their births. As
indicated, this research did not attempt to identify these means precisely
because that topic was theoretically irrelevant. The only theoretically
relevant question was what happened to actual fertility levels. I infer
that the family planning services that have existed on Barbados
(whether through the Barbados Family Planning Association or
through other sources) have been at least moderately (and perhaps very)

successful in making it possible for the Barbadian women who wanted to limit births to do so.

These data also clearly reveal that the provision of such services did not make women *want* to limit their births. Women who wanted large families because, for them, children functioned effectively as resource channel gatekeepers, had large families. Women who wanted small families because, for them, children could not function effectively as resource channel gatekeepers, had small families. The provision of family planning services should not be expected to lead to fertility declines. Reductions in fertility require an opening and diversification of the prevailing resource structure in ways that reward women's individual skills and initiatives. The Barbadian women who still have relatively large numbers of children will continue to do so until they, too, have access to means by which they can chart their own course independently of their children.

SUMMARY

This chapter tested the hypothesis that the Barbadian fertility transition has been a simple function, on the micro level, of changes in women's view of the moral economy of childbearing and parent-child relationships. Only three factors have borne centrally on the fertility of Barbadian women: (1) the early onset of sterility, (2) the duration of different forms of spousal union, and (3) women's view of moral economy. The first factor dictates whether or not the other factors operate. Involvement in spousal unions generates a birth trajectory that is conditional on women's view of moral economy. Test of a model of these relationships accounted for more than 60% of the variance in fertility and exhibited a standard error of the estimate of only 1.196 on a range of fertility from 0 to 9. Examination of residual plots revealed that there were no significant outliers and that residuals were normally and homogeneously distributed. Model coefficients effectively generated the high fertility levels of the 1950s and the low fertility levels of the 1980s.

This model was systematically tested against a range of alternative hypotheses:

(1) main effects of the components of the model interaction variables,
(2) effects stemming from the inclusion of women younger than 30 in the data base used for estimating the coefficients,
(3) uncaptured historical trends,

    (4) effects of exposure to urban values and life-styles,
    (5) effects of exposure to international values and life-styles,
    (6) effects of the influence stemming from exposure to formal educational institutions, and
    (7) possible family planning service effects.

The model estimates remained unchanged in all tests. These tests revealed only one additional factor that explained variance in Barbadian fertility: delays in childbearing that stemmed from increasingly long attendance at school.

However, whereas the model variables doubled the explanatory power of union duration variables uncontrolled for the birth trajectory effects of moral economy, the education variable did not contribute important additional explanatory power. The results of these analyses demonstrated that the model developed at the beginning of the chapter is robust in the face of challenges from alternative hypotheses and constitutes a parsimonious and very accurate summary of Barbadian fertility. On the micro level, the Barbadian fertility transition stemmed simply from increases in the prevalence of a moral economy of childbearing and parent-child relationships that views children not as capital investments, but as consumption expenditures.

—8—

A MACRO-LEVEL MODEL OF BARBADIAN FERTILITY TRANSITION

THE MODEL

Chapters 3, 5, and 7 revealed that the high fertility Barbados experienced in the 1950s reflected women's (accurate) belief that bearing children constituted an investment activity.

Chapters 4, 5, and 7 revealed that the low fertility in Barbados in the 1980s reflected the converse (and accurate) view that childbearing constituted a consumption activity.

Chapters 4 and 6 revealed that childbearing changed from an investment to a consumption activity, both objectively and in the moral economy that rationalizes one or the other reproductive pattern, when daughters saw that it was realistic to plan for future goals beyond finding a mate and bearing children.

Chapters 4 and 6 also revealed that children could no longer function effectively as resource channel gatekeepers, and thus daughters saw that it was realistic to make such plans, after the Barbadian economy experienced a structural discontinuity marked by decline in the importance of sugar and rise in the importance of industrial manufacturing and tourism.

Hence, at the macro level, the Barbadian fertility transition should be accounted for almost solely by variables that measure the three principal dimensions of recent Barbadian economic history: (1) the growth of a diversified industrial manufacturing sector, (2) the growth of tourism, and (3) the sharp discontinuity with the previous 320 years of Barbadian history, represented by decline in importance of the sugar industry. Chapter 4 argued, and Chapter 6 provided empirical support, for the view that fertility should vary positively with general economic well-being. A macro-level model of transition thus must also include a measure of the Barbadian population's material well-being if it is clearly to discriminate between fertility transition and nontransition fertility fluctuations owing to economic factors.

MODEL SPECIFICATION

When we link the historical and ethnographic data in Chapters 3 and 4 with the reasoning outlined here, we arrive at the following model:

$$Y = \beta_0 + \beta_1 X_1 + \beta_2 X_2 + \beta_3 X_3 + \beta_4(D{*}X_2) + \beta_5(D{*}X_3) + \beta_6(D{*}X_4) + \epsilon$$

Where: Y = period total fertility
        X_1 = material well-being
        X_2 = job opportunities in the manufacturing sector
        X_3 = job opportunities represented by tourist spending
        X_4 = structural change in the sugar industry
        D = structural discontinuity in the Barbadian economy

Model specification stipulates that, after structural discontinuity in the Barbadian economy, fertility is a linear function of material well-being, job opportunities in the manufacturing sector, and job opportunities represented by tourist spending:

$$\beta_1(X_1) + \beta_2(X_2) + \beta_3(X_3)$$

I would expect that the effect of real wages would remain unaltered by structural discontinuity.

The historical data reviewed in Chapter 4 revealed that Barbadian sugar producers came under selective pressure by international markets during the 1950s. That pressure selected for structural change and mechanization in the industry, and should have subjected employees, like their employers, to selection on the basis of personal performance and competence. Ironically, sugar may have been the first Barbadian economic sector to offer new and competitive employment opportunities that eliminated children's gatekeeper functions. Increases in employment and tourism during the 1950s may have merely alleviated employment shortages and inadequacies in other economic sectors. Thus, prior to structural discontinuity in the Barbadian economy, fertility may fall with changes in the sugar industry, but will increase with growth in manufacturing and tourism. The effect of manufacturing prior to structural discontinuity would be estimated as

$$\beta_2(X_2) + \beta_4(X_2)$$

Likewise, the effect of tourism prior to structural discontinuity would be estimated as:

$$\beta_3(X_3) + \beta_5(X_3)$$

The effects of increases in material standards of living, and of increases in industrial manufacturing employment and tourist spending prior to 1960, are not necessarily manifested in fertility *decisions*. Although the findings presented in Chapter 6 suggested that increases in real income have been accompanied by increases in the proportion of women who view childbearing as an investment activity, this variable also may capture important effects on fecundity. Similarly, increases in employment in manufacturing and tourisms are likely to capture effects on fecundity rather than effects manifested in intentional fertility behavior, at least prior to 1960. Census data (e.g., Forte and Zaba, 1985) clearly reveal that the number of women who have borne no children increases regularly with age among women in older cohorts.

The observed levels of primary sterility found among the oldest cohorts may reflect a high incidence of venereal disease. The incidence of gonorrhea in the Caribbean is thought to have been very high historically. The discovery of penicillin, which came only after World War II, meant effective treatment for the disease, and the increases in fertility experienced by all Caribbean islands after World War II are widely ascribed to this factor.

Attempts to measure the incidence of gonorrhea on Barbados have proven futile thus far. Venereal diseases have not been reportable on the island and examination of the archived annual reports of the Director of Medical Services reveal only (1) spotty and inconsistent data on reported cases of gonorrhea in public health clinics (which are not comparably reported by different facilities), (2) the number of gonococci smears analyzed by the bacteriology department, (3) and the number of patients admitted to the general hospital with salpingitis or pelvic inflammatory disease (the means by which gonorrhea creates blocked fallopian tubes and thus bears on fertility). These data, however, suggest that the incidence of gonorrhea may have increased during the early part of the 1950s when fertility was increasing—the number of tests conducted by the bacteriological department increased from 201 in 1950 to 900 in 1954 and fell only to 724 in 1955; the number of women admitted to a hospital for salpingitis or pelvic inflammatory disease displays no clear pattern, for 296 women were admitted in 1950, 248 were admitted in 1952, 311 were admitted in 1953, 106 were admitted in 1955, but 235 were admitted in 1957, the last year for which such data were available.

It remains plausible that the incidence of gonorrhea fell over this period, but there may be another factor that contributed to the increases in fertility Barbados experienced over this period—improvements in nutrition and reductions in the level of strenuous activity undertaken by Barbadian women. Barbadian infant mortality was very high as late as the 1950s. Examination of the listed causes of death reveal, as one might suspect, the complex of malnutrition-gastrointestinal disease-respiratory disease associated with poverty. The factors responsible for infant mortalities surely also capture nutritional deprivation for women, a large proportion of whom were employed as field laborers. Wilmsen (1986) presents evidence that nutritional deprivation that occurs jointly with high levels of strenuous activity may have an interaction effect that sharply reduces fertility. Increases in material standard of living brought about by increases in real wages and increased opportunities for employment outside the sugar plantations can be expected to have generated increased female fecundity because they moderated or eliminated such an interaction.

This research cannot, of course, evaluate these possibilities. Here I merely observe that increases in fertility that stem from these factors do not necessarily—indeed, probably do not—stem from *intentional* changes in behavior. By contrast, the competition and mechanization within the sugar industry that selected employees on the basis of increased levels of technical skill and performance would be expected to reduce the importance of children as resource channel gatekeepers, and thus they would be expected to reduce fertility through intentional changes in behavior. Barbados' transition to replacement-level fertility, however, should come about with the subsequent growth in both manufacturing and tourism and concomitant growth in Barbados' residentiary sector.

THE VARIABLES

The Dependent Variable

The dependent variable is the natural logarithm of period total fertility rates estimated for the years 1950 through 1980. These rates were estimated from the random sample of 436 women described in the appendix. The rates computed for the period 1950-1955 understate actual period fertility because they exclude women who bore children in the last half of their reproductive years. The figures used for this analysis are corrected by the addition of age-specific fertility rates computed as an average of the period age-specific fertility for the years 1955-1960.

Independent Variables

The first independent variable (X_1) is an index of real wages for the period 1949 through 1980 (1980 = 100) constructed by the Central Bank of Barbados, and provided me by courtesy of Dr. DeLisle Worrell, the Research Director of the Bank, and by Clyde Mascoll, an Economist in the Central Bank's Research Department.

The second independent variable (X_2) measures manufacturing as an index of the proportion of the Barbadian labor force employed in manufacturing (1980 = 100). The basic data are found in Cox (1982: 60). These figures exclude both workers in sugar factories and workers employed in small-scale cottage industries. The basic data consist of percentage figures for 1946, 1960, 1966, 1970, 1976, and 1979. Points missing in this time series were assumed to be a function of constant growth rates between the years for which percentages are available. The data for 1980 were estimated as a one-year extension of the rate of growth for the period 1976-1979.

The third independent variable (X_3) measures tourism, an index of the level of tourist spending in Barbados. The basic data consist of a continuous time series in real Barbadian dollars for the years 1961-1980, and are found in Phillips (1982: 127). Data points missing for the years 1949-1960 were estimated using an instrumental variable approach. Tourist arrival data are available for the period 1956-1980. There is a very strong linear relationship (r = .920) between an index of tourist arrivals (1980 = 100) and the level of tourist spending for the first eight years for which spending data are available. There is also a strong linear relationship between the index of tourist arrivals and the manufacturing index. I estimated a model that specified the index of tourist arrivals as a linear function of the manufacturing index and used the solution ($\hat{Y}$ = 2.822 + 1.442X; r^2 = .939) to estimate the missing values for the index of tourist spending.

The fourth independent variable (X_4) monitors the increasing importance of skilled labor and individual performance in the sugar industry as an index of real wages in the sugar industry (1980 = 100).

After World War II the sugar industry came under increased pressure to increase productivity. One response was to mechanize production. This change required increased skill and performance levels at a time when tourism and manufacturing began to draw labor away from sugar production. To attract the necessary labor, real wages in the sugar industry rose at a time when real wages for the economy as a whole fell. The basic data are found in Haynes (1982: 89) and consist of data points for 1946, 1950, 1955, 1960, 1962, 1965, 1968, 1970, 1973, 1975, 1978, and 1980. Missing values for this series were estimated on the assumption that there was a constant growth rate (negative or positive) between the years for which data were available.

The fifth independent variable (D) measures structural discontinuity in the Barbadian economy as a dummy variable that equals 1 if the time period is 1960 or before, and 0 otherwise. The structural change represented by the growth of tourism and manufacturing and the decline in importance of sugar began in the mid-1950s and was reasonably complete by 1965. The year 1960, however, appears to be the best choice of a point that marked the first time that sugar no longer dominated the Barbadian economy (see Worrell, 1982).

MODEL SOLUTION

Table 8.1 reveals that the model just described accounts for about 97% of the variance in fertility over the period 1950 through 1980. Figures 8.1 and 8.2 trace out three-year moving average time series for the dependent variable and the model estimate, respectively. The model clearly yields estimates that accurately reproduce Barbadian fertility history since 1950.

The Durbin-Watson test reported in Table 8.1 indicates that no significant autocorrelation is present. The normal probability plot of residuals in Figure 8.3 reveals a normal distribution and no outliers. The plot of the studentized residuals by the estimate in Figure 8.4 reveals an approximately homogeneous scatter of error. Two variations on the Park-Glejser test for heteroscedasticity were applied: (1) one assumed that the squared residuals were a multiplicative function of the independent variables; (2) the other assumed that the absolute values of the residuals were an additive function of the independent variables. Neither test yielded evidence of heteroscedasticity.

Table 8.2 presents eigenvalues, condition indices (the square root of the ratio of the largest eigenvalue to each of the others), and variance

TABLE 8.1
Macro-Level Model of Barbados' Fertility Transition

Dependent Variable: LnTFR		N: 31		Squared Multiple R: .969	
Adjusted Squared Multiple R: .961				Standard Error of Estimate: 0.050	

Variable	Coefficient	STD. Error	STD. Coef.	T	P (2 Tail)
Constant	1.58989	0.16137	0.00000	9.85232	0.00000
Real wages	0.00665	0.00126	0.59160	5.28290	0.00002
Manufacturing	-0.01033	0.00158	-0.87641	-6.52372	0.00000
Tourism	-0.00434	0.00119	-0.55453	-3.64486	0.00129
		Prior to 1960			
Manufacturing	0.10406	0.02405	7.52365	4.32733	0.00023
Tourism	0.05677	0.01418	0.98930	4.00223	0.00052
Sugar industry real wages	-0.05245	0.01197	-8.44790	-4.38104	0.00020

Analysis of Variance

Source	Sum-of-Squares	DF	Mean-Square	F-ratio	P
Regression	1.89748	6	0.31625	125.27012	0.00000
Residual	0.06059	24	0.00252		

Durbin-Watson D statistic: 2.105
First order autocorrelation: -.053

proportions (the proportion of the variance of the estimate accounted for by each principal component associated with each of the preceding eigenvalues). One of the eigenvalues is approximately zero and another is very close to zero. These low values suggest that the model contains some redundancy. As is apparent in Table 8.1, however, all the regression standard errors are small.

Aggregate time series data such as those employed here almost always contain a good portion of multicollinearity. The fact that several variables load highly on the factors with the largest condition indices indicates its presence. However, no condition index is particularly high and there appears to be little multicollinearity effect on the model. As we shall see later, the addition of other variables does not significantly alter either the model coefficients or their standard errors. The stability of the model coefficients and their standard errors in the presence of control factors suggests that the model usefully summarizes the processes that

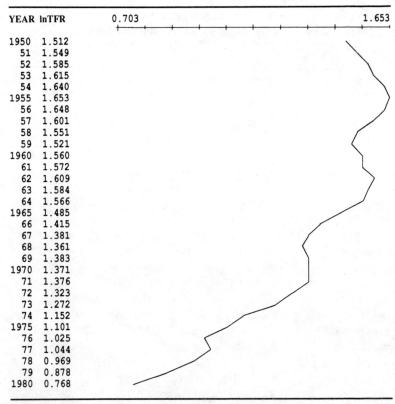

YEAR	lnTFR
1950	1.512
51	1.549
52	1.585
53	1.615
54	1.640
1955	1.653
56	1.648
57	1.601
58	1.551
59	1.521
1960	1.560
61	1.572
62	1.609
63	1.584
64	1.566
1965	1.485
66	1.415
67	1.381
68	1.361
69	1.383
1970	1.371
71	1.376
72	1.323
73	1.272
74	1.152
1975	1.101
76	1.025
77	1.044
78	0.969
79	0.878
1980	0.768

Figure 8.1.   Smoothed time series for LnTFR.

generated Barbadian fertility history over the 31 years from 1950 through 1980.

FINDINGS

These findings, like those for the micro-level model of Barbadian fertility transition developed in Chapter 7, constitute a serious challenge to standard demographic transition theory that interprets fertility transition as part of a broader set of changes in a population's social institutions and standard of living. If fertility transition actually is part of a general response to industrialization and urbanization and consequent rising standards of living, an index of economic well-being should display an inverse relationship with fertility. However, if fertility

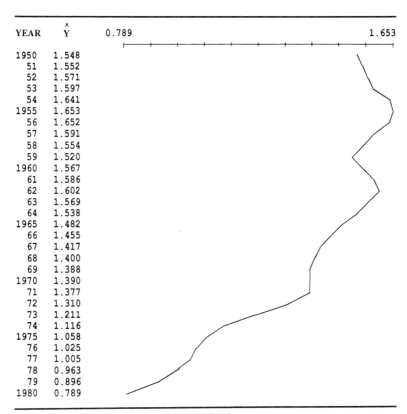

YEAR	$\hat{Y}$
1950	1.548
51	1.552
52	1.571
53	1.597
54	1.641
1955	1.653
56	1.652
57	1.591
58	1.554
59	1.520
1960	1.567
61	1.586
62	1.602
63	1.569
64	1.538
1965	1.482
66	1.455
67	1.417
68	1.400
69	1.388
1970	1.390
71	1.377
72	1.310
73	1.211
74	1.116
1975	1.058
76	1.025
77	1.005
78	0.963
79	0.896
1980	0.789

Figure 8.2. Smoothed time series of the model estimate.

transition is a phenomenon that is qualitatively distinct from fertility declines that occur because of depressed economic conditions, an index of economic well-being should distinguish one source of fertility decline from the other. There should be a positive relationship between fertility and increases in economic well-being. This positive relationship should hold both in pretransition cohorts, for whom children constitute a source of wealth, and in posttransition cohorts, for whom children constitute a consumption expenditure. The pretransition cohort is distinguished from the the posttransition cohort in that, in the former, the positive relationship between material well-being and fertility is mutually determined. Children both contribute to that rising material well-being and stem from the increases in fecundity that accompany rising material well-being. The results presented here clearly support this line of reasoning, contrary to standard transition theory.

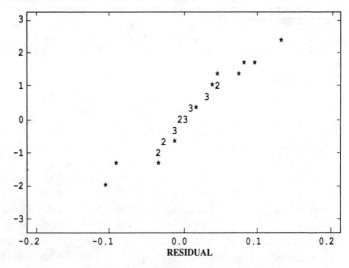

Figure 8.3. Normal probability plot of model residuals.

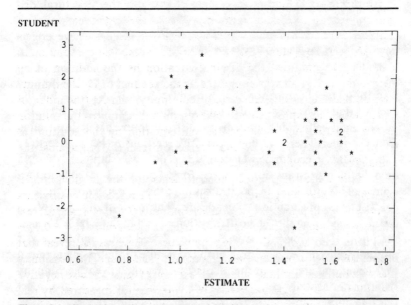

Figure 8.4. Studentized residuals by the model estimate.

TABLE 8.2
Eigenvalues, Condition Indices, and Variance Proportions

Eigenvalues of Unit Scaled X' X

1	2	3	4	5	6	7
4.659	2.132	0.125	0.065	0.016	0.002	0.000

Condition Indices

1	2	3	4	5	6	7
1.000	1.478	6.095	8.445	17.016	51.818	194.781

Variance Proportions

	1	2	3	4	5	6	7
Constant	0.000	0.000	0.004	0.004	0.001	0.946	0.044
Real wage	0.000	0.000	0.001	0.012	0.125	0.812	0.050
Manufacturing	0.000	0.000	0.000	0.000	0.282	0.698	0.019
Tourism	0.000	0.002	0.044	0.102	0.084	0.740	0.028
Discontinuity 1	0.000	0.000	0.000	0.001	0.000	0.000	0.999
Discontinuity 2	0.000	0.001	0.057	0.047	0.005	0.036	0.854
Discontinuity 3	0.000	0.000	0.000	0.000	0.000	0.002	0.998

However, some questions remain. First, did the structural discontinuity in the Barbadian economy change the effect of real wages on fertility? Second, did real wages in the sugar industry have effects beyond 1960? To evaluate the first question, I computed the solution to a model that modified the original equation by the addition of an interaction term that was computed as the product of D (the dummy variable that identified structural discontinuity) and X_1 (the index of real income). To evaluate the second question, I computed the solution to a model that modified the original equation by the addition of variable X_4, and thus tested the interaction term $(D*X_4)$ against the main effects of the sugar industry variable.

In both tests, the regression coefficients for the original model variables did not change in significant ways. The regression coefficients for (1) real wages prior to structural discontinuity (t = –0.604) and (2) real wages in the sugar industry after structural discontinuity (t = + 0.779) were associated with high probability values. These results reveal that neither addition to the model was empirically valid. Test of the possibility that structural discontinuity affected the intercept value was also negative (t = –0.534). Thus as the standard of living rose (as measured by real wages) so did fertility, and this was true for both pre-and posttransition cohorts. Thus the increases in real wages that Barbados experienced over the period 1950-1980 reduced the rate at which period total fertility declined after 1960, once fertility transition began.

These findings support the analysis of Barbadian economic history presented in Chapters 3 and 4. Increases in manufacturing and tourism increased fertility prior to structural discontinuity in the Barbadian economy. As indicated earlier, and as was implicit in the micro-level findings presented in the previous chapter, these effects almost certainly reflect changes in fecundity rather than changes in decisions. After structural discontinuity, however, the effect of increases in these variables was manifested in fertility decisions to reduce fertility. The Barbadian fertility transition can be accounted for almost wholly by structural discontinuity and the opening and diversification of the Barbadian economy.

CONTROL VARIABLES

But is it really possible that fertility transition is explained so simply, that it merely reflects the opening of new and competitive resource access channels? As indicated in Chapter 1, standard transition theory stipulates that fertility decline should follow from reductions in infant mortality. However, the infant mortality variable performs no better here than it did when we tried to use it (in Chapter 6) to account for changes in moral economy. When infant mortality was entered into the model individually and simultaneously with the model variables, model estimates were unaffected, there was no evidence of multicollinearity, and the resulting t-statistic was -0.209 ($p = .836$).

Surely, however, education plays a role in fertility decline? The analyses reported in previous chapters, of course, suggest not. Examination of the micro-level effects of education on changes in moral economy reported in Chapter 6 revealed that increasing levels of education were accompanied by slight reductions in the value of a woman's moral economy index but that changes in moral economy clearly had a more substantive influence on the level of education women eventually obtained. Moreover, at the macro level, increases in women's participation in Barbadian educational institutions bore no relationship to changes in moral economy. Historical declines in the proportion of women who viewed childbearing as an investment activity were almost completely explained by increases in employment in industrial manufacturing and by increases in tourist spending. The micro-level analyses reported in Chapter 7 revealed that education reduced individual fertility only to the extent that women going through school delayed childbearing to do so.

Nevertheless, education may display important *macro-level* effects on fertility. Standard demographic transition theory stipulates that education plays a central role in fertility transition. The reasons that education *should* play an important role in transition are legion and the inverse relationship between educational attainment and fertility transition is the most consistently reported correlation in the literature. Indeed, Jack Caldwell's Westernization hypothesis contends that the growth of mass education is the single determinant of the onset of fertility decline.

Similarly, surely the provision of family planning services has been important in Barbadian fertility decline. The analysis of micro-level family planning service effects on fertility in the previous chapter revealed that the provision of such services either by the Barbados Family Planning Association or by private retailers may have permitted Barbadian women to plan their births effectively, but that they had no demonstrable dampening effect on fertility: women who wanted large families planned their children, spaced their births, and intentionally terminated their reproductive careers when they had enough children—but they continued to have large families. Nonetheless, replacement-level fertility requires the intentional and sharp truncation of reproductive careers. Contraception and abortion are necessarily implicated when women intentionally and sharply truncate their reproductive careers. The Barbados Family Planning Association (BFPA) is widely hailed as having run a model program in the Eastern Caribbean. The BFPA's activities have been viewed (e.g., Nag, 1971) as instrumental in bringing about fertility decline and, if not actually initiating transition, then at least significantly facilitating transition.

I examined several control variables to assess these possibilities.

Education

The first set of variables consists of four measures of education. First, I use the arithmetic mean number of years of formal schooling for succeeding cohorts of women aged 20-24 (see Chapter 4). This variable measures the potential impact that the *level* of educational attainment might have on fertility. Several alternative constructions of this variable were explored, including several lag computations. None provided a superior fit with the period total fertility time series.

Second, I use the proportion of women in succeeding 20- to 24-year-old age cohorts who had completed secondary school (see Chapter 4). This variable is a measure of the potential impact that the *prevalence* of education might have on fertility and, thus constitutes a measure of the spread of *mass education* in Caldwell's terms.

Examination of scatterplots revealed that there appeared to be a nonlinear relationship between these measures of education and fertility. Caldwell (1980) and others have argued that the relationship between education and fertility *should* exhibit a threshold effect. The pattern apparent in scatterplots (not included) suggested that education has no impact on fertility below a threshold level. Beyond that level, education may have a clear, inverse linear relationship with fertility.

To evaluate possible threshold effects, I created truncated measures of both educational level and educational prevalence. I determined threshold levels empirically by using a nonlinear maximum-likelihood estimation procedure. I then recoded the original measures of education as: 0 if the threshold had not been reached, and as (X – the threshold level) to indicate how far beyond the threshold value the mean level of education and the proportion of women who completed secondary school had progressed.

Family Planning

The second set of control variables consists of measures of family planning services availability. I measured the influence of the BFPA in ways that are based on significant events in the history of the association: (1) its opening in Bridgetown in 1955, (2) its establishment in parishes throughout the island in 1966, and (3) its establishment of a Community Based Distribution of Contraceptives project in 1975 (Nair, 1982). Data on new acceptors (1982: 15) suggest that at each of these expansions the BFPA experienced a significant increase in its influence. If this reading is correct, then the influence of the BFPA should be captured by an ordinal score of 0 prior to its formation, and by successive increments that indicate the BFPA's increased influence at each successive expansion. I used this approach to create three measures that might tap the impact of family planning services on fertility.

First, I recorded each significant expansion of BFPA services as a dummy variable: BFPA1, where 1 = years in which the BFPA Bridgetown office was opened, and 0 otherwise; BFPA2, where 1 = years in which the BFPA had spread outside Bridgetown, and 0 otherwise;

and BFPA3, where 1 = years in which the Community Based Distribution of Contraceptives project was ongoing, and 0 otherwise.

Second, I created an index of the influence of the BFPA by assigning each significant expansion of services an increase in scale: 0 prior to formation, 1 for each year after the BFPA's establishment in Bridgetown, 2 for each year after BFPA's expansion to the parishes, and 3 for each year after BFPA's establishment of the Community Based Distribution of Contraceptives Project.

Third, I took the ordinally scaled index of family planning influence and assigned influence weights at each successive expansion. At its opening I assigned a rank of 1 for the first two years; I assigned 2, 3, 4, and so on for successive increases in influence after this period; I assigned the highest of these levels for the remainder of the period until the next expansion of services. I repeated this procedure for each of the two subsequent service expansions. Thus this measure assumes an initial period for adjustment, a subsequent period of increasing influence, and a period of influence that remains at a high level but does not increase until the next period of BFPA expansion.

Education and Family Planning Effects

Table 8.3 summarizes tests of the hypothesis that education and family planning services have had important macro-level effects on the Barbadian fertility transition. I avoided atheoretical approaches such as stepwise regression in all tests, and I tempered my judgment about multivariate models with considerations of the potential effects of multicollinearity. In all tests, control variables were entered simultaneously with the model variables. I examined the effects of each control variable individually so that I could avoid having to reject education or family planning variables simply because of multicollinearity problems. My approach involved two steps. First, I constructed models of the Barbadian fertility transition based solely on the education and family planning variables. Second, I took the variables that appeared to be plausible determinants of transition and tested them against the model variables.

Table 8.3 is divided into two sections that correspond with the two sets of tests subsequently carried out against the model variables. The first set of tests systematically examined the individual effects of each important control variable when it was added to the equation simultaneously with the model variables. The second set of tests examined the

TABLE 8.3
Education and Family Planning Effects

Dependent Variable: LnTFR		Bonferroni Adjustment for α: $.05/16 = .003$		
Independent Variables:	STD. Coef.	T	P (2-Tail)	R² Change
Tests for Individual Effects				
Educational level	.329	.893	.381	+.001
Educational level threshold	-.109	-.836	.412	+.001
Educational prevalence	-.584	-2.094	.047	+.005
Educational preva threshold	-.368	-1.977	.060	+.005
BFPA in parishes	-.083	-0.797	.433	+.001
BFPA project	-.103	-1.215	.237	+.001
Family planning index #1	-.057	-0.441	.663	.000
Family planning index #2	-.356	-1.236	.229	+.002
Tests for Interactive Effects				
Educational prevalence*				
family planning index #1	-.191	-1.372	.183	+.002
Educational prevalence*				
family planning index #2	-.366	-2.208	.038	+.005
Truncated ed. prevalence*				
family planning index #1	-.182	-1.572	.130	+.003
Truncated ed. prevalence*				
family planning index #2	-.261	-2.240	.035	+.006
Educational level*				
family planning index #1	-.062	-.441	.663	.000
Educational level*				
family planning index #2	-.350	-1.231	.231	+.002
Truncated ed. level*				
family planning index #1	-.105	-1.052	.304	+.001
Truncated ed. level*				
family planning index #2	-.167	-1.654	.112	+.003

possibility that there were interaction effects such that the effect of education on Barbadian fertility has been contingent on the provision of family planning services or, conversely, that the effect of family planning services has been contingent on women's educational level. These tests were conducted using all possible interactions between measures of education and the two family planning index variables.

Plainly, the 16 tests reported here were carried out while I conducted a fishing expedition. One cannot trust probability levels generated in this way. Consequently, I adjusted alpha with the Bonferroni procedure by dividing a standard alpha value of .05 by 16. Probabilities that fall at or below the result (.003) can be confidently used to reject the Null Hypothesis. The results in Table 8.3 reveal that it was impossible to reject the Null Hypothesis for any of the 16 tests.

Moreover, these tests revealed only one multicollinearity effect. This exception involved both the truncated and the untruncated measures of educational prevalence (the proportion of secondary-school leavers). Whenever one or the other of these variables were entered in the equation there was a disturbance with the tourism variable.

This disturbance might be explained by arguing that the two variables measure much the same effect. If this interpretation is chosen, the disturbance can be eliminated by dropping one or the other variable. However, this choice has important theoretical implications. This research would be suspected of fudging if it dropped the education variable. Conversely, the theoretical implications of the model would be obscured if the tourism variable was dropped, for then (1) the model would be consistent with Caldwell's claim that Westernization contributes to fertility decline, because Westernization should be the product of formal schooling; with the modernization hypothesis that claims that something about education contributes to fertility decline; and also with the resource access hypothesis, in that the education variable could be merely capturing the effect of the diversification in the economy represented by tourism.

The resource access hypothesis suggests another explanation for the disturbance. As indicated in Chapter 2 and elsewhere (Handwerker, 1986a), education should contribute to fertility transition only when it is accompanied by increasing material rewards. In the contemporary world, an increasingly open and competitive resource structure *creates* increasing returns to education. The micro-level analysis in Chapter 7 revealed that women's educational attainment was influenced in substantial ways by their view of the moral economy of childbearing and parent-child relationships. We would expect that changes in moral economy would influence women's educational attainment only if formal schooling constituted an important resource access channel. If this hypothesis and the findings of Chapter 7 are correct, on Barbados we would not expect education to affect fertility through a measure of growth in manufacturing because women have not been subject to widespread selective hiring on the basis of educational attainment in that sector. Employees have been most subject to such selection in the tourist industry and in residentiary sector activities supported by tourism. Perhaps an interaction term between the educational prevalence variable and the tourism variable will capture such effects.

Tests for main effects and the interaction term yield low t-statistics for all terms: for the educational prevalence variable, $t = +0.031$; for the tourism variable, $t = -0.383$; and for the interaction term, $t = -1.161$. A test that substituted the truncated measure of educational prevalence for

TABLE 8.4
Modified Macro-Level Model of
Barbados' Fertility Transition

Dependent Variable: LnTFR		N: 31		Squared Multiple R: .975	
Adjusted Squared Multiple R: .969				Standard Error of Estimate: 0.045	
Variable	Coefficient	STD. Error	STD. Coef.	T	P (2 Tail)
Constant	1.701	0.114	0.000	14.949	0.000
Real Wages	0.005	0.001	0.409	5.736	0.000
Manufacturing	-0.010	0.001	-0.872	-8.058	0.000
Educational prevalence*					
Tourism	0.008	0.002	-0.430	-4.720	0.000
		Prior to 1960			
Manufacturing	0.094	0.021	6.800	4.421	0.000
Tourism	0.051	0.013	0.895	4.029	0.000
Sugar industry	-0.048	0.011	-7.652	-4.462	0.000

Analysis of Variance

Source	Sum-of-Squares	DF	Mean-Square	F-ratio	P
Regression	1.909	6	0.318	156.448	0.000
Residual	0.049	24	0.002		

Durbin-Watson D statistic   2.539
First order autocorrelation   -.300

the untruncated variable yielded nearly identical results (respectively, $t = -.175, +.377$, and -1.078). The finding that the t-statistic is highest for the interaction term reveals that the interaction term best fits the data and does capture an effect of education on the Barbadian fertility transition.

A REVISED MODEL

Table 8.4 presents the solution to a revised model that substitutes the interaction between tourism and education for the original tourism variable. The interaction term used in this model was constructed with the untruncated educational prevalence variable. Use of the truncated educational prevalence variable yields nearly identical results. The relatively low probabilities associated with the interaction of educational prevalence variables with the second family planning index variable in Table 8.3 raise the possibility that there may be a residual interaction effect with the family planning variables. To evaluate this possibility, I entered simultaneously with the model variables the family planning index, both alone and in interaction with both the untruncated and the truncated measures of educational prevalence. The t-statistics (respectively, t = –0.264, –.312, and –.319) revealed that there was no such effect.

A comparison of Table 8.1 with Table 8.4 reveals that the regression coefficients and the standard errors of the basic model variables are not significantly affected by the addition of the interaction term. Examination of residuals reveals that the modified model duplicates the findings of the original: the estimates are normally distributed, there are no outliers, and the plot of studentized residuals by the estimate reveals an approximately homogeneous scatter of error. The first-order autocorrelation is noticeably higher for the revised model, but a plot of autocorrelations (not included) revealed no statistically significant serial correlation.

Comparison of the standard error of the estimates for the original and the revised model reveals that the addition of the (tourism*educational prevalence) interaction term yields a negligible improvement in fit (+.006). Such a small improvement in predictive value suggests that adding the interaction term may be unduly redundant. However, one can estimate historical trends in Barbadian period total fertility with either the original or the revised model with inconsequential differences in results.

However, this finding concerning the interaction term is significant— it allows us to discriminate among the modernization, Westernization, and resource access hypotheses on the basis of explanatory import. This finding reveals that education has contributed to the Barbadian fertility transition *in ways that have been contingent on the opening and diversification of Barbadian resource structure.* Education influences fertility transition only insofar as increases in education are accompanied by increasing material rewards. This finding thus constitutes another demonstration that the results of both micro and macro levels of analysis, based on very different data bases, yield consistent findings about the underlying determinants of the Barbadian fertility transition.

SUMMARY

This chapter tested the macro-level hypothesis that the Barbadian fertility transition has been a simple function of the opening of new and competitive resource access channels. The Barbadian economy experienced a major structural discontinuity around 1960 when the sugar industry, which had dominated the economy for more than 300 years, was restructured under competitive pressure from world sugar markets, and the Barbadian government encouraged the growth and expansion of industrial manufacturing and tourism, both of which have been subject to sharp competitive pressure in world markets. Fertility transition occurred when industrial manufacturing and tourism emerged as the most important sectors in the Barbadian economy. Measures of these variables and of the structural discontinuity in the economy accounted for about 97% of the variance in estimated period total fertility rates. The model very accurately reconstructs the trends in Barbadian period fertility from 1950 through 1980.

This macro-level model was systematically tested against a variety of alternative hypotheses, including

(1) main effects of interaction term components,
(2) effects of increases in material well-being as measured by an index of real wages,
(3) effects of declines in infant mortality,
(4) effects of increasing levels of education attained by Barbadian women,
(5) effects of the increasing prevalence of high levels of education among Barbadian women, and
(6) effects of the Barbados Family Planning Association.

Without exception, these tests revealed that no control variable had a significant influence on the Barbadian fertility transition. With one exception, estimates of the model variables remained unchanged in these tests.

The one exception was a disturbance between tourism and the prevalence of secondary education. Examination of the sources for this disturbance revealed that, because the tourism sector and economic sectors supported by tourism have subjected both employers and employees to selection on the basis of educational qualifications, the increasing prevalence of secondary-school leavers in Barbados has contributed to the Barbadian fertility transition by interacting with the growth of tourism. This finding is consistent with and clarifies micro-level findings presented in Chapters 6 and 7: (1) increasing levels of education slightly reduce the degree to which women view childbearing as an investment activity, but the emergence of new, competitive resource access channels creates a realistic basis for women to plan a future independent of men and children; (2) the emergence of these resource access channels sharply reduces the proportion of women who view childbearing as an investment activity and thus stimulates women to take fuller advantage of the available educational opportunities to attain increasingly higher levels of education; (3) fertility declines partly because such women delay childbearing while in school, but also and more importantly because such women have taken the view that childbearing is a consumption activity that must be balanced by their other life goals. These findings are consistent with the deductions outlined in Chapter 2 and elsewhere: Education, by itself, does not contribute to fertility transition in important ways. Education has contributed to Barbadian fertility transition only via the opening of new, competitive resource access channels.

—9—

POPULATION, POWER,
AND DEVELOPMENT

Between the 1950s and the 1980s, Barbadians "developed" in all ways connoted by the term. The level of real wages doubled and infant mortality fell from well over 100 to around 30. The proportion of women aged 20-24 who completed secondary school rose from about 3% to more than 50%, and the mean level of completed schooling for those women rose from about 8 years to nearly 12. Whereas in the 1950s, Barbadian family relationships were characterized by sharp spousal and generational inequalities, in the 1980s, younger Barbadian women experienced family relationships characterized by a growing ideology of and behavioral equality. Whereas in the 1950s Barbadian women experienced fertility levels restricted only by constraints on their own fecundity and by constraints on sexual activity implicit in their spousal unions, in the 1980s, younger Barbadian women bore children at a rate less than half that of their mothers and grandmothers. Period total fertility rates fell from around 5.0 in the mid-1950s to a low of about 2.0 in 1980.

These observations make it easy to interpret the Barbadian fertility transition as a classic instance in which widespread modernization or Westernization, coupled with an effective family planning program, brought about a dramatic fertility decline. Close examination of ethnographic data, both macro- and micro-level data, and both period and cohort fertility, however, reveal that the standard interpretation simply is not correct.

Prior to 1960, the Barbadian economy was characterized by an uncompetitive and oligopolistic resource structure the primary effect of which was to allocate opportunities largely on the basis of personal relationships, and these on the basis of sex, class and color. For the majority of the Barbadian population, this structure created a fundamental conflict between the interests of men and women in which the only way each could optimize their access to key resources was to exploit the weaknesses and dependencies of the other.

Childbearing was a singularly important means women could use to gain access to the resources on which their material welfare depended. In a woman's youth, children legitimated her claims for income from men. In her middle age, children provided financial support that could make her independent of spousal support that required her subservience. In her old age, financial support from children meant the difference between abject poverty and a moderate, or even comfortable, level of living.

In the 1950s, men could not win either with their spouses or with their children. Men were pressured to get a job to bring in money to help their mothers. To get a steady job, to find additional work, or to get better jobs, men needed contacts with other men. Within the middle and upper classes, contacts were provided by one's family. Within the lower class, the vast majority of Barbadians, men needed to establish their reputation and character. Men gained and maintained a good reputation if they exploited their women by demanding of them sexual and domestic services and children, and by spending their time in the company of men and other women. As they responded rationally to the resource structure in which they were enmeshed, men invited complaints and criticisms from their women and alienated their children. Women, in the meantime, drilled into the children not only how much they sacrificed and how hard they had to work to raise them properly, but also that their labors were made only that much worse because they had no companion (a reliable spouse) to help them. Family hardships thus became perceived as owing to the fact that a child's father, and men generally, simply were irresponsible.

Men were peripheral to the processes of family life and, "naturally," children came "to cling" to their mothers who indoctrinated them into thinking that they owed their mothers for the sacrifices she made to raise them well. Because childbearing entailed only investment expenditures, women experienced fertility levels limited only by constraints on their fecundity and by constraints on sexual activity implicit in their spousal unions.

Between 1955 and 1965, the Barbadian economy underwent a major structural discontinuity marked by decline in the importance of sugar and the ascendancy of industrial manufacturing and tourism. The economic well-being of these sectors was subject to selection on the basis of quality and cost factors set in international markets. Consequently, employment and upward mobility in these sectors, and in sectors supporting manufacturing and tourism, came to be subject to selection on the basis of qualifications and performance rather than personal relationships with employers.

The opening of new and competitive resource access channels thus was accompanied by a shift in the means by which both men and women could best optimize resource access. Young men, unlike their fathers and grandfathers, were not placed in a position in which they had to exploit their women and alienate their children to respond rationally to the resource structure. Young women, unlike their mothers and grandmothers, could find work that permitted them an independence from men. Relationships between young men and women came to be characterized by companionate qualities that their parents and grandparents experienced only rarely.

Thus by the 1980s, Barbadian women came to be independent agents who were able to chart their own courses in life in ways that had been denied their mothers and grandmothers. In the presence of competitive employing organizations that, consequently, have increasingly emphasized both employer and employee productivity, children could no longer serve effectively as resource access channels. Children thus became consumer durables—albeit very special ones—and bearing children became a consumption activity in which parents had to choose between children or television sets and videos. Because parents have special obligations to their children—once they are born—that can and do take precedence over many (and perhaps all) other consumer choices, it has become morally wrong that *bearing* children itself take precedence over a woman's personal goals and dreams.

Hence, on the micro level, Barbadian fertility has been a function of birth trajectories set by different forms of spousal union interacting with women's view of children as investment or consumption activity. The Barbadian fertility transition has been a simple function of increasing proportions of women who view childbearing as a consumption activity. The increasing proportion of women who take this point of view has been a simple function of the extent to which Barbadian women have been able to control their lives by using new and competitive resource access channels. Hence, at the macro level, the Barbadian fertility transition has been a simple function of structural discontinuity in the economy that marked the emergence of a open and diversified resource structure.

Ordinary least-squares regression analyses confirmed the claims, derived empirically from ethnographic data and deduced from the resource access hypothesis, that prior to fertility transition on Barbados (1) young women's income was significantly enhanced by childbearing and (2) older women's income increased with completed fertility. Statistical models provide estimates of the actual amount of additional income childbearing provided women at different ages.

Two-stage least-squares regression analysis of a pair of simultaneous equations revealed that, at the individual level, women's view of childbearing as a consumption or an investment activity has been influenced by education, and that women's participation in the Barbadian educational system has been influenced by their perception of childbearing. Model estimates indicate that the effect of women's perception of childbearing on their schooling have been substantively more important than educational effects on their view of childbearing. Thus, whereas completed secondary education still left women in even the youngest cohorts only ambiguously committed to the view that childbearing was a consumption activity, if women took the view that childbearing was an investment activity their expected level of completed education was below the level of a secondary school education. Moreover, when the macro-level effects of educational attainment, educational prevalence, real incomes, and infant mortality levels was tested against the effects of industrial manufacturing and tourist spending, historical declines in the proportion of women who view childbearing as an investment activity is shown to have been a simple function of the opening of new and competitive resource access channels measured by the latter two variables. This analysis revealed that rising real wages *increased* the proportion of women who viewed childbearing as an investment activity, and thus slowed the historical decline that was brought about by the opening of new and competitive resource access channels.

Micro-level and macro-level models of the Barbadian fertility transition were developed on the basis of ethnographic and historical research. The micro-level model accounted for about 62% of the variance in individual fertility. The macro-level model accounted for about 97% of the variance in period total fertility rates from 1950 through 1980 and very accurately reproduced the historical trends in Barbadian fertility. These models were systematically tested against specifications consistent with the viewpoints of both standard demographic transition theory and Caldwell's wealth flows alternative. The micro-level model was tested against (1) main effects of the components of the model interaction variables, (2) effects stemming from inclusion of women younger than age 30 in the data base for estimating the coefficients, (3) uncaptured historical trends, (4) effects of exposure to urban values and life-styles, (5) effects of exposure to international values and life-styles, (6) effects of participation in the Barbadian educational system, and (7) the impact of the Barbados Family Planning Association. The macro-level model was tested against (1) main effects of pertinent interaction terms, (2) the effects of increases in material well-being (using both a measure of real wage rates and infant mortality levels as indexes), (3) effects of increasing levels of education and the adoption of Western values of egalitarianism and opportunity, (5) effects of increasing proportions of women who had completed secondary school, and (6) the impact of the Barbados Family Planning Association. The macro-level model demonstrated that rising real incomes actually *increased* fertility between 1950 and 1980, and thus reduced the rate at which the Barbadian fertility transition took place.

Specifications consistent with either standard demographic transition theory or wealth flows theory failed to exhibit statistically significant results. On the micro level, tests revealed that education has not affected birth trajectories, as it should have if either the modernization hypothesis or the Westernization hypothesis were correct. Moreover, education led to only minimal reductions in fertility. Those reductions occurred only because women delayed childbearing while they were in school. On the macro level, tests revealed that Caldwell's mass education variable reduced period age-specific fertility rates only by interacting with a measure of the tourism-related employment where both employment and advancement have been subject to selection on the basis of educational qualifications and perspectives.

POPULATION ISSUES IN THE CARIBBEAN

In the Caribbean, Barbados (together with Puerto Rico and Cuba) represents the low end of a fertility spectrum, at the opposite end of which lie Belize and Haiti. Despite the exceptions represented by Belize and Haiti, the islands of the Caribbean share a recent history of fertility increase and decline—increases following World War II, and declines that began at various times between the mid-1950s and the mid-1970s. Fertility on Montserrat began declining about the same time as on Barbados, but fertility on other islands began declining later: in Grenada, St. Kitts-Nevis, and Trinidad, and Tobago by the early 1960s; in Jamaica, Antigua, and St. Vincent by the late 1960s; in the U.S. and British Virgin Islands, St. Lucia, and Dominica, after 1970. Once begun, fertility decline has been consistent and, occasionally, precipitous. For instance, since 1970 total fertility on St. Lucia has fallen 1.5% annually from its high of nearly 7.0. Excepting Barbados, Antigua, Cuba, Montserrat, and Puerto Rico, however, fertility has remained considerably above replacement levels. In 1980, total fertility on St. Lucia and St. Vincent hovered around 4.2—not much lower than total fertility recorded for several pretransition European villages—and total fertility on other islands ranged between 3.0 and 4.0.

TABLE 9.1
Cohort Age-Specific Fertility for Barbadian Teenagers, 1950-1980

	Pre-1955	1955-1959	1960-1964	1965-1969	1970-1974	1975-1979
ASFR 15-19	.151	.129	.104	.095	.074	.079
Index	1.000	.854	.689	.656	.490	.523

On islands like Barbados that have experienced a completed fertility transition, the population issues of most concern include (1) the prospect that fertility may fall so low that the island might face either long-term population decline or the possibility of being inundated by migrants, and (2) high teen-age pregnancy rates (e.g., Clipson, 1981). Table 9.1 reveals that teenage fertility in fact fell dramatically on Barbados over the last 30 years, and it appears to have done so as well on other islands (see Guengant, 1985). Nonetheless, there appears to be a small group of high-fertility women that persists in the midst of a low-fertility society. Clipson's research and review of the literature suggests that the teenagers who are getting pregnant today do so under circumstances that differ little from those that their mothers and grandmothers experienced prior to 1960. The circumstances that brought about the Barbadian fertility transition may have bypassed a significant minority of women, a situation that may also explain high teenage fertility in the United States. It is important to determine if this is the case, and what might be done about it if it is. To answer these questions, we need to know in detail how young women think of childbearing at the beginning of their reproductive years and why they think that way, how their ideas change as they mature, the variables that influence these changes, and the path through which these variables exert their influence.

For most of the Caribbean, however, the pertinent population issue centers on the large gap between mortality that has fallen to very low levels and fertility that may have declined but is still high and may continue that way for many years into the future. Significant gaps between birth and death rates raise the specter of overpopulation and ecological imbalance. As Guengant (1985: 15) points out, fears of imminent overpopulation may be more apparent than real. The 1980 census returns indicated that, by the 1970s, 11 of the 25 major countries of the region had achieved either close to zero or negative population growth and only 3 of the remaining 14 countries had growth rates in excess of 2% annually. Nonetheless, the population structure on most islands is characterized by sharp age imbalances; typically, 40%-50% of

Caribbean populations are under age 15. Extremely high levels of emigration both follow from and may exacerbate the economic dependence of this region on North America and Europe (see Marshall, 1982). Even if fertility falls to replacement levels next year, the proportion of young people on the islands promises dangerously high levels of unemployment within the next decade, especially if opportunities for emigration contract.

Concern with population in the Caribbean is not new, of course (see Roberts, 1957). Population concerns emerged in the seventeenth century with the establishment of a plantation economy and underpinned the development of the Atlantic slave trade. Emancipation changed the particular expression of population concerns but, with the exception of Barbados (which, as Sir Arthur Lewis, 1950, observed, was "fully peopled in the seventeenth century and [has] been complaining about overpopulation for nearly three centuries"), the primary objective remained that of assuring a stable or growing labor force. The labor disturbances of the 1930s, however, placed metropolitan concerns about population-resource relationships in the Caribbean in a new light. The subsequent Moyne Commission report brought home the fact that Caribbean economies were not providing, and perhaps might not provide in the foreseeable future, adequate employment to their growing populations.

Because many of the region's difficulties have been conceptualized in Malthusian terms, as a population problem, family planning programs often are proposed as solutions. Until recently, however, "population" has not been a development issue worthy of explicit policy. Although the Moyne Commission Report was issued following World War II, by 1980 the only Caribbean countries that had adopted official population policies to reduce fertility were Barbados, the Dominican Republic, Jamaica, Puerto Rico, and Trinidad and Tobago (Nortman and Hofstatter, 1980). Although privately sponsored efforts to reduce the birth rate were initiated in 1925 in Puerto Rico, by 1939 in Jamaica, and by 1955 in Barbados, official government population policies supporting family planning efforts were not adopted until the late 1960s and early 1970s (Barbados in 1967, the Dominican Republic in 1968, Jamaica in 1966, Puerto Rico in 1970, Trinidad and Tobago in 1967; see Harewood, 1968). Haiti and Cuba both make family planning technologies available, but not officially for population control purposes. Their policies also are of recent date: 1971 for Haiti, and the early 1960s for Cuba. It was not until 1986 that St. Lucia formalized any population policy. Even under pressure from international donor organizations, most countries in the Eastern Caribbean still have no explicit population policies.

In the face of public apathy and of opposition from the Church and other politically influential organizations, family planning programs in the Caribbean owe their origin primarily to local voluntary organizations, to activities of the International Planned Parenthood Federation, and to activities of donor organizations, such as the United Nations Fund for Population Activities (UNFPA) and the United States Agency for International Development (USAID). With the notable exception of the Barbados Family Planning Association, whose establishment in 1955 coincided with the origins of the Barbadian fertility transition and whose significant expansions coincided with significant reductions in the birth rate, Caribbean family planning efforts have not yielded clear successes. The problems of the Puerto Rican and Jamaican family planning programs in the 1950s stimulated significant research efforts (Stycos, 1955; Blake, 1961). Despite private efforts dating to 1956 and government support since 1967, in 1980, Trinidad and Tobago's total fertility still remained above 3.0 (Guengant, 1985). A hint of the difficulties faced in Trinidad and Tobago is found in a 1970 KAP survey (Harewood, 1978) that revealed that 65% of the women whose ideal family size was 5 or greater reported being aware of a significant relationship between population and Trinidad and Tobago's economic difficulties. We may infer that these women believed that their fertility did not bear on the islandwide population problem.

Indeed, there is little circumstantial evidence and *no* clear evidence that family planning programs have had any influence at all on Caribbean fertility rates. For instance, in a detailed examination of Jamaican fertility, focusing on the Parish of St. Ann, that used census data from 1946, 1960, and 1970, Sinclair (1974) found expected inverse relationships between fertility and both educational attainment and contraceptive effort, but was able to account for a statistically insignificant 17% of the variance in parish fertility for the island. The evidence for Barbados itself, which often is held up to other islands as an example of what an effective family planning program can accomplish (e.g., Slavin and Bilsborrow, 1974), is scanty. A 1980-1981 contraceptive prevalence survey carried out by the BFPA revealed that only about 31% of all women sampled had *ever* made use of BFPA services; less than half of all women who had used contraceptive methods had *ever* made use of BFPA services (Nair, 1982: 98).

Findings such as these raise fundamental questions about the efficacy of Caribbean family planning programs. These questions are now being addressed by operations research teams funded by USAID that seek to design more efficient methods of extending the influence of existing family planning programs.

However, if the findings of this study of Barbados are on the right track, the Caribbean does not face a population problem. It faces a problem of power relations. Family planning programs should not be expected to bring about fertility transition because they can neither create the jobs, nor provide the education necessary for many jobs that would permit women to achieve meaningful control over their own lives. The "right" to have a small family is not a real option for women who are dependent for basic material well-being on their children. Such women use family planning services: (1) to determine why they have such difficulty getting pregnant (Handwerker, 1986c), (2) to avoid pregnancy, but only during their school years (Handwerker, 1986c), (3) to permit couples to resume their sexual relationship during periods that, traditionally, required abstinence (Caldwell and Ware, 1977), or (4) to have 9 children but to avoid having 15 (e.g., in Barbados and see also Brainard and Overfield, 1986). They don't use family planning services to sharply curtail their family sizes. The human right to have small families exists as a meaningful, legitimate expectation only when women can realistically expect to achieve and maintain an independence from their children. It is these women for whom smaller family sizes represent not only a viable option, but perhaps a prerequisite for realizing their hopes and dreams. It is these women who use birth control to significantly lower their fertility. Of course, once women experience these changes in power and opportunities and marital fertility declines to very low levels, it is as hard to raise fertility as it appeared to be in order to initiate fertility transition, as Hungary has recently found (Simonelli, 1986).

It does not follow that donor funding for family planning programs should be reduced, for those programs offer women help that goes far beyond assistance in controlling their births. Through a family planning program, women often can avoid the expense of seeing a medical doctor, or can consult an M.D. at accessible rates; the people they see more often than not are other women, who offer encouragement, emotional support, and perhaps professional counseling, in ways that respect their integrity; perhaps most importantly, family planning programs offer women means to circumvent the control over their lives exercised by men and the extensions of men's power manifested in formal governmental and church organizations.

It also does not follow that the optimal mix of funding for family planning programs and socioeconomic development varies with the level of development or that funding for family planning programs should correspond with a country's level of development, as Easterlin and Crimmins (1985: 189-191) propose. For example, Barbara Pillsbury (1986) points out that the severe circumstances of Bangladesh, which is one of the poorest and most densely populated regions of the world, mean that women's (and families') welfare can be improved immensely if family planning services are offered, even if the use of these services would not bring about fertility transition. By contrast, Barbados was relatively well off even in the 1950s. Funding for the Barbados Family Planning Association achieved some important development goals, but it had no perceptible influence on the Barbadian fertility transition.[1] The Barbadian fertility transition and the emergence of egalitarian social relationships followed as direct consequences of structural change in the Barbadian economy, as did these changes in England (Chapter 2), Sicily (Schneider and Schneider, 1984a, 1984b), Sweden, and Japan (Mosk, 1983).

It *does* follow that effective policy decisions require a more sophisticated understanding of development if they are to provide an optimal mix of services, facilities, costs, and personnel training appropriate for the needs of different populations. Such a perspective requires a clearer understanding of the determinants of contraceptive usage.

Clearly, if fertility is to decline to near or below replacement levels, some combination of contraception and abortion must be applied. Yet it is not clear that the fertility declines that have occurred elsewhere in the Caribbean reflect the liberating influences documented for Barbados. We have good reason to believe that oppressive economic conditions will lower fertility (e.g., the findings of this research; also see Hum and Basilevsky, 1978, and Wrigley and Schofield, 1981). Oppressive economic conditions also may raise infant mortality if effective contraception or abortion are not available (see Scrimshaw, 1978).

However, declines in fertility that stem from these conditions do not constitute the phenomenon of fertility transition. Jack Harewood (1981a), a respected West Indian demographer, has recently suggested that "to the extent that the increased use of contraception has contributed to the recent decline of fertility in the Caribbean, both the national problems of development and the personal problems of family improvement have been responsible" (p. 44; cf. Diaz-Briquets and Pérez, 1987, for Cuba). Fertility surely will skyrocket when, or if, conditions improve if an island's fertility decline is not a result of the liberating development processes that have been experienced on Barbados.[2]

These questions in turn raise one of the most perplexing theoretical and policy issues in the social sciences, namely, the source or sources of fertility transition and the social changes that precipitate it.

ADAM SMITH, CHARLES DARWIN, AND KARL MARX

In *The Wealth of Nations,* Adam Smith created an image of people and society that has profoundly influenced all subsequent thought about both. This image, of people who competitively pursue their own best interests and improve the well-being of society in the process, has given rise to the presumption that human history is decided by purposeful, rational thought and action. This view has become an essential assumption of contemporary social science and the modernization hypothesis it uses to interpret social and demographic change in the contemporary world. But Adam Smith's image is incomplete, and we have failed to recognize significance in this fact.

For example, when we presume that human history is the outcome of purposeful human action, we construct explanations that take the following form: (1) if people make assumptions $A_1, A_2, A_3, \ldots A_n$, (2) within the set of constraints $C_1, C_2, C_3, \ldots C_n$, (3) they will conform to behavioral pattern B. Such models usefully describe equilibrium states (e.g., the rationale for high or low fertility, see Mosk, 1983). Clearly defined equilibrium states then can be used to identify disequilibrium states when empirical tests reveal that equilibrium conditions are not met (e.g., Varian, 1984: 1-5). But the observation that an equilibrium model does not match empirical reality does not tell us why.

The theory outlined in this book leads to the conclusion that social change entails discontinuity and, hence, to a change in system states. This conclusion should not be surprising, but it does underline the central weakness of equilibrium descriptions, whether they are formal mathematical models or qualitative Parsonian or ethnographic descriptions of value- consensus—*they cannot be used to explain changes in system states.* Equilibrium descriptions beg the central issue. Transition from one state to another comes about only through changes in assumptions or constraints or both. Adam Smith's conception of people and society takes assumptions and constraints as given; it cannot tell us the circumstances under which they may change or the direction change may take.

Adam Smith's conception of people and society is incomplete in another way, equally important—it underestimates our capacity to muddle our affairs and to mistake our best interests. Thus the conception of human history as the product of human foresight, intentions and rationality appears to be more utopian than realistic. It is not at all clear that human rationality can effectively sort through problems of even moderate complexity (e.g., Hogarth and Reder, 1987); this does not bode well for economic theories of fertility (see Crosbie, 1986). It is clear that we regularly blind ourselves to effective courses of action even when we have at our disposal enough information to identify them, as Barbara Tuchman pointed out in her book, *The March of Folly* (1984). Even if we are prescient, the complexities of power relationships make it virtually impossible to direct the course of human events in ways we might like (e.g., Skocpol, 1979). A Darwinian theory encompasses these issues and so takes us beyond them because it recasts the entire argument.

In *The Origin of Species* (1859), Darwin argued that Nature simply exists—as a physical system that operates impersonally by reference to discernible principles, and without regard to the intentions, purposes or rationality of the organisms subject to those principles. In Darwin's view, the direction of change is decided by material events and circumstances completely independently of intentions or of purposeful, rational thought or action. The driving force of evolution is an interaction between innovations and selective *criteria* that are dictated by the properties of living things.

Darwin thus created a revolutionary image of life. The contrast between a Malthusian view and a Darwinian view perhaps is clearest if we imagine a Petri dish to which we add one bacterium. From a Malthusian perspective, the bacterium becomes bacteria, all of which will ultimately die because all the resources will ultimately be consumed. From a Darwinian perspective, the bacterium becomes bacteria which, by mutation and selection, become a myriad of new species that consume, along with uncounted other possibilities, the Petri dish itself.

Our knowledge of the genetics of living things reveals that, although existing species may be "discrete" in one sense or another, all species share a common ancestor. This means that all current species are merely the end points of a continuous growth trajectory for the population of life forms as a whole. The history of life on earth has revealed an infinite supply of resources over any finite long-term, not because environmental conditions elicit specific innovations, but because selection creates relatively advantageous means for using resources. The innovations that may differentiate the offspring of common parents, which selection may concentrate into different species, change the definition of what constitutes a resource or the means used to acquire resources, and creates new niches in the environment of our earth. So may new ideas.

As Barnett shows (e.g., 1953), over the life of an individual, his or her brain automatically generates the systems of understanding and meaning that anthropologists call "culture." These systems of ideas must be integrated and must change in ways that maintain an internal coherence not because the world possesses an inherent order and coherence, but because new ideas can be created only by combining elements of prototype memory traces. Because they are integrated, ideas also must be symbolic—any one idea must evoke another, or others. These systems are unique to each individual because no two people take precisely the same path through life. These systems can be shared, at least insofar as people can share equivalent experiences and thus can build similar prototype memory traces. This will be the case most likely, but not exclusively, among the people who live together and interact frequently. But because people must create their understanding of a changing world only from prototype memory traces that have been built up over the course of a unique life history, learning is a creative, highly personal act, and cultural sharing is only partial.

People use cultural constructs to guide their behavior, but what they do is not mechanically dictated by what they think. What people do becomes part of the environment that they perceive and, by becoming part of it, changes it. What people perceive thus changes over time at least partly because of their own activities. Our brains take these perceptions and integrate them with prototype memory traces in ways that create new ways of understanding the world in which we live. This interplay between our ideas about the world, how we act in it, and a world that changes simply because we do act—what we might call "cultural dynamics"—creates the most distinctive characteristic of human life—it regularly changes in new and unexpected ways.

The modernization paradigm was created as we tried to come to grips with how we are different from our forebears. In the process, we may have lost sight of how much we share with them. Men and women do not think and act in ways that are fixed by socialization or convention. Their childhood and adult experiences provide cultural prototypes that they can use to construct and negotiate social relationships in particular social interactions, subject to selective constraints. They love, they hate, they get drunk, and they display devotion. They may act out of greed or they may sacrifice their own interests for the sake of others. They make mistakes and they doggedly pursue courses of action for principle, or whim, even when they know they will suffer.

However, what men and women believe and do changes in predictable ways when there are changes in resources or in the costs attached to particular resources and resource access channels. Changes in resource access costs come about when people create new ways to think about and act in the world, when ecological parameters change, and when populations grow, decline, or when they experience change in their age or sex structure or in their fertility, mortality, or migration parameters (see Fig. 9.1).[3] The behavioral strategies that optimize or improve resource access change accordingly. Many conceptual and behavioral innovations prove, in retrospect, to be mistaken. Other innovations create new resources or resource access channels and so change the costs attached to both. Technical innovations in energy use, transportation, information processing and dissemination, agriculture, construction, and manufacturing (see, e.g., Braudel, 1979; Barnett, 1961) radically changed the cost structure of resource access and thus constitute the core of the contemporary world social revolution. Selection eliminates innovations that interfere with the process of resource acquisition and concentrates those innovations that improve or optimize resource access. Consequently, human beliefs and behavior change whenever conceptual and behavioral innovations, or changes in climatic, edaphic, or biotic parameters change the cost structure of resource access. Social change thus reflects changes in resources or resource access channels, and thus reflects changes in the power relationships captured by the variable K.

These conclusions lead to a new way to think about the revolution in social relationships, and the transition to replacement-level fertility, which marks this period in human history. The distinctive qualities of the contemporary world social revolution reflects fundamental change in the costs that attach to resources and to means *women* can use to gain access to resources. These changes thus reflect a fundamental change in *women's* power relationships with men, their children, and their parents.

Marx, of course, directly addressed these issues of historical change in power and resource access, and his central conclusions were correct. Although Marx often is thought of as presenting an analysis of social and economic forms that is antithetical to equilibrium analyses (those of symbolic anthropology, Parsonian sociology, or Neoclassical economics), the core of Marx's theory is compatible with equilibrium analyses, and complements them. Thus Marx made the following essential claims: [4]

(1) the means by which people can best access resources determines what they do and what they believe,

(2) historical change is driven by conflict between gatekeepers who wish to consolidate and extend their position and resource seekers who wish to subvert the position of gatekeepers,

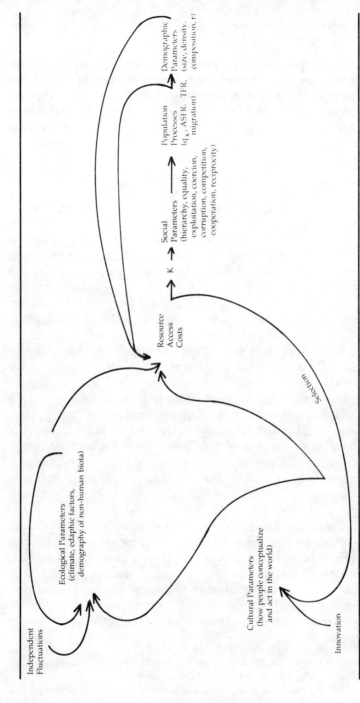

Figure 9.1. Population, power, and evolution: A model of system interdependencies.

(3) conflict between resource gatekeepers and resource seekers, not harmony, is normal and inevitable, and

(4) this reflects objective material conditions.

If we take as our central premise that all life requires regular inputs of energy and nutrients, it follows that selection must favor behavior that optimizes or improves resource access. If we substitute the concept of selection for the concept of rational actors derived from Adam Smith, we create the theory of power outlined in this book. Marx's essential claims thus follow as logical consequences of a definition of life.

Moreover, we transform Marx's ideas for we free them from a variety of nineteenth-century intellectual impedimentae—for example, the conceptualization of feudalism, capitalism, and socialism as mutually exclusive social formations, the Spencerian conception of a unilinear evolution of social and economic formations, and the pipe dream of a world without gatekeepers. We also free Marx's ideas from a variety of other intellectual impedimentae—for example, the propensity to reify concepts (such as "class") and to attribute intentionality to concepts that cannot so act, the failure to recognize that explanations that appeal to intentions (e.g., "class consciousness") as key factors in social change cannot comprehend the social processes they seek to analyze, the failure to recognize the selection-induced "market" forces that drive those processes, and the propensity to beg the question of historical analysis by substituting simplistic and static typologies for an analysis of the selection-induced processes that drive cultural evolution and social change. The concepts of *gatekeeper* and *resource seeker* reconceptualize the concept of *class* in ways that make it possible to conduct empirical analyses that discriminate power relationships very finely, and that encompass the face-to-face interactions and individual thought and behavior through which cultural evolution and social change take place. The resource access hypothesis thus establishes a testable foundation for Marx's ideas and makes it possible to conduct explicit and empirically grounded analyses. This foundation also makes it possible to clarify policy issues in ways that the conventional modernization paradigm cannot.

A NEW POLICY DIRECTION

In their book, *The Fertility Revolution* (1985), which develops the standard modernization hypothesis of fertility transition, Richard

Easterlin and Eileen Crimmins point out that standard theory informs policy only ambiguously. Adherents to standard modernization theory include at one extreme "those who see family planning programs [which reduce regulation costs] as the answer [to the question of how to reduce fertility and population growth in today's less developed countries]; at the other are those who advocate socioeconomic development to increase motivation for fertility control" (Easterlin and Crimmins, 1985: 11) People committed to the view that family planning programs are essential simultaneously commit themselves to population policies that advocate the commitment of substantial amounts of aid for building strong family planning programs. People committed to the other extreme may take the view that fertility will fall even if we do nothing.

Both options to which policy discussions are thus channeled by standard theory impede development. They do so because they expect family planning programs to meet goals they cannot achieve and they ignore the genuine developmental impact that family planning programs can and do have. If we observe underused programs and little change in fertility, or very slow declines in fertility, many years after family planning programs are established, as we do commonly, the principal policy alternatives are reduced to: (1) throw money at the family planning program, which simultaneously reduces the funds available for improving formal educational programs or for job creation, or (2) cut funding and thus curtail the important development role that family planning programs play. The latter option becomes increasingly likely as it becomes clearer (e.g., Easterlin and Crimmins, 1985: 24-25) that family planning programs cannot have a significant impact on fertility.

As indicated earlier, Easterlin and Crimmins's own policy recommendations are plausible only because they are consistent with the modernization paradigm. Moreover, Easterlin and Crimmins cannot provide clear guidelines for development policy because their conclusions beg the central questions: What, among all that the term *modern* encompasses, do we need more of, and why? What facet or facets of "socioeconomic development" create women who are motivated to reduce fertility in ways that bring about fertility transition? Yet, without being able to discriminate between the ends that one or another policy tool can be reasonably expected to accomplish, policy discussion is unnecessarily confused, and policy decisions can be expected to reward consultants but to provide questionable development assistance for recipients.

Women can use family planning programs for many purposes, only a few of which are associated with reductions in fertility. Family planning programs are not the only sources of fertility control technologies.

Women use fertility control technologies for many reasons and in ways that may or may not reduce their fertility. In severe economic circumstances, contraception and abortion may substitute for infanticide, which until recently was one of the few effective ways to limit family size (see Scrimshaw, 1978; Simonelli, 1986, touches on these issues for Hungary). When economic circumstances improve, however, we can expect fertility to rise. Contraception and abortion bring about fertility transition only when power relations between men and women and between parents and children are altered in fundamental ways, and this occurs only when women are freed from dependency on their children. Informed policy clearly needs to discriminate among these options, and to do so it requires better information about the processes that facilitate or impede one or another development goal. This information can be provided only if background analyses focus on the moral economy of particular places and times—the power relationships and the resource access costs on which those relationships are predicated.

Contemporary human development is characterized by cultural and social changes that have been common to all of the revolutions that have marked human history—it is a fundamental change in power and resource access. The current transformation is marked primarily by increasing equality, both between women and men and between generations. This transformation is also marked by conflict, both between men and women and between generations; by a depersonalization of social relationships in which the formation and maintenance of social relationships shifts from being an investment to a consumption activity; and using social relationships to justify material assistance shifts from being morally right to being morally wrong. These changes in social relationships and morality thus constitute a revolution in the ways in which individual women and men and entire generations relate to one another. These changes precipitate a revolution in reproductive behavior.

The Barbadian data reveal that women who in the 1950s were dependent on men and children have been replaced in the 1980s by women who are able to chart their own courses in life, independently of their children and independently of men. This change marked a dramatic change in women's freedom and thus in their ability to enjoy a greater measure of what have come to be known as "human rights." Barbadian women have participated in processes that not only have markedly increased their material standard of living but have freed them from constraints on their potential.

These data clearly demonstrate that these changes are not the product of a "modernization" process that consists of highly interdependent changes in many areas of social and economic life. On the contrary, these changes are clearly linked with historical changes in only two dimensions of social life (power and resource access) and in only two variables: education and jobs. Increases in women's participation in Barbadian educational institutions provided an ideological foundation for an egalitarianism in spousal relationships that was very rare in the 1950s. However, increasing education has not been linked directly with the dramatic decline in fertility Barbados experienced between 1950 and 1980. The Barbadian fertility transition has been a function of structural discontinuity in the economy that was accompanied by the creation of new and competitive resource access channels. The policy message of these data is clear: If the objective is to achieve fertility transition, do not expect results from increased levels of literacy, industrialization, education, urbanization, or from well-run and well-financed family planning programs. You have to change the cost structure of resource access. You may do so directly. Alternatively, you have to provide good jobs, for women as well as men, that reward individual skills and performance.

NOTES

1. Mauldin and Berelson (1978) adduce support for the position that family planning effort plays a clear role as a determinant or a facilitator of fertility decline. This conclusion is contingent on the validity of their measurement of the effectiveness of family planning program effort. If their treatment of Barbados, which they classified as having a "strong" family planning program (the BFPA) effort, is typical of their treatment of other countries, their conclusion has no empirical foundation.

2. To wit—the sharp rise in real incomes in the late 1940s and 1950s and the difficulties women faced in freeing themselves from dependency on their children and husbands that jointly produced the U.S. "baby boom" (see Harris, 1981, Margolis, 1984).

3. The more general Darwinian theory of population is outlined in Handwerker (1988b).

4. Marx made many other claims, of course. Most of these other claims have proved to be empirically inaccurate (e.g., the labor theory of value, conceiving feudalism and capitalism to be mutually exclusive) or theoretically inadequate (e.g., thinking that there could be stages of social and economic change). Marx, after all, wrote in the nineteenth century and was influenced both by inadequate historical and comparative data and by the conceptual frameworks that were widely accepted by his contemporaries.

Appendix
Issues of Methods and Data

The data reported in this study were collected over the course of six months of fieldwork on Barbados, West Indies. I was in the field from July through September 1985 and from June through August 1986. The sample data reported in this book were collected in 1985.

This research was an outgrowth of research focused on power and social relationships that I had the opportunity to carry out in Liberia, West Africa, in 1984 (Handwerker, 1987). Although corruption was the substantive problem I addressed in the West African research, my approach to this problem was grounded on previous research on high fertility, and one of the implications of the conclusions I drew about corruption was a theory about fertility transition.

Prior to coming to Barbados I wrote up a preliminary version of this theory, tested it with country-level data collected by the World Bank, and examined its fit with the existing literature on West Indian family organization (Handwerker. 1986a). When I arrived in Barbados I was working in a culture area in which I had never conducted field research, but I had a theory from which I deduced behavior and perspectives that *had to exist* if the theory was correct. The very first questions I asked yielded data consistent with my deductions. Answers to all subsequent questions revealed that behavior and perspectives that theoretically had to exist did in fact exist. My research experience on Barbados (and later on St. Lucia) was extremely powerful, both intellectually and emotionally. That experience was also intellectually frightening: Was I seeing only what I wanted to see?

This chapter addresses four key issues bearing on this question. First, is it really possible to study "fertility transition" on an island or do the unique demographic characteristics of island populations vitiate any general claims that such a study may make? Second, what data were collected, how were they collected, and are the measurement and sampling errors in the data sufficiently small and unbiased to make analysis worthwhile? Third, how much confidence can we place in the retrospective data on which this study relies? Fourth, and finally, is cumulative fertility to age 30, which is the dependent variable in a micro-level model of the Barbadian fertility transition developed in Chapter 7, a valid indicator of transition?

ISLAND DEMOGRAPHY

Although the possibility that islands may possess unique demographic characteristics may have been raised first by an anthropologist—by Raymond

Firth in his classic studies of the Polynesian island of Tikopia—over the past decade a number of demographers have come to believe that island populations do exhibit special characteristics that make them unsuitable for testing general hypotheses concerning fertility transition. If this is so, of course, a study of fertility transition on one or a set of Caribbean islands would be *sui generis*; we could not generalize the findings of this research, or any research carried out on small populations, to other times and places.

It is clear that island populations do possess some distinctive demographic characteristics. These appear to be unique, however, not to island status but to the size of the land area people can occupy (e.g., Monaco, Luxembourg, and Switzerland compare favorably with many islands in the Eastern Caribbean and the Pacific Basin) and to the size of the populations, which tend to be smaller on average than the populations of continental countries (as do the populations of Monaco, Luxembourg, and Switzerland). Cleland and Singh (1980) point out that small populations that occupy small land areas are likely to suffer greater proportional damage from natural disasters than larger populations occupying larger land masses; the small relative size of populations means that emigration and immigration of even moderate absolute size can radically alter age-sex ratios in ways that significantly alter childbearing and mating patterns (see, e.g., Marino, 1970) and can make demographic indices like the Crude Birth Rate invalid indicators of underlying fertility processes. Cleland and Singh also suggest that the clear bound on land area represented by the ocean (or political boundaries) may lead to greater awareness of the potential dangers of rapid population growth and so lead to a greater propensity to adopt strategies that would establish a population-resource balance (for Switzerland, see Netting, 1984); and that a combination of small land area and small population may lend itself to greater national cohesion, may minimize the distortion of centrally originated policy, and may facilitate the distribution of goods and services (e.g., contraceptives and family planning services).

For these and other reasons one might suspect that fertility transitions on islands exhibit distinctive patterns and that island populations may undergo transition earlier than continental populations—witness the early transitions undertaken by Sri Lanka, Taiwan, Singapore, Hong Kong, and Barbados. Island status, of course, does not appear to explain why fertility transition on Sicily and England occurred at roughly the same time as the transition in continental Europe as a whole (including the small countries), why fertility transition in France appears to have been initiated some 80 years prior to transition on these islands, and why Ireland's fertility decline lagged so far behind other countries in Western Europe. Similarly, island status does not clearly explain why the Pacific Basin islands exhibit much higher levels of fertility than do the islands of the Caribbean, nor why, within the Caribbean, there has been such diversity in levels and patterns of fertility decline. Nonetheless, one can raise the question of whether size or island status have effects on fertility transition that would make it impossible to test adequately a general theory of transition.

Cleland and Singh (1980) believe that their findings lend support to such a view. They review early studies (e.g., Mauldin and Berelson, 1978) and conclude that these studies "provide empirical grounds for believing that islands may possess distinctive demographic features that cannot be attributed entirely to their more advanced economies" (p. 971). They point out that the simple island/non-island dichotomy (or an extended trichotomy) used by early studies may serve descriptive purposes but is inadequate for more analytic understanding, and their article examines separately the effects on transition of both island size and the colonial role of islands as plantation economies. They go on to analyze recent data from the Caribbean and the Pacific Basin and conclude that, although the Pacific Basin data reveal no linkages between island status and declines in fertility, the Caribbean data do reveal a linkage between island status and declines in fertility that is independent of socioeconomic factors.

Cleland and Singh's (1980) study is important because it moves beyond simple zero-order relationships examined by earlier studies. Anyone with a reasonable degree of statistical sophistication recognizes that zero-order relationships can tell us next to nothing about the empirical world—such relationships can disappear, or even reverse themselves, once control variables are included in the analysis. Cleland and Singh's analysis demonstrates that, in the Caribbean as in the Pacific, there is *no* relationship between size(area)/island status and declines in fertility.

Cleland and Singh examine the relationship between size and declines in fertility partly by computing correlation coefficients between these variables and partly by computing partial correlations for these variables using mortality and a variety of socioeconomic variables for controls. *Every* test of these coefficients reveals a *high probability* of its being found merely by chance.

Cleland and Singh excuse their findings with the observation that all the correlation coefficients have the "correct" sign. This is merely wishful thinking. Just by chance correlation coefficients can attain small or large sizes and both "correct" and "incorrect" signs. Statistical tests are useful because, if their assumptions are met, they tell us the probability of finding the observed result merely by chance. If their associated probability level is (as in Cleland and Singh's findings) higher than an appropriate alpha rejection region, we have no grounds for concluding that the correlation coefficients measure empirically real relationships. Thus, even if we accept the limitations of data that Cleland and Singh do, their analysis reveals only that relationships between indicators of island status and fertility are merely what one would expect by random sampling fluctuation.

To summarize, the often strongly held beliefs about the supposed special characteristics of islands and their effect on fertility transition have *no* empirical support. On the contrary, the evidence that has been adduced supports the view that there is no relationship at all between island status and the nature of fertility transition. I infer that the claims supported by this study are applicable to the study of fertility transition in continental populations.

FIELD METHODOLOGY

Intentions

My 1985 field trip to the Eastern Caribbean was conceived of as an exploratory period to evaluate the prospects for carrying out an interisland comparative analysis of both historical and cross-sectional variance in reproductive behavior. The purpose of this project was to test the idea, proposed by Jack Caldwell (e.g., 1982) that the long-term and apparently "permanent" decline of fertility to very low levels reflected a change in the morality of childbearing and parent-child relationships of women and (perhaps) their mates, which, I suspected (e.g., Handwerker, 1986a) stemmed from changes in resource structure that increased the returns to individual skills and abilities and meant that children could not serve as resource channel gatekeepers. I thought that it would be useful to combine an in-depth study of one island with a comparative analysis based on aggregate data.

I traveled first to Barbados to establish ties with the Institute of Social and Economic Research at the Cave Hill campus of the University of the West Indies. I intended to spend a few weeks on Barbados and then spend the bulk of my time on Dominica, which had appeared to be the most promising field site for the in-depth research.

My first weeks on Barbados were spent largely talking with Dr. Joycelin Massiah, Dr. Graham Dann, and other staff and faculty at the University of the West Indies; Neville Selman, who has long experience with family planning programs in the Eastern Caribbean and who was then overseeing USAID's activities in this area; Angela Cropper, who was then head of IPPF activities in the Eastern Caribbean (and now is a Director of CARICOM); and catching up with recent research results. These conversations and my reading led to the conclusion that an analysis of aggregate data would be superfluous and that the best strategy would be to conduct an interisland comparison that examined relationships between historical macro-level changes in resource structure and micro-level historical and cross-sectional variance in reproductive behavior on a set of islands that were selected to span the range of fertility histories in the Eastern Caribbean (see Guengant, 1985). In these detailed analyses I wanted to collect data on:

(1) the relative responsibilities and expectations of, and perceived wealth flows between, mothers and children, fathers and children, siblings, spouses/mates, and both friends and extended kin; and the rationale that justifies these structural relationships.

(2) the importance of spousal and parent-child bonds relative to bonds to other kin, and the importance of parental obligations to children relative to children's obligations to parents; the importance of personal relationships relative to

relationships created by educational attainment in making accessible or constraining individual material well-being.

(3) variation in the cultural specification of these social relationships, and their rationale, by sex, age, household composition, developmental stage of the household, educational and occupational status, social class, and nature of the marital/sexual union (e.g., visiting, consensual, legal).

(4) culturally specified linkages between these parameters and norms concerning who should bear children, when childbearing should start, what is a desirable interval between children, and when in social aging childbearing should cease; the desirability of avoiding childbearing at specified periods and how that goal is best accomplished (including selection of birth control options); the desirability of parental status; marital/union status; the locus of reproductive decision making; and the relative egalitarianism of spousal relationships.

(5) the sources (and relative importance) of ideas and techniques of family limitation; parents' perceptions of educational, occupational, and emigration opportunities and constraints over the decades of the 1950s, 1960s, and 1970s, and their recollections of events and processes that influenced their fertility behavior; the relative importance of personalized social relationships in creating individual material well-being; and how access channels to key resources may have changed and may be changing.

The bulk of these data, of course, needed to be collected through directed and open-ended interviews and participant-observation with both men and women, purposely selected to represent all social classes except, possibly, the elite. To maximize the rate and quality of responses, I anticipated making contact and establishing close relationships with a small number of people who then might be able to introduce me to others. I wanted to be able to identify clearly which social relationships and aspects of reproductive behavior have changed, and which have not. To facilitate this identification process, I wanted to examine and contrast the views of women (and men) from two cohorts: (1) those whose childbearing ended prior to the initiation of Barbados' sustained fertility decline, and (2) those whose childbearing began only after the initiation of Barbados' sustained fertility decline. Subsequent to these enquiries, and to test formally the hypotheses I was working with, I intended to conduct an islandwide survey of women. To supplement data collected in informal circumstances and in a survey, I wanted to review archival material and government documents and to speak with professionals with practical experience in areas covered by this research.

I began enquiries on Barbados to assess the feasibility of this strategy. These enquiries went far better than I had any reason to expect. My few months on the island yielded more data than I had been able to collect in much longer field periods in West Africa.

I settled in a house just south of Bridgetown near Carlisle Bay in the parish of St. Michael. As a single male in the field I found ready acceptance by men. Most women, however, were clearly nervous about my intentions and many of my questions. The arrival of my wife and two youngest daughters greatly eased my acceptance by women. But the most important step toward the success of this project was the hiring of three women research assistants. These women ranged in age from 21 to 34 and represented both posttransition and midtransition age cohorts.

Field Training

Training for these research assistants extended over several weeks. During the first week we sat and discussed the project and the questions I was interested in answering. We outlined responses to different questions and used this period to examine problems of informant recall. We talked about their responses to questions bearing on the data outlined previously and about how their mothers and fathers thought now and in the past. I began to compare systematically what people reported about family and fertility behavior in the 1950s with the reports that Greenfield (e.g., 1961, 1966) published based on his work on the island during this period. We worked initially from a long question schedule I had put together from my earlier reading and eventually worked out a short interview form that could be used in the field without severely taxing respondents' patience and without asking questions that might be unduly embarrassing. Each research assistant practiced administering the question schedule. Mannerisms and question phrasing that led to biased responses were identified and eliminated.

Each research assistant conducted trial interviews once an initial interview form was worked out. After about 40-50 pretest interviews had been completed, further ambiguities, unnecessary questions, and questions that were not eliciting valid responses were identified and eliminated. Changes in eliciting strategy allowed us to collect accurate data on some subjects that previously were being measured with much error, but acceptable corrections for other questions were not found. Such questions were deleted from the final question schedule. The pretested interview form was subsequently administered to randomly selected women who were aged 20 through 64 in 1985. Initially, I merely wanted to assess the feasibility of conducting such a survey, and we interviewed about 100 women. The survey went so well and so rapidly that we extended the initial sample frame to the entire island. The completed sample size was 436 women.

Sample Selection

Accessible voter registration lists made it possible to select a simple random sample of all registered Barbadian voters. This ready-made sampling frame was not used because it would have been too expensive in time and money to find particular respondents, and because it contained an unknown bias in eliminating women who were not registered voters.

Instead, I created a small-scale grid over a map of the island and randomly selected grid clusters. Within each grid I randomly selected an interview starting point. In all parishes outside St. Michael, that constitutes the metropolitan area of Bridgetown, interview "starting points" were communities; within St. Michael (and occasionally within heavily built-up Christ Church), "starting points" were street intersections. Respondents consisted of one woman in each house containing women of the appropriate ages. The sample was stratified on the basis of age. Initially, respondents consisted of the first woman encountered. As the sampling limits for each age cohort were reached, respondents consisted of the first woman in a household whose age matched cohorts, the sample size for which had not yet been reached. The variability in the sample size for these cohorts stems from a combination of circumstances. Variable sample sizes originated because the rapidity with which interviews were collected from women of given cohorts varied with the age composition of the area being sampled and, once the survey was well underway, research assistants reported to me only once per week. The determining factor, however, was that I ran out of money to add interviews for the cohorts with small samples. Because of the small number of women 60-64 interviewed, I collapsed the last two cohorts.

Research assistants carried with them a letter of introduction and explained to each potential respondent the purposes of the questions and the uses to which the data would be put. Except for women from the highest income class (over about BDS\$65,000 annual income; US\$1.00 = BDS\$1.99), the number of women who chose not to participate in the survey was negligible. The grids were small and, with the exception of three households in which more than one woman insisted on being interviewed (1.6% of the total sample), the probability of selecting any one woman for interview was approximately equal to the probability of selecting any other woman for interview. Thus the completed sample approximates a simple random sample of women in a series of age cohorts from 20-24 through 55-64, excluding women in the highest income class.

Survey Question Schedule and Sample Characteristics

The final question schedule consisted of five major sections. The first section asked for information concerning the respondent's age ($\overline{X}$ = 39.7 years, SD = 12.0 years), current marital status (78.9% were currently involved in one or another form of sexual/marital union), the number of children the woman's mother had (a maximum of 17, $\overline{X}$ = 6.030, SD= 3.295), and a series of questions concerning the moral economy of childbearing, parent-child, and spousal relationships. These latter questions provide a basis for quantifying contrasts between pretransition and posttransition age cohorts along the moral dimensions identified by Caldwell (1982).

Two of these questions proved crucial for differentiating pre- and post-transition cohorts: (1) Do you think children *owe* their parents more than their parents owe them, or that parents owe their children more than their children owe their parents? and (2) Should getting pregnant and having children take

TABLE A.1
Sample Strata

Cohort	20-24	25-29	30-34	35-39	40-44	45-49	50-54	55-64
N of cases	38	70	56	69	51	43	42	67
Mean age	22.158	26.943	31.643	36.609	41.765	47.093	52.000	58.985
Standard deviance	1.405	1.578	1.394	1.467	1.350	1.509	1.249	2.750
Standard error	0.228	0.189	0.186	0.177	0.189	0.230	0.193	0.336

precedence over personal goals (having children *is* my personal goal), or should reaching personal goals (e.g., a career) take precedence over having children? The first question is one Caldwell identifies as discriminating between pre- and posttransition cohorts; the importance of the second question emerged in the course of my interviews on Barbados. Both questions were scored on a three-point scale: zero if the response indicated that children constituted a net economic loss to parents, 2 if the response indicated that children constituted a net economic gain to parents, and 1 if the response indicated a balance between these extremes. I had employed the first question in West Africa both in surveys and in informal interviews and consistently found that the question was readily understandable and tapped a crucial dimension of the moral economy of parent-child relationships. I found the same to be the case in Barbados. The second question tapped an equally crucial dimension of the moral economy of childbearing on Barbados. The opportunities implicit in this question have not been realized in West Africa. Consequently, its importance never emerged explicitly in my West African research. I created an additive scale of these variables to form an index of the micro-level transformation in moral economy ($\overline{X} = 2.205$, SD = 1.324) that theory stipulated should differentiate pretransition from posttransition women. Reinterviews with a 10% sample of respondents indicate a reliability rate for the questions bearing on moral economy of just over 90%.

The second and third sections of the question schedule consisted of a pregnancy history and a marital history, respectively. Barbadian informants are highly competent with numbers, ages, and dates. Whereas in West Africa it is necessary to create age-calendars to estimate dates and ages, it was not necessary to do so in this research even for the oldest respondents. During interviews, we were careful to pay attention to and to enquire about what appeared to be unusually long birth-intervals or intervals without a mate and to examine responses for possible inconsistencies. These data appear to be subject to only minor and random recall inaccuracies.

Table A.2 reveals patterns of union durations, as measured by the average proportion of a year spent in different forms of marital unions over the course of the reproductive period, that are consistent with the literature. The average period spent in legal unions is very low in the beginning of the reproductive period, rises sharply in the late twenties, and continues to rise thereafter. The

TABLE A.2
Duration of Union by Reproductive Age

	15-19	20-24	25-29	30-34	35-39	40-44	45-49
Legal marriage							
N of cases	436	430	377	310	251	191	143
mean	0.017	0.133	0.358	0.480	0.542	0.564	0.587
standard deviation	0.096	0.290	0.448	0.490	0.493	0.489	0.487
standard error	0.005	0.014	0.023	0.028	0.031	0.035	0.041
Consensual unions							
N of cases	436	430	377	310	251	191	143
mean	0.036	0.154	0.232	0.229	0.193	0.173	0.154
standard deviation	0.142	0.308	0.387	0.398	0.382	0.372	0.353
standard error	0.007	0.015	0.020	0.023	0.024	0.027	0.029
Visiting unions							
N of cases	436	430	377	310	251	191	143
mean	0.419	0.533	0.320	0.170	0.135	0.115	0.074
standard deviation	0.347	0.405	0.410	0.345	0.325	0.314	0.252
standard error	0.017	0.020	0.021	0.020	0.021	0.026	0.021
Not in union							
mean	.528	.180	.009	.121	.130	.148	.185

average period spent in consensual unions is low at the beginning of the reproductive period, rises to a peak in the late twenties and early thirties, and falls slowly until the end of the reproductive period. The average period spent in visiting unions is very high in the earliest portion of the reproductive years but peaks in the early twenties and falls consistently until the end of the reproductive period. Women between 15-19 years spend, by far, the least time in sexual unions. The time spent in sexual unions peaks in the late twenties and declines slowly through the rest of the reproductive period.

These women reported 1,418 pregnancies and 1,328 live births. Pregnancy loss components were: natural abortions, 3.6% (a maximum of 4); induced abortions, 1.6% (a maximum of 5); and stillbirths, 1.2% (a maximum of 2). On average, these women experienced 3.046 live births (SD = 2.572; a range from 0 to 14). Their aggregate total fertility rate was 3.82 (see Table A.3). Seven older women volunteered (1.6% of the sample) that their absence of pregnancies and births was owing to their own sterility and this information was coded as a separate variable.

Interviews revealed no unusual birth intervals that could not be accounted for either by the use of contraception or by the absence of a mate. Data on the number of live births thus appear to be very accurate. However, women appeared to be hesitant to talk about intentional abortions. It is possible that the data slightly understate the number of intentional abortions and consequently

TABLE A.3
Aggregate Age-Specific Fertility

	15-19	20-24	25-29	30-34	35-39	40-44	45-49
ASFR	.1156	.1926	.1974	.1385	.0914	.0236	.0048
Coale-Trussell parameters		1.000	1.025	.719	.474	.122	.025

Sum of ASFR = .7639, TFR = 3.8195

slightly understate the number of pregnancies. Because the key dependent variable in the subsequent analysis is the number of live births, however, this error has little bearing on the analyses presented next.

A total of 81 of the children born alive died before 1 year of age (qo = .06099). Overall, 64 women in the sample had never had a child. Of the mothers, only 14.5% experienced an infant death. Of the mothers who had experienced an infant death, 72.7% had had only one infant who died. One woman, however, reported 7 infant deaths.

Figure A.1 reveals that women reported mean breast-feeding periods that averaged around 7 months ($\overline{X}$ = 6.966). However, there was a large amount of variance in the data (SD = 5.104) and one woman reported that she breastfed her one child for 54 months.

Section four consisted of a series of questions that probed who the respondent lived with (her principal residence or residences), her level of personal income per week, and who contributed to her income (using a list of possible sources as a memory aid) for up to four periods of her life: ages 15-19, ages 20-24, ages 25-29, and currently (for 1985). Significant changes that occurred during these periods were recorded and subsequently coded. Questions concerning sources of income and principal residence(s) elicited ready, confident responses and reinterviews yielded reliability rates of about 90%. However, approximately 100 women were unable to provide income estimates in which they had confidence. When women were not confident about estimates of the income they received, or when conversions from shillings to Barbadian dollars could not be made, we recorded missing data. Missing data were recorded for some women in all cohorts, but the the most frequent sources of missing data were women in the oldest cohorts when they were asked about income they had received when they were young. Weekly incomes for all women who reported 1985 incomes (N = 345) ranged from BDS$5 (BDS$250 annually) to BDS$1250 (BDS$62,500 annually). The mean weekly income was BDS$233.59 (about BDS$11,700 annually) and the standard deviation was BDS$175.43.

Table A.4 reveals patterns of support consistent with the available literature. For women in their late teens, the single most frequently cited source of income (assisting two-thirds of these women) is their mothers. Fathers contributed to the support of 54.9% of these women, but 48.3% contributed to their own support and 32% received income from husbands or boyfriends. Support from

	Months	Fractions and Count
	0	0000000000000000
	1	00055
	2	000000000002223355555555666
Quartile: 3.5	3 H	0000000000000000000000000000000000000033555555667
	4	00000000000000223345555566788
	5	0000000000000000000000022555555578
Median: 6.0	6 M	000000000000000000000000000000000000000000002345555556667778
	7	0000000000001335555556666777
	8	00000000000024455566666666668
Quartile: 9.0	9 H	0000000000000000000000000000002333566688
	10	00002233455555
	11	2267
	12	0000000000000235
	13	028
	14	000167
	15	00004
	16	007
OUTSIDE VALUES		
	18	0000
	22	67
	24	00000
	26	6
	54	0

Figure A.1. Stem and leaf plot of the mean period of lactation: N = 369.

fathers drops significantly in the early twenties and almost disappears by the late twenties. Contributions by mothers also decline, but frequencies remain much higher than for fathers. The proportions of women who receive income from husbands or boyfriends increases sharply in the early twenties, as does support from these women's own employment. As of 1985, 68% of the women interviewed were employed (SD = .467). Women with older children reported various levels of support from varying numbers of their children. A small number of such women, however, reported that as many as five sons and five daughters were contributing financial assistance on a regular basis.

Of course, incomes (and sources of income) rise and fall significantly over short periods of time with a variety of factors and may do so many times over the five-year periods to which these questions were addressed. Responses to the question of income sources probably leave out sources whose contributions were minor. Such error does not affect conclusions drawn in this study. Of greater concern is potential error in reported weekly income estimates. Reports of current (1985) income are not subject to significant memory errors and only one reported income estimate was not consistent with incomes reported by other women of the same age, occupational class, and educational level (it was too low). This datum was deleted from the data base. However, error variance in reports of weekly income levels during women's late teen years and twenties can be expected to increase directly with age.

TABLE A.4
Sources of Income During the Early Reproductive Period

Source of Support	Proportion of Women Receiving Support from Source		
	15-19	20-24	25-29
Mother	.676	.346	.139
Father	.549	.249	.066
Former spouse	.007	.063	.117
Current spouse	.320	.781	.872
Brother	.097	.054	.037
Sister	.044	.037	.061
Grandparent	.108	.051	.011
Other*	.156	.129	.077
Public sector assistance	.000	.068	.089
Remittances	.182	.203	.213
Job	.483	.758	.785

Includes: MZ, MB, FZ, mother's husband, and foster parent.

Most respondents confidently estimated averages for these periods. These averages showed consistent and expected patterning with the sources of income and economic class from which respondents came. Reinterviews yielded reliability rates just over 80%. Figure A.2 illustrates these relationships between class and income level in a box-plot of current personal weekly income (from all sources) by economic class. The parentheses mark 95% confidence intervals around the median. Thus the box-plot reveals significantly higher levels of income for professionals, managers, and white collar workers than for people of other economic classes. The overlap between incomes reported for professionals and for white collar workers reflects the fact that women have moved into professional positions relatively recently and, consequently, tend to receive pay at the low end of the professional salary range.

Income estimates for the early portion of women's reproductive career were corrected using the retail price index constructed by the Central Bank of Barbados (eight significant digits). The resulting real weekly income levels for the ages 15-19 and 20-24 were plotted and only a few outlying estimates were detected. These outliers were recoded as missing values. Error variances in the corrected data base are within acceptable bounds, the error that is present appears to be randomized, and these data constitute useful indicators of economic well-being relative to other women of the same age at the same historical period. Weekly income is a critical dependent variable in some analyses reported in this study (Chapter 5). However, models that use imperfectly measured dependent variables still yield unbiased and consistent parameter estimates and all statistical tests will apply. Hence, the remaining error variance for weekly incomes will not distort the conclusions drawn in this study.

Section 5 consisted of questions concerning the number of years of formal schooling for the respondent ($\bar{X} = 10.413$, SD = 2.302, ranging from 4 to 20 years) and her parents, religious affiliation (56.8% claimed membership in standard

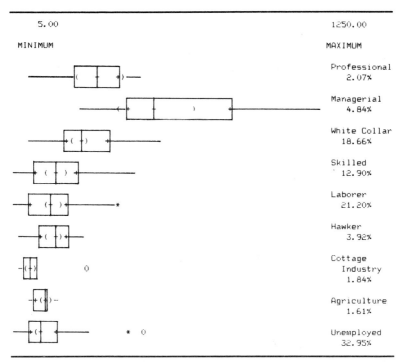

Figure A.2. Box-plot of current (1985) weekly income by occupational class.

Christian churches, mainly Anglican; 32.4% claimed membership in fundamentalist Christian churches; .7% were Rastafarians; 10.1% claimed no religious affiliation), the number of years the respondent spent in Bridgetown or in Bridgetown's metropolitan area, on another island, on the South or Central American mainland, or in North America or Europe, before they were aged 30, and the current household composition. Only 137 women knew the level of their mothers' schooling and only 85 women knew the level of their fathers' schooling. Although there was a very high proportion of missing data for these questions, the reliability of questions in this section, as in earlier sections, was very high (over 90%). Error in these responses is likely to be minor and random.

HOW GOOD ARE THE RETROSPECTIVE DATA?

Any study of fertility transition must examine changes in behavior and perspectives over time. Each of the several strategies that we can use to study fertility transition entails using data that are inaccurate in various ways, for which adjustments of one kind or another are necessary. The strength of one or another approach does not hinge on whether or not the data are accurate in any absolute sense, for inaccuracies are a fact of research life and constitute a problem of adjustment so that accuracy is sufficient for one's purpose; within the limits of acceptable inaccuracy, such error merely obscures one's results. I believe that the problem of data adequacy is more important than the problem of data inaccuracy.

One way to approach the study of fertility transition is to use historical records, as I do in Chapter 2. The major limitation of this approach is the inability to demonstrate clearly that real and determinant empirical relationships exist between model variables at the micro level at which fertility transition works itself out. Individual-level data of sufficient precision simply do not exist in the historical record.

Another approach to the study of fertility transition is to use panel or time-series data on contemporary countries, such as the data base prepared by the World Bank. I used such data in an earlier test of theory (Handwerker, 1986a) and had anticipated conducting a more finely tuned test of theory using regional data for the Caribbean as a whole. Such a test would be better than one that is based on country-level data. However, even if such data were readily available (they aren't), such a test still would not permit one to demonstrate clearly that real and determinant empirical relationships exist between model variables at the micro level at which fertility transition works itself out. Individual-level data simply do not exist in aggregate data bases.

The other viable strategy for studying fertility transition—the only option that holds the potential to test for real and determinant empirical relationships between model variables at the micro level—is to use retrospective data collected from individual informants.

Ideally, of course, we would want to base such tests on carefully crafted long-term field studies. Such studies are inordinately expensive, however, and cannot be justified given the current absence of well-formulated theory. More important, an understanding of fertility transition has important implications for development policy and spending and profound implications for human welfare. Measurement imperfections exist in all data bases. Measurement imperfections in retrospective data bases can be controlled as well as such imperfections in other data bases and, because the potential inaccuracies are more apparent, in some ways better. Well-crafted studies in which independent and dependent variables are measured with error may generate biased parameter estimates, but estimates that are biased in only negligible ways because the error variance is both randomized and small. Such studies that are based on retrospective data are currently the only means we have for adequately addressing (i.e., identifying linkages between macro-level determinants and the micro-level processes through which transition manifests itself) these policy and human welfare issues.

Possibly the most important reason for using retrospective data, however, is that they allow valuable analyses that otherwise cannot be made, namely simultaneous historical and cross-sectional comparisons. The research strategy employed in this study takes full advantage of this potential. The data base was constructed in such a way that it can be used to estimate historical trends in fertility, marital patterns, breast feeding, educational levels and prevalence, and sources of income, employment, and income levels. The data base was constructed in such a way that we can also make cross-sectional comparisons for these variables at different historical periods—so that we can compare, for instance, the marital and fertility patterns during women's early reproductive period (ages 15-29) both for the 1950s and for the 1970s. This form of analysis makes it possible to contrast pretransition and posttransition cohorts and provides insight into characteristics of fertility transition that otherwise remain hidden.

The problems inherent in using retrospective data from informants do not, for these reasons, disappear. We all know that memories are faulty, that for various reasons what people tell us is not perfectly accurate, and that memory decays exponentially over time. In a major review paper, Bernard et al. (1984) have recently called attention to the problem of informant accuracy and, after reviewing a vast amount of literature on the problem, come to the frightening conclusion that "The results of all of these studies leads to one overwhelming conclusion: On average, about half of what informants report is probably incorrect in some way" (p. 503).

This does not mean that retrospective data cannot or should not be confidently used for analysis any more than it means that census results— or intercensus estimates—cannot or should not be confidently used for analysis. It does mean that we need to be careful in how we use such data and that we have some reason for thinking that our data are sufficiently accurate for our purposes. I present some reasons for thinking that the data used for analysis in this report generally are both reliable and accurate.

I employed several strategies to assess the accuracy of my data. First, I asked Barbadians to identify questions to which people might respond inaccurately intentionally. Such questions either were not asked or are identified in the preceding review. Interviews were, with few exceptions, conducted in private and anonymously. Inaccuracies still enter the data base, of course. To identify inaccuracies further, I employed interviewing strategies (e.g., memory aids, requesting information on the most recent events first, attention to unusually long birth intervals, repeated questions) to minimize memory error. Pretests of the question schedule eliminated unnecessary questions, identified ambiguities in wording, and led to better approaches to data collection. Question selection was crucial. The acceptable level of error variance in estimates of former income levels is largely owing to the fact that we asked not about the level of income flows from particular people at particular times, but about sources of income and aggregate income averages over five-year periods. Had we asked about particular income flows at particular times we probably would have received many responses, but the level of precision to these responses would have been spurious. The more general question takes advantage of people's tendency to estimate in round numbers and yields less precise but much more accurate (i.e., less error variance) information. Finally, I examined the statistical patterns that emerged in the completed data base. The previous literature on Barbados and on the West Indies generally provides patterns one would expect in any set of survey data. Expected patterns were present. Plots of data for which there were good reasons for suspecting significant levels of inaccuracy and possible bias (e.g., recollections of weekly income levels) revealed some data that clearly were out of line with the body of responses. Such data were recoded as missing.

Finding patterns consistent with the existing literature leads me to think that the error variance for nearly all variables is both small and randomized. The corrections that were applied to the critical variables that were subject to potentially devastating levels of measurement inaccuracy, such as income levels, maintain error variance within acceptable limits.

Studies such as this one cannot, in themselves, either entirely avoid the problem of measurement inaccuracy or precisely measure the real impact of such error. Replicative studies are necessary for estimating both. In that regard, this research has had the benefit of two sources of data on key issues. Comparison of my data with those collected independently and at prior historical periods lends credence to the view that there is only inconsequential error in the present data base and that conclusions drawn from those data are valid.

The first source of comparative data consists of data reported by Sidney Greenfield, based on research undertaken in the mid-1950s in the parish of St. George. In addition to the formal survey interviews, both I and the research assistants carried out further informal interviews with both men and women throughout the 1985 field period. These data continued to support and added depth to the outline of historical ethnography that was constructed prior to initiating the survey. Chapter 3 revealed that retrospective data on behavior and beliefs in the 1950s that were collected in 1985 confirmed the patterns reported by Greenfield. In addition, several respondents volunteered compliments on the questions we asked them. They were particularly pleased with the questions on moral economy because those questions addressed issues about which they had had great concerns, and they viewed those questions as very important to understanding the changes in family and fertility on Barbados over the last 30 years. These compliments and the correspondence between Greenfield's data and my own lead me to think that the contrasts drawn next between pre- and posttransition cohorts are both valid and very accurate.

The second source of comparative data consists of census and intercensus estimates of total fertility rates over time. A three-year moving average of total fertility rates was presented in Chapter 1 as revealing the historical changes in fertility experienced by Barbados between 1950 and 1980. These estimates are based on a sample that excludes three groups of women who participated in the fertility processes at earlier historical periods: (1) women in the highest income group, (2) women who have since died and (3) women who have since migrated. If these excluded groups of women are not random samples of the population that has been sampled for the present study, my sample will yield biased estimates of historical fertility and may yield a distorted picture of historical fertility processes. The first two sources of error may contribute slight overestimates of historical fertility. The third source of error contains counterbalancing biases and generally appears not to bias estimates of historical fertility. Exclusion of these groups does not distort conclusions concerning historical fertility processes.

The exclusion of women in the highest income group may slightly inflate sample estimates of historical fertility because such women probably have had fewer children, on average, than the women sampled. Because the size of this population component has been small, however, such inflation is likely to be small. Similarly, because illness associated with death can be expected to reduce fecundity we would expect that accurate fertility histories reported by surviving women would slightly overestimate historical fertility levels. Because Barbadian mortality levels are very low, especially for the principal childbearing years of 15-35, the effect of this bias is also likely to be small. Finally, since women in both of these groups would have been subject to the same macro-level processes as the women sampled, we can expect that their historical fertility processes could not be differentiated from the processes experienced by the women sampled.

There are a priori grounds for thinking that the exclusion of emigrant women could contain biases that balance each other. Thus on the one hand, it is possible that women with small families found it easier to emigrate than did women with large families; on the other hand, women with large families may have received a greater push to emigrate than had women with small families. I infer that excluding migrant women does not significantly bias historical estimates of fertility. Moreover, the reproductive performance of sampled women who migrated and later returned to the island cannot be discriminated from the reproductive performance of nonmigrants: fertility of both migrants and nonmigrants respond to the same independent variables. I infer that the exclusion of migrants will not lead to distorted conclusions about historical fertility processes.

In sum, there are several reasons for thinking that sample estimates overestimate historical fertility parameters, but only in negligible ways: (1) the exclusion of women in the highest income class constitutes only a small proportion of the population, (2) the low mortality rates on Barbados mean that attrition owing to death can bias fertility estimates in only minor ways, and (3) migrants appear to be a random sample of the population sampled by this study. Moreover, because all excluded groups have been subject to historical fertility processes identical to those of the sampled women, their exclusion would not affect study conclusions concerning Barbadian historical fertility processes.

On an island that has experienced as much migration as Barbados over this period, intercensus estimates contain an undetermined amount of error, and total fertility rate estimates based on such data necessarily are subject to much error. A comparison of period total fertility estimates from my sample data and from census data, however, reveals a very close correspondence. In 1960, census data yield an estimated TFR of 4.7 and sample data yield an estimated TFR of 4.7; in 1970, census data yield an estimated TFR of 3.3 and sample data yield an estimated TFR of 3.9; in 1980, census data yield an estimated TFR of 2.1 and sample data yield an estimated TFR of 2.0. The differences between estimates based on census data and estimates based on my sample of 436 women can easily be explained as random sampling fluctuations.

CUMULATIVE FERTILITY TO AGE 30: THE MICRO-LEVEL DEPENDENT VARIABLE

Chapter 7 presents a micro-level model of fertility transition in which the dependent variable is cumulative fertility to age 30. The use of this variable, rather than completed fertility (at age 45 or 50), has the singular advantage that we can explore the determinants of both cross-sectional (e.g., why, at time t, women have 0-9 children) and historical (why, both at time t and at time $t+25$, women have 0-9 children) variance in fertility simultaneously. Thus such a variable makes it possible to test the claim that all Barbadian cohorts have been subject to the same fertility processes and to explore any differences that emerge. However, the validity of this measure of fertility is contingent on two considerations: (1) cumulative fertility to age 30 must be a good predictor of completed family size, and (2) cumulative fertility to age 30 must validly indicate the historical trends that comprise fertility transition. Evidence for the first contingency is a demonstration that completed family size covaries closely with cumulative fertility to age 30. Evidence for the second contingency is a demonstration that historical declines in fertility at later portions of the reproductive span are accompanied by historical declines in cumulative fertility to age 30.

Figure A.3 demonstrates that completed family size covaries both consistently and very closely ($r = .85$) with cumulative fertility to age 30 for the oldest cohorts for whom such a relationship should be weakest.

Guengant's (1985) time plots of period age specific fertility ratios for the Caribbean region provide evidence for the second contingency. These plots demonstrate that, on Barbados and throughout the Caribbean, period age-specific fertility ratios for the early portion of the reproductive span declined simultaneously with declines in age-specific fertility ratios for the later portions of the reproductive span. Table A.5 presents age-specific fertility ratio indexes for Barbadian cohorts from 1950-1954 through 1975-1979 for the age ranges 15-19 through 40-44. The age-specific fertility ratio index expresses cohort fertility at a given point in the reproductive span as a proportion of the age-specific fertility of the pre-1950 cohort. This table reveals, as expected, that cohort fertility transition was initiated when women began to restrict their fertility in the latter portions of their reproductive years. This table also reveals, however, that declines in age-specific fertility ratios during the early portions of the reproductive span generally correspond with declines in age-specific fertility during the later portions of the reproductive span. Thus trends in cohort cumulative fertility to age 30 are sensitive indicators of the historical trends that have marked the Barbadian fertility transition.

COMPLETED FAMILY SIZE

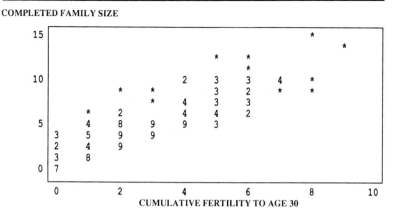

Figure A.3.   Completed family size by cumulative fertility to age 30.

SUMMARY AND QUALIFICATION OF FINDINGS

This chapter has addressed four key questions bearing on the credibility of the data used for this study. First, is it really possible to study "fertility transition" on an island, or do the unique demographic characteristics of island populations vitiate any general claims that such a study may make? Second, what data were collected and are the measurement and sampling errors in the data sufficiently small and unbiased to make analysis of the data base worthwhile? Third, just how much confidence can we place in the retrospective data on which this study relies? Fourth, and finally, is cumulative fertility to age 30 a valid measure of fertility transition? The credibility of the data withstand scrutiny on all questions.

First, the concerns over the supposed unique characteristics of island demography seem to stem from beliefs that are held with a strength inverse to the supporting evidence. There is no credible evidence supporting the view that islands possess unique characteristics that vitiate attempts to test general hypotheses concerning fertility transition on their populations. On the contrary, the evidence adduced actually supports the view that there is no relationship between island status and characteristics of fertility decline.

Second, the data collected in this study surely contain some measurement errors and sampling biases. However, the survey questions elicited reliable data and key variables appear to be valid measures of key historical changes in Barbadian family and reproductive behavior. The sampling strategy yielded a simple random sample of Barbadian women in a series of age cohorts, excluding women from the very highest income group. Because the sample excludes women in the very highest income group and women who died, estimates of

TABLE A.5
Cohort Age-Specific Fertility Indexes

Age	Pre-1955	1955-59	1960-64	1965-69	1970-74	1975-79
15-19 ASFR	.151	.129	.104	.096	.074	.079
ASFR index	1.000	.854	.689	.636	.490	.523
20-24 ASFR	.234	.220	.186	.132	.146	.158
ASFR index	1.000	.940	.795	.564	.624	.675
25-29 ASFR	.228	.259	.159	.121	.176	
ASFR index	1.000	1.136	.697	.530	.772	
30-34 ASFR	.179	.094	.087	.083		
ASFR index	1.000	.525	.486	.464		
35-39 ASFR	.110	.055	.045			
ASFR index	1.000	.500	.409			
40-44 ASFR	.024	.011				
ASFR index	1.000	.458				

historical fertility levels may be slightly overstated. However, since these women would have been subject to the same macro-level processes as the women sampled, their exclusion should not distort the picture of historical fertility processes and trends outlined in this study. The exclusion of migrants appears to have no impact on the conclusions that can be drawn from the data base.

Third, retrospective data are notoriously suspect for measurement inaccuracies. However, close examination of the data reveals patterns consistent with the existing literature and leads me to think that the error variance for nearly all variables is both small and randomized. Critical variables subject to potentially devastating levels of measurement inaccuracy, such as recollected income levels, were carefully examined. The corrections that were applied to these variables maintain error variance within acceptable limits. Comparison of the results of this field study with data collected independently and in prior historical periods suggest that retrospective inaccuracies are negligible and do not distort the conclusions of this study.

Fourth, and finally, cumulative fertility to age 30 is both a highly accurate predictor of completed family size and a sensitive indicator of the historical trends that have marked the Barbadian fertility transition. This variable is a valid indicator of fertility transition.

Academics like to add disclaimers in their conclusions. This saves us the embarrassment of being found wrong by later studies and adds an appropriately serious tone to analyses such as those presented in earlier chapters. For instance, one might point out that no model-building exercise, and no hypothesis test, can ever be definitive by itself. There may be hidden measurement errors that have led to distorted results. Education and family planning measured in other ways might reveal strong effects. There might be an alternative specifications that yield a still better fit to Barbadian fertility history. In short, the theory and analyses presented in earlier chapters might be wrong.

On the positive side, however, the analyses conducted in this book follow from the ethnographic data, and are mutually consistent even when, as in the macro-level analyses, model independent variables were measured by other people at other times and places. Further, these results are consistent with the findings of a number of studies, including an analysis that used country-level data from the World Bank (Handwerker, 1986a). Barbados provides an unusually good case study because fertility transition is an historically recent event that occurred very rapidly. Direct qualitative and quantitative information on family relationships and childbearing activities could be collected from pretransition, midtransition, and posttransition cohorts. This research measured nearly all variables stipulated by alternative theories. Moreover, this research has had the benefit of comparative data collected from the 1950s to the present day both by ethnographers and government ministries. These data have been used to judge the accuracy of informant recall data and to help assess the level of error variance and bias in survey data collected in 1985. The survey itself consists of a simple random sample of women in a series of five-year cohorts of women who were aged 20-64 in 1985 and who belonged to all but the highest income class (greater than BDS$65,000 annual income).

The data base used for this study appears to contain only negligible biases and small, randomized error variances. Findings based on these data should be highly credible. But as in any such study, it is impossible to say that the data base contains absolutely *no* unrecognized measurement and sampling biases that would severely distort the findings presented here. It is unrealistic to expect the results presented in earlier chapters, the analyses from which they stem, or, for that matter, any other results, to be perfect; they need to be used with an appropriate level of caution.

Having made appropriate qualifications, academics also promptly ignore them. If we didn't think the variables sufficiently valid and the measurements sufficiently accurate and unbiased we wouldn't (shouldn't) have analyzed them in the first place. To judge if the results presented really here are on the mark, we need replicative studies—perhaps a restudy of Barbados, but certainly studies of other islands, other regions, and other time periods.

References

Adams, Henry (1957) Mont-Saint-Michel and Chartes. New York: Heritage.

Alexander, Paul (1986) "Labor expropriation and fertility: Population growth in nineteenth century Java," pp. 249-262 in W. Penn Handwerker (ed.) Culture and Reproduction. Boulder, CO: Westview.

Axelrod, Robert and William D. Hamilton (1981) "The evolution of cooperation." Science 211: 1390-1396.

Banks, J. A. (1981) Victorian Values. London: Routledge & Kegan Paul.

Barnett, Homer G. (1953) Innovation. New York: McGraw-Hill.

Barnett, Homer G. (1961) "The innovative process." Kroeber Anthropological Society Papers 25: 1-25.

Barnett, Homer G. (1983) Qualitative Science. New York: Vantage.

Bernard, H. Russell, Peter Killworth, David Kronenfeld and Lee Sailer (1984) "The problem of informant accuracy: The validity of retrospective data." Annual Review of Anthropology 13: 495-518.

Blake, Judith (1961) Family Structure in Jamaica. New York: Free Press.

Bledsoe, Caroline (1980) Women and Marriage in Kpelle Society. Stanford: Stanford University Press.

Bledsoe, Caroline (1988) "People and wealth among the Mende of Sierra Leone." (unpublished)

Bledsoe, Caroline and Uche C. Isiugo-Abanine (forthcoming) "Strategies of child fosterage among Mende grannies in Sierra Leone," in Ronald Lesthaeghe, (ed.) African Reproduction and Social Organization.

Bloch, Marc (1961) Feudal Society, Vol. 2. Chicago: University of Chicago Press.

Bolton, J. L. (1980) The Medieval English Economy 1150-1500. London: J. M. Dent.

Bongaarts, John (1982) "The fertility inhibiting effects of the intermediate fertility variables." Studies in Family Planning 13: 179-189.

Bongaarts, John (1983) The proximate determinants of natural marital fertility, pp. 103-138, in R. A. Bulatao and R. D. Lee (eds.) Determinants of Fertility in Developing Countries, Vol. 1. San Francisco: Academic Press.

Boyd, Robert and Peter J. Richerson (1985) Culture and the Evolutionary Process. Chicago: University of Chicago Press.

Bradley, Candice (1987) "Women, children, and work." Ph.D. dissertation, University of California, Irvine.

Brainard, Jean M. and Theresa Overfield (1986) "Transformation in the natural fertility regime of Western Alaskan Eskimo," pp. 112-124 in W. Penn Handwerker, (ed.) Culture and Reproduction. Boulder, CO: Westview.

Brana-Shute, Gary and Rosemary Brana-Shute (1980) The Unemployed of the Eastern Caribbean: Attitudes and Aspirations. U.S. Agency for International Development (Contract #AID/LAC-C-1395).

Braudel, Fernand (1979) The Wheels of Commerce. Vol. 2: Civilization and Capitalism 15th-18th Century. New York: Harper & Row.

Briggs, Asa (1983) A Social History of England. New York: Viking.

Brody, Eugene B. (1981) Sex, Contraception, and Motherhood in Jamaica. Cambridge, MA: Harvard University Press.

Bulatao, R. A. and R. D. Lee [eds.] (1983a) Determinants of Fertility in Developing Countries, Vol. 1. San Francisco: Academic Press.

Bulatao, R. A. and R. D. Lee (1983b) Determinants of Fertility in Developing Countries, Vol. 2. San Francisco: Academic Press.

Burnett, John (1982) Destiny Obscure. Autobiographies of Childhood, Education and Family from the 1820s to the 1920s. New York: Penguin.

Caldwell, J. C. (1980) "Mass education as a determinant of the timing of fertility decline." Population and Development Review 6: 225-255.

Caldwell, J. C. (1982) Theory of Fertility Decline. San Francisco: Academic Press.

Caldwell, J. C. and Helen Ware (1977) "The evolution of family planning in an African city: Ibadan, Nigeria." Population Studies 33: 487-507.

Cavalli-Sforza, L. L. and M. W. Feldman (1981) Cultural Transmission and Evolution. Princeton: Princeton University Press.

Charlton, Thomas H. (1978) "Teotihuacan, Tepeapulco, and obsidian exploitation." Science 200: 1227-1236.

Charlton, Thomas H. (1984) "Production and exchange: Variables in the evolution of a civilization," pp. 17-42 in Kenneth G. Hirth (ed.) Trade and Exchange in Early Mesoamerica. Albuquerque: University of New Mexico Press.

Clark, Edith (1966) My Mother Who Fathered Me (2nd ed.). London: Allen & Unwin.

Cleland, John G. and Susheela Singh (1980) "Islands and the demographic transition." World Development 8: 969- 993.

Cleland, John and Christopher Wilson (1987) "Demand theories of the fertility transition: An iconoclastic view." Population Studies 41: 5-30.

Cleveland, David (1986) "The political economy of fertility regulation: The Kusasi of Savanna West Africa (Ghana)," pp. 263-293 in W. Penn Handwerker (ed.) Culture and Reproduction. Boulder, CO: Westview.

Clipson, Paul T. (1981) Adolescent Fertility in the English-Speaking Caribbean. Regional Development Office/Caribbean, U.S. Agency for International Development.

Coale, Ansley J. (1984) "The demographic transition." The Population Debate: Dimensions and perspectives. Papers of the World Population Conference, Bucharest, 1975. New York: United Nations.

Coale, Ansley J. and T. James Trussell (1974) "Model fertility schedules." Population Index 40: 185-258.

Coale, Ansley J. and T. James Trussell (1975) "Erratum." Population Index 41: 572-573.

Coale, Ansley J. and Susan Cotts Watkins [eds.] (1986) The Decline of Fertility in Europe. Princeton: Princeton University Press.

Cochrane, Susan (1979) Fertility and Education. World Bank Staff Occasional Papers, No. 26. Baltimore, MD: Johns Hopkins University Press.

Colson, Elizabeth (1974) Tradition and Contract. Chicago: Aldine.

Comaroff, John L. and Simon Roberts (1981) Rules and Processes. Chicago: University of Chicago Press.

Copelman, Dina M. (1986) "A new comradeship between men and women: Family, marriage and London's women teachers, 1870-1914," pp. 175-194 in Jane Lewis (ed.) Labour and Love. Oxford: Basil Blackwell.

Cowgill, George L. (1983) "Rulership and the Ciudadela: Political inferences from Teotihuacan architecture," pp. 313-344 in Richard M. Leventhal and Alan L. Kolata (eds.) Civilization in the Ancient Americas. Albuquerque: University of New Mexico Press.

Cox, Winston (1982) "The manufacturing sector in the economy of Barbados 1946," pp. 47-80 in DeLisle Worrell (ed.) The Economy of Barbados, 1946-1980. Bridgetown: Central Bank of Barbados.

Crosbie, Paul V. (1986) "Rationality and models of reproductive decision-making," pp. 30-58 in W. Penn Handwerker, (ed.) Culture and Reproduction. Boulder, CO: Westview.

Czap, Peter, Jr. (1983) "A large family: The peasant's greatest wealth: Serf households in Mishino, Russia, 1814-1858," pp. 105-152 in Richard Wall, Jean Robin and Peter Laslett, (eds.) Family Forms in Historic Europe. Cambridge: Cambridge University Press.

Darwin, Charles (1966) The Origin of Species (1859). Cambridge, MA: Harvard University Press.

Davidson, Maria (1978) "Female work status and fertility in urban Latin America." Social and Economic Studies 27: 481-506.

Davis, Kingsley (1963) "The theory of change and response in modern demographic history." Population Index 29: 345-366.

Davis, Kingsley and Judith Blake (1956) "Social structure and fertility: An analytic framework." Economic Development and Cultural Change 4: 211-235.

Davis, William (1973) Social Relations in a Philippine Market. Berkeley: University of California Press.

de Albuquerque, Klaus, Paul D. Mader and William F. Stinner (1976) "Modernization, delayed marriage and fertility in Puerto Rico: 1950 to 1970." Social and Economic Studies 25: 55-65.

Diaz-Briquets, Sergio and Lisandro Pérez (1987) "The demography of revolution," pp. 409-436 in Irving Louis Horowitz (ed.) Cuban Communism (6th ed.). New Brunswick, NJ: Transaction Books.

Dirks, Robert and Virginia Kerns (1976) "Mating patterns and adaptive change in Rum Bay, 1823-1970." Social and Economic Studies 25: 34-54.

Dorjahn, Vernon R. (1986) "Temne fertility," pp. 321-349 in W. Penn Handwerker, (ed.) Culture and Reproduction. Boulder, CO: Westview.

Dyhouse, Carol (1986) "Mothers and daughters in the middle-class home c. 1870-1914," in Jane Lewis, (ed.) Labour and Love. Oxford: Basil Blackwell.

Easterlin, Richard A. (1978) "The economics of sociology and fertility: A synthesis," pp. 57- 134 in Charles Tilly (ed.) Historical Studies of Changing Fertility. Princeton: Princeton University Press.

Easterlin, Richard A. (1983) "Modernization and fertility," pp. 562- 586 in R. A. Bulatao and R. D. Lee (eds.) Determinants of Fertility in Developing Countries, Vol. 2. New York: Academic Press.

Easterlin, Richard A. and Eileen M. Crimmins (1985) The Fertility Revolution. Chicago: University of Chicago Press.

Forte, Alyson and Basia Zaba (1985) Preliminary Analysis of the 1980 Census Data. 1980-1981 Population Census of the Commonwealth Caribbean, Barbados, Vol. 3.

Gittins, Diana (1982) Fair Sex. New York: St. Martin's.

Gittins, Diana (1986) "Marital status, work and kinship, 1850-1930," pp. 249-267 in Jane Lewis (ed.) Labour and Love. Oxford: Basil Blackwell.

Gonzales, Nancie L. Solien (1969) Black Carib Household Structure. Seattle: University of Washington Press.

Goode, William J. (1963) World Revolution and Family Patterns. New York: Free Press.

Greenfield, Sidney (1961) "Socio-economic factors and family form." Social and Economic Studies 10: 72-85.

Greenfield, Sidney (1966) English Rustics in Black Skin. New Haven: College & Universities Press.

Grigg, D. B. (1974) The Agricultural Systems of the World. Cambridge: Cambridge University Press.

Guengant, Jean Pierre, in collaboration with Dawn I. Marshall (1985) Caribbean Population Dynamics: Emigration and Fertility Challenges. Conference of Caribbean Parliamentarians on Population and Development, Heywoods, Barbados. U.S. Agency for International Development.

Hagelberg, G. B. (1985) "Sugar in the Caribbean: Turning sunshine into money," pp. 85-126 in Sidney W. Mintz and Sally Price (eds.) Caribbean Contours. Baltimore, MD: Johns Hopkins University Press.

Hamilton, Cicely (1909) Marriage as a Trade. New York: Moffat, Yard.

Hanawalt, Barbara (1986) The Ties That Bound. New York: Oxford University Press.

Handwerker, W. Penn (1973) "Kinship, friendship and business failure among market sellers in Monrovia, Liberia, 1970." Africa 43: 288-301.

Handwerker, W. Penn (1979) "Daily markets and urban economic development." Human Organization 38: 366-377.

Handwerker, W. Penn (1983) "The first demographic transition." American Anthropologist 85: 5-27.

Handwerker, W. Penn (1986a) "The modern demographic transition." American Anthropologist 88: 400-417.

Handwerker, W. Penn (1986b) Culture and reproduction: Exploring micro/macro linkages," pp. 1-28. in W. Penn Handwerker (ed.) Culture and Reproduction. Boulder, CO: Westview.

Handwerker, W. Penn (1986c) "'Natural fertility' as a balance of choice and behavioral effect: Policy implications for Liberian farm households," pp. 90-111 in W. Penn Handwerker (ed.) Culture and Reproduction. Boulder, CO: Westview.

Handwerker, W. Penn (1987) "Fiscal corruption and the moral economy of resource acquisition." Research in Economic Anthropology 9: 307-353.

Handwerker, W. Penn (1988b) "The politics of fertility transition: Severing ties of dependence in England." (unpublished)

Handwerker, W. Penn (1988c) "Population, power and evolution. (unpublished)

Handwerker, W. Penn (in press) "The origin and evolution of culture." American Anthropologist.

Harewood, Jack (1968) "Population trends and family planning activity in the Caribbean." Demography 5: 874-893.

Harewood, Jack (1978) "Female fertility and family planning in Trinidad and Tobago." Mona, Jamaica: Institute of Social and Economic Research.

Harewood, Jack (1981) "Introduction and background," pp. 39-48 in Susan Craig, (ed.) Contemporary Caribbean, A Sociological Reader, Vol. 1. Port-of- Spain, Trinidad: College Press.

Harris, Marvin (1966) "The cultural ecology of India's sacred cattle." Current Anthropology 7: 51-59.

Harris, Marvin (1981) American Now. The Anthropology of a Changing Culture. New York: Simon & Schuster.

Hayden, Brian (1981) "Subsistence and ecological adaptations of modern hunter/gatherers." in Robert S. O. Harding and Geza Teleki (eds.) Omnivorous Primates. New York: Columbia University Press.

Hayden, Brian (1986) "Resources, rivalry and reproduction: The influence of basic resource characteristics on reproductive behavior," pp. 176-195 in W. Penn Handwerker (ed.) Culture and Reproduction. Boulder, CO: Westview.

Hayden, Brian, Morley Eldridge, Anne Eldridge and Aubrey Cannon (1985) "Complex hunter-gatherers in interior British Columbia," pp. 181- 199 in T. D. Price and James Brown, (eds.) Prehistoric Hunter-Gatherers. New York: Academic Press.

Hayden, Brian, M. Deal, A. Cannon and J. Casey (1986) "Ecological determinants of women's status among hunter/gatherers." Human Evolution 1: 449-474.

Haynes, Cleviston (1982) "Sugar and the Barbadian economy 1946-1980," in DeLisle Worrell (ed.) The Economy of Barbados 1946-1980. Bridgetown: Central Bank of Barbados.

Heer, David M. (1983) "Infant and child mortality and the demand for children," pp. 369-87 in R. A. Bulatao and R. D. Lee (eds.) Determinants of Fertility in Developing Countries, Vol. 1. New York: Academic Press.

Henry, Frances and Pamela Wilson (1975) "The status of women in Caribbean societies." Social and Economic Studies 24: 165-(198.

Horowitz, Michael (1967a) "A decision model of conjugal patterns in Martinique." Man 2: 445-453.

Horowitz, Michael (1967b) Morne-Paysan. New York: Holt, Rinehart & Winston.

Houlbrooke, Ralph A. (1984) The English Family 1450-1700. London: Longman.

Hogarth, Robin M., and Melvin W. Reder [eds.] (1987) Rational Choice. The Contrast between Economics and Psychology. Chicago: University of Chicago Press.

Hum, Derek and Alexander Basilevsky (1978) "Economic activity and cyclical variation in birthrates: Some new evidence for Jamaica." Social and Economic Studies 27: 197-203.

Karch, Cecilia A. (1979) The Transformation and Consolidation of the Corporate Plantation Economy in Barbados: 1860-1977. Ann Arbor: University Microfilms.

Karch, Cecilia (1981) "The growth of the corporate economy in Barbados: Class/race factors, 1890-1977," pp. 213-241 in Susan Craig, (ed.) Contemporary Caribbean, A Sociological Reader, Vol. 1. Port-of-Spain, Trinidad: The College Press.

Levine, David (1977) Family Formation in an Age of Nascent Capitalism. New York: Academic Press.

Lewis, Sir Arthur (1950) "The industrialization of the British West Indies." Caribbean Economic Review 2: 1-61.

Lewis, Jane (1984) Women in England 1870-1950. Bloomington: Indiana University Press.

Lowenthal, David (1957) "The population of Barbados." Social and Economic Studies 6: 445-501.

MacFarlane, Alan (1978) The Origins of Individualism in England. Cambridge: Cambridge University Press.

MacFarlane, Alan (1986) Marriage and Love in England 1300-1840. Oxford: Basil Blackwell.

MacNeish, Richard S. (1978) The Science of Archaeology. North Scituate, MA: Duxbury.

MacNeish, Richard S. (1981) "Tehuacan's Accomplishments" in Jeremy A. Sabloff (ed.) Supplement to the Handbook of Middle American Indians. Vol. 1: Archaeology. Austin: University of Texas Press.

Marino, Anthony (1970) "Family, fertility, and sex ratios in the British Caribbean." Population Studies 24: 159-172.

Margolis, Maxine L. (1984) Mothers and Such. Views of American Women and Why They Changed. Berkeley: University of California Press.

Marshall, Dawn I. (1982) "The history of Caribbean migrations." Caribbean Review 11: 6-9, 52- 53.

Mascoll, Clyde (1985) "Wages, productivity and employment in Barbados 1949-1982." Economic Review of the Central Bank of Barbados 12: 10-23.

Massiah, Joycelin (1982) "Women who head households," pp. 62-130 in Joycelin Massiah, (ed.) Women and the Family. Vol. 2: Women in the Caribbean Project. Cave Hill, Barbados: Institute for Social and Economic Research (Eastern Caribbean), University of the West Indies.

Massiah, Joycelin (1984) Employed women in Barbados: A demographic profile, 1946-1970. Institute of Social and Economic Research (Eastern Caribbean) Occasional Paper No. 8. University of the West Indies, Cave Hill, Barbados.

Mauldin, W. Parker and Bernard Berelson (1978) "Conditions of fertility decline in developing countries, 1965-75." Studies in Family Planning 9: 90-147.

Meacham, Standish (1977) A Life Apart. Cambridge, MA: Harvard University Press.

Mintz, Sidney (1964) "The employment of capital by market women in Haiti," in Raymond Firth and B. S. Yamey (eds.) Capital, Savings, and Credit in Peasant Societies. Chicago: Aldine.

Mintz, Sidney and Eric R. Wolf (1950) "An analysis of ritual co-parenthood (Compadrazgo)." Southwestern Journal of Anthropology 6: 341-368.

Millon, Rene (1976) "Social relations in ancient Teotihuacan," pp. 205-248 in Eric R. Wolf (ed.) The Valley of Mexico. Albuquerque: University of New Mexico Press.

Millon, Rene (1981) "Teotihuacan: City, state, and civilization," pp. 198-244 in Jeremy A. Sabloff, (ed.) Supplement to the Handbook of Middle American Indians. Vol. 1: Archaeology. Austin: University of Texas Press.

Mosk, Carl (1983) Patriarchy and Fertility, Japan and Sweden 1880-1960. New York: Academic Press.

Murphy, William P. (1980) "Secret knowledge as property and power in Kpelle society: Elders versus youth." Africa 50: (193-207.

Murphy, William P. (1981) The rhetorical management of dangerous knowledge in Kpelle brokerage." American Ethnologist 8: 667-685.

Murphy, William P. (1988) "Rhetoric and dialectic of consensus in Mende political discourse." (unpublished)

Nair, Neal Kar (1982) Fertility and Family Planning in Barbados. Bridgetown: BFPA.

Nag, Moni (1971) "The Influence of conjugal behavior, migration, and contraception on natality in Barbados," pp. 105-123 in Steven Polgar (ed.) Culture and Population. Cambridge, MA: Schenkman.

Netting, Robert McC. (1984) Balancing on an Alp. Cambridge: Cambridge University Press.

Newton, Velma (1984) The Silver Men. Institute of Social and Economic Research, University of the West Indies, Mona, Jamaica.

Nortman, Dorothy L. and Ellen Hofstatter (1980) Population and Family Planning Programs (10th ed.). New York: Population Council.

Notestein, Frank (1945) "Population: The long view," pp. 36-57 in T. W. Schultz (ed.) Food for the World. Chicago: University of Chicago Press.

Otterbein, Keith (1965) "Caribbean family organization." American Anthropologist 67: 66-79.

Petersen, Jeanne (1984) "No angels in the house: The Victorian myth and the Paget women." American Historical Review 89: 677-708.

Phillips, Edsil (1982) "The development of the tourist industry in Barbados 1956-1980," pp. 107-140 in DeLisle Worrell (ed.) The Economy of Barbados 1946-1980. Bridgetown: Central Bank of Barbados.

Pillsbury, Barbara (1986) "Family planning and human rights in Bangladesh: The case of sterilization." Paper presented at the 87th annual meeting of the American Anthropological Association, Philadelphia.

Powell, Dorian, Linda Hewitt and Prudence Wooming (1978) Contraceptive Use in Jamaica. Institute of Social and Economic Research, University of the West Indies, Mona, Jamaica.

Power, Eileen (1975) Medieval Women. Cambridge: Cambridge University Press.

Prior, Mary (1985) "Women and the urban economy: Oxford 1500-1800," pp. 93-117 in Mary Prior (ed.) Women in English Society 1500-1800. London: Methuen.

Quadagno, Jill S. (1982) Aging in Early Industrial Society. New York: Academic Press.

Richardson, Bonham C. (1985) Panama Money in Barbados, 1900-1920. Knoxville: University of Tennessee Press.

Rindos, David (1985) "Darwinian selection, symbolic variation, and the evolution of culture." Current Anthropology 26: 65-88.

Rindos, David (1986) The evolution of the capacity for culture: Sociobiology, structuralism, and cultural selectionism." Current Anthropology 27: 315- 332.

Roberts, G. W. (1955) "Some aspects of mating and fertility in the West Indies." Population Studies 8: (199-227.

Roberts, G. W. (1957) The Population of Jamaica. Cambridge: Cambridge University Press.

Robinson, Warren C. (1987) "The time cost of children and other household production." Population Studies 41: 313-323.

Ross, Ellen (1986) "Labour and love: Rediscovering London's working-class mothers, 1870-1918," pp. 73-98 in Jane Lewis, (ed.) Labour and Love. Oxford: Basil Blackwell.

Ross, Eric B. (1986) "Potatoes, population, and the Irish famine: The political economy of demographic change," pp. 196-220 in W. Penn Handwerker, (ed.) Culture and Reproduction. Boulder, CO: Westview.

Sanders, William T. (1976) "The agricultural history of the basin of Mexico," pp. 101-160 in Eric R. Wolf, (ed.) The Valley of Mexico. Albuquerque: University of New Mexico Press.

Sanders, William T. Jeffrey R. Parsons and Robert S. Santley (1979) The Basin of Mexico. New York: Academic Press.

Sanders, William T. and Robert S. Santley (1983) "A tale of three cities: Energetics and urbanization in pre-Hispanic central Mexico," pp. 243-291 in Evon Z. Vogt and Richard M. Leventhal, (eds.) Prehistoric Settlement Patterns. Albuquerque: University of New Mexico Press.

Schneider, Jane and Peter Schneider (1984a) "Demographic transition in a Sicilian rural town." Journal of Family History 9: 245-272.

Schneider, Jane and Peter Schneider (1984b) "The demographic transition of landpoor peasants in a Sicilian rural town: A study of class and family." Paper presented to the 85th meeting of the American Anthropological Association, Denver, CO.

Schumann, Debra A. (1986) "Fertility and historical variation in economic strategy among migrants to the Lacandon Forest, Mexico," pp. 144-158 in W. Penn Handwerker, (ed.) Culture and Reproduction. Boulder, CO: Westview.

Scrimshaw, Susan C. M. (1978) "Infant mortality and behavior in the regulation of family size." Population and Development Review 4: 383-404.

Sheppard, Jill (1977) The "Redlegs" of Barbados. Millwood, New York: KTO Press.

Simonelli, Jeanne M. (1986) "Policy, power, and reproductive behavior in Hungary." Presented at the 87th annual meeting of the American Anthropological Association, Philadelphia.

Sinclair, Sonja S. (1974) "A fertility analysis of Jamaica: Recent trends with reference the Parish of St. Ann." Social and Economic Studies 23: 588-636.

Skocpol, Theda (1979) States and Social Revolutions. Cambridge: Cambridge University Press.

Slater, Mariam (1977) The Caribbean Family. New York: St. Martin's.

Slater, Miriam (1984) Family Life in the Seventeenth Century. London: Routledge & Kegan Paul.

Slavin, S. L. and R. E. Bilsborrow (1974) "The Barbados Family Planning Association and fertility decline in Barbados." Studies in Family Planning 5: 325-332.

Smith, Adam 1776 [(1937)] An Inquiry into the Nature and Causes of the Wealth of Nations. New York: Modern Library.

Smith, M. G. (1962) West Indian Family Structure. Seattle: University of Washington Press.

Smith, Raymond T. (1956) The Negro Family in British Guiana. London: Routledge & Kegan Paul.

Smith, Richard M. (1981) "Fertility, economy and household formation in England over three centuries." Population and Development Review 7: 595-622.

Sternberg, Robert J. (1985) Human intelligence: The model is the message." Science 230: 1111-1125.

Stoffle, Richard A. (1972) "Industrial employment and inter-spouse conflict: Barbados, West Indies." Ph.D. dissertation, University of Kentucky.

Stycos, J. Mayone (1955) Fertility and Family Planning in Puerto Rico. Westport, CT: Greenwood.

Stycos, J. Mayone and Kurt W. Back (1964) The Control of Human Fertility in Jamaica. Ithaca, New York: Cornell University Press.

Tacitus (1948) Tacitus on Britain and Germany (H. Mattingly, trans.). Baltimore, MD: Penguin.

Varian, Hal R. (1984) Microeconomic Analysis (2nd ed.). New York: Norton.

Wall, Richard (1985) "Work, welfare and the family: An illustration of the adaptive family economy," pp. 261-294, in Richard M. Smith and Keith Wrightson (eds.) The World We Have Gained. Lloyd Bonfield, Oxford: Basil Blackwell.

Ward, Barbara (1960) "Cash or credit crops." Economic Development and Cultural Change 2: 148-163.

Weil, Peter (1986a) "Agricultural intensification and fertility in The Gambia (West Africa)," pp. 294-320 in W. Penn Handwerker (ed.) Culture and Reproduction. Boulder, CO: Westview.

Weil, Peter (1986b) "Men's masking and ritual in the 19th and 20th century adaptive processes of the Mandinka of Senegambia: Art history and culture history." Presented at the 29th annual meetings of the African Studies Association, University of Wisconsin, Madison.

Wilmsen, Edwin N. (1986) Biological determinants of fecundity and fecundability: An application of Bongaarts' model to forager fertility," pp. 59-89 in W. Penn Handwerker, (ed.) Culture and Reproduction. Boulder, CO: Westview.

Wilson, Peter J. (1973) Crab Antics. New Haven, CT: Yale University Press.

Woods, R. and C. W. Smith (1983) "The decline of marital fertility in the late nineteenth century: The case of England and Wales." Population Studies 37: 307-325.

Woods, R. I. (1987) "Approaches to the fertility transition in Victorian England." Population Studies 41: 283-312.

Worrell, Delisle, ed. (1982) The Economy of Barbados 1946-1980. Bridgetown: Central Bank of Barbados.

Wrigley, E. A. and R. S. Schofield (1981) The Population History of England, 1541-1871. Cambridge: Harvard University Press.

Wrigley, E. A. and R. S. Schofield (1983) "English population history from family reconstitution: Summary results 1600-1799." Population Studies 37: 157-184.

INDEX

About the Author

W. Penn Handwerker received his Ph.D. from the University of Oregon in 1971 and is Professor of Anthropology at Humboldt State University on California's north coast. His principal theoretical and research interests center on human population ecology, especially the political economy of development. He has conducted field research in West Africa, primarily in the Republic of Liberia, on migration and social organization (1968), food production and marketing (1969-1970), the determinants of high fertility (1977-1978), and management and corruption in the agricultural sector (1984). He has published widely on this research and has edited the book *Culture and Reproduction: An Anthropological Critique of Demographic Transition Theory*. He is developing the more general theory of power, population, and evolution left implicit in this book, and is editing a collection of papers under the title *Births and Power: The Politics of Reproduction*. He also plans to extend the fieldwork reported here to study further aspects of women's power in the Eastern Caribbean.